TWILIGHT AND WALLFLOWERS

by

Jean Arnold

These memories are for my son, Lynn
and my grandchildren and great-grandchildren

And are dedicated to my wonderful Maurice and Bronwyn.
'There is a land where those who loved when here shall meet to love again'

And in loving memory of my brother, Ferg, with whom I shared a childhood which he enriched beyond measure

Peacock Publications
2008

© Lena Jean Arnold 2007
First edition 2007
Revised edition 2008
All rights reserved

This book is copyright. Apart from any fair dealings for the purposes of private study, research, criticism or review, as permitted under the *Copyright Act*, no part may be reproduced by any process without written permission. The right of Lena Jean Arnold to be identified as the moral rights author has been asserted by her in accordance with the *Copyright Amendment (Moral Rights) Act 2000* (Commonwealth).

All sketches by Maurice Arnold
   Front cover photo:
      Left to right: Kath; Mother; Ferg; Pat; Jean and
        Pauline. 1935
   Back cover photo:
      Left to right: Leon's cousin with her daughter; Pauline;
      Kath; Pat; Mother and Jean, at New Brighton c1940.

Inquiries to: larnold@optushome.com.au

Printed by:
Peacock Publications
38 Sydenham Rd, Norwood, South Australia 5067

Arnold, L J (Jean), 1930-.
Twilight and Wallflowers.
National Library of Australia Card Number & ISBN 1 921008 90 3

      1. Arnold LJ, (1930-) – Childhood and youth
      2. Colomendy Camp – evacuation – Biography
      3. Barton-upon-Humber – Biography
      4. Liverpool (UK)   I. Title

CHAPTER ONE

We lived at No. 32 but it would have made no difference had we lived at No.12 or 17, all the houses were the same. We couldn't have lived at No.13 because the Liverpool Corporation, sensitive to people's superstitions, had no No.13. But they couldn't fool us - we knew the people in No.15 should really have been in No.13 and we felt they were very unlucky because of this. The dark forces couldn't be fooled.

When we first moved to No.32 in 1935 there were Mother and five of us siblings, Pauline, Pat, Ferg, Kath and me. My Father, Cyril, had died on 15th September 1932. My brother Deryk had died shortly before on 1st August and Kath's twin, Maureen, less than three years before that. We were all living in Nottingham then but went to Liverpool after my Father's death so Mother, who had been born and raised there, could be near her parents and other relatives.

We lived first at Scarisbrick Drive, Norris Green. I was too young to go to school but Ferg and Kath went. Ferg remembers me standing at the gate hitting the schoolchildren as they passed and then dashing inside - I remember this too. Of course he copped it in my place. Mother remembers how territorial I was. If the even younger child from next door went up our path (we shared an entry to the back) I would gently lead her out again and re-direct her firmly up her own path. Otherwise no-one seems to remember too much about me when I was young - Kath and Ferg were busy being young themselves and the older two sisters, Pauline and Pat, had other things to think about. Pauline does remember when we were still living at Scarisbrick Drive, seeing me sitting on the kerb looking ashen and very undernourished and thought to herself that I might not grow up. T.B. was very much on people's minds in those days due to the fact that so many people had it. My Father had died of T.B. so we were always conscious of it.

Otherwise, apart from hitting schoolchildren, my only memory of Scarisbrick Drive is being left all alone one night and screaming and screaming when I woke up in the dark, though not dark enough not to be able to make out my Father's sailor's trunk under the window - a sinister looking thing. And then Mother came in - she had heard me from across the road where she had been visiting with Mr & Mrs Pickles.

The Wireless Inspector

Mr and Mrs Pickles became legendary in our house because Mr Pickles had taken the wireless up into the loft when the government inspector had called to see if he had a licence for it, and while his wife was telling the inspector that they didn't have a wireless, Mr Pickles' foot came through the ceiling. It was also said they kept hens up in the loft, but this could have been an embellishment of the story. We liked this story - it was very much a 'them and us world' in which I grew up.

My earliest memory before that was going into a room, coming out again and pulling the door shut by a scarf which was on the door handle. Mother confirmed this years later. When my Father was seriously ill and still at home, she put a scarf on the bedroom door so that we children who were too small to reach the handle could pull the door to after us. This would have been in Nottingham.

I can vaguely remember when we moved to No. 32 in May 1935. I was pushed down the road in a goat-chair; though I imagine the real name was probably go-chair, they were always referred to as goat-chairs. The next thing I was being taken to school. This was Colwell Road School. I hated it from the first day and until the day I left. My first day was ruined by the teacher, Miss Archer, who screamed and carried on because I had put up my hand when she had said, "Who wants milk?" and after I had drunk it she had come around to collect the halfpenny or penny for it and I hadn't had any money. I probably didn't like milk before then but I certainly have never liked it since, or teachers for that matter.

Another thing I learnt on that first day of school, apart from the fact that there is no such thing as a free milk, was that I had no sense of direction. I was always getting lost finding my way back home. The road from the corner leading to home forked and I invariably took the wrong one, which meant Ferg or Kath lost their lunchtime going in search of me. Many times, instead of going up Kings Drive, I went up Fincham Road. Often, when I was in the school, I couldn't find my way to the classroom in spite of it coming off one long straight corridor - I kept forgetting which end my classroom was. I would walk up and down sobbing. Once Kath saw me from her classroom - all classrooms had windows looking out onto the corridor and also onto the outside world on the opposite side of the classroom. She burst into tears when she saw me and was told off for it. It was that sort of school. You always just got yelled at. I had a trick when I was a child of being able to 'blur' my eyes without anyone being aware I was doing so. If I were being told off I would blur my eyes so I didn't have to see the person doing it. On one occasion, having been sent to school, I returned home again. Mother was out but when she returned and saw me looking out of the window, she promptly took me back to school again and had to ring the bell, the outer gate to the schoolyard being locked after nine a.m.

The Missing Classroom

My memories of this awful school were that it smelled of chalk and sour milk and the horrible headmistress who smelled of mothballs. She was a tall, gaunt woman with grey hair and a cold-looking red-blotched face. If you were late twice you had to watch the child who had been late three times being caned across the hand. She would bring the cane down with a terrifying whack. Later, when I had been late twice, I had to watch a girl who had been late three times being caned. It was so terrifying that I started to get up very early to be at school about an hour before time.

Boys and girls were in separate classes right from Infant School but shared the same playground. The building was U-shaped, the central wing forming the Infant School, the classrooms for boys in one half and the classrooms for girls in the other half. Double doors led from one to the other but only teachers were allowed to pass through them. In Junior School the boys were in the furthest part of the school away from the girls facing each other on opposite sides of the 'U' and each had their own playground. In Infant School boys and girls had the same playtime and early on I was chased by one of the boys who peed on me. There were extensive playing fields which stretched endlessly and where we had our PT lessons which were usually rounders, passing the beanbags, or vaulting over a wooden horse.

Infant School was for ages five to seven, and Junior School from eight to eleven. Senior School was at another school altogether, a quarter of a mile away. We did not wear a school uniform as such in any of the years. In those days stockings were held up by elastic bands, older girls sometimes having a suspender belt. Most girls wore a Liberty Bodice over their singlets and under their outer clothing. Boys wore short trousers with braces summer and winter and only went into long trousers when they went to Senior School.

The school-day started with the 'reading of the register' - a very large book with our names written in alphabetical order. When the teacher called our name we would respond with "present" and we would be marked off. If anyone were absent for more than a few days and the school had not been informed of the reason, then a Truant Officer was sent to their home. A note to the teacher was required whenever a pupil was absent.

We were examined at intervals by the school nurse. If we were found to have nits or vermin, we were given a note to take home. These notes were always distributed by the teacher after we had returned to the classroom so everyone knew that you had received a 'note' and it was a cause of great shame. You were then re-examined later to see if you were free of infestation. I know all this as I once received a note. Mother combed our hair every night with a fine toothcomb and washed our hair once a week with Derbac soap. There was a clinic in the area where we were sent if we needed follow-up treatment for anything. The school nurse once referred me there as I had catarrh. We also went if we needed any dental work. Kath once had to have a tooth pulled and it left her with a dread of the smell of rubber - they had given her gas, administered by placing a rubber mask over the face. I once had it but it didn't bother me.

We had lessons in 'reading, writing and arithmetic'. In arithmetic we added, subtracted, divided and multiplied, resolved 'problems' and learnt all the tables off by heart. Reading and writing were taught simultaneously. After learning the alphabet, we graduated to forming words and then on to reading. In Infant School I received a prize for coming top in reading and was given a book which was called 'Saved by a Bear'. It was about a little girl in Canada whose Christian and surname, coincidentally, were the same as mine.

I'll never forget the pleasure of seeing my name printed in a book. After we had read a book, we had to be able to say what it was about before we could go on to the next book and you were made to feel important because you had to go to the headmistress who would give approval for your continuing on to the next book.

One series of books we were required to read was Milly Molly Mandy. Milly Molly Mandy's life was so totally divorced from the reality that we children knew, that all it did was make us long for such a world. We could identify far more with William Brown who was always getting up to mischief and being told off for being scruffy, but he wasn't a school textbook. My favourite reading was Rupert Bear, also not a school textbook, but I had a number which had been given as gifts. I never could pronounce the word 'ogre' though. We had a few books at home - one had stories of the Arabian Nights, such as Sinbad the Sailor. I was repulsed by one picture in this book of someone piggy-backing on someone else's back and refusing to let go. When I read about Aladdin and his genie, I hopefully went around for a while rubbing the curtain rings hoping one of them would produce a genie.

In one class in Infant School I sat next to a girl called Theresa. She shocked me in the first couple of days of our acquaintance by sneezing so that it splattered horribly all over her exercise book - she didn't have a handkerchief. To this day I am a bit obsessive about always carrying a handkerchief. Also Theresa and I had a fight over a ruler - we didn't own anything ourselves, all pens, rulers, exercise books, etc., belonged to the school, being handed out as they were required during the day and then collected again when we had finished with them. There was only one ruler to each desk of two and both of us wanted it at the same time. It broke and for the rest of that year the teacher made each of us use one of the broken halves. It was that sort of school. In later years I took a photograph of the school and showed it to my brother, Ferg. He remarked that it looked more like a penal institute, to which I replied, that was just what it was.

This was before the days of ballpoint pens so we had an inkwell on each desk and our pens were the 'nib' type. I think we all consumed our fair share of ink - sometimes licking the nib. The ink was only powder and water and obviously not poisonous. We used ordinary lead pencils in school, never the indelible puce pencils in which the lead became a fluorescent purple when you wet it. These we sometimes had at home. There was a large pencil sharpener in the classroom, but you only got to turn the handle of this to sharpen the pencils if you were lucky enough to be chosen by the teacher. When the teacher read to us we had to put our hands on our heads. On one occasion I had a splitting headache when it was 'hands-on-heads' time and I cried when I got home. Pauline put a warmed cloth dipped in vinegar on my forehead to ease the ache. (Was this a carry over from 'Jack & Jill', Jack having his head mended with vinegar and brown paper when he fell down and broke his crown whilst fetching a pail of water?)

There was a lot of discrimination in the school - in my case I was discriminated against because I didn't have a father. The girls could be very spiteful. They would say to each other in my presence, "Where did your dad take you over the weekend?" and I was so envious. It just didn't feel the same to say, "My mum took me to so-and-so." So I just remained quiet and felt worthless. It was never "daddy" and "mummy" - always "me dad" and "me mam," though we never said "mam," Mother would have had a fit. She made sure we never sank to the depths in which we found ourselves.

It was a rough area - two or three times I was set upon on my way to school. Mother would also warn us not to take sweets from strange men. If we were lost and needed to know the way, we were only to ask a policeman. Those were the days when Bobbies walked the beat. Mother's brother, Billie, worked for the Liverpool Corporation and he said that the rent-collectors didn't like to collect in our area. There was one house where they hadn't been able to collect the rent for a long time because when the collector called, the householder would bellow that he'd paid rent for so many years and therefore owned the house and he wasn't going to pay rent any more.

I can remember almost all the teachers I had, if not their names. Most of them have left no impression, one way or another, two were awful. During one year Kath had Miss Hosendorf. There were opposing opinions on her, she was either liked enormously or not at all. I never had her as a teacher but she stands out as she wore fancy jacquard-patterned stockings. One teacher, however, was exceptionally nice, and that was Miss de Jong. All the pupils liked her. There was Miss Clark who read beautifully and you really became absorbed in the story she was reading - hands-on-heads notwithstanding.

There was only one black child in the school, we thought she was lucky because she was different. There was also a girl who was backward. It was said that a wardrobe fell on her. Sometimes she would just aimlessly roam up and down the corridor.

Then there was Pansy. I thought the name Pansy was the nicest I had heard and wished that it had been mine. In a world of Gerties, Sarahs, Dorothys, Ritas, Iris', Ethels, Bettys, Beryls, Jeans, Joans and Janes, the name Pansy was poetry indeed. Pansy herself was well off in our terms. But one day, coming from tap-dancing, she was run over and after that she had to be pushed around in a long pram. Her mother brought her to school once to see everyone. Another girl Iris is remembered, not only because she was a very nice girl, but also because she had a double row of upper teeth.

Third-pint bottles of milk were served during mid-morning to each pupil who could pay. Later when it became free, I had to drink it too - I never liked milk. Bringing in the milk crate each morning wasn't considered such a great thing for the teacher to ask you to do, but I was asked to do this on a couple of occasions. The really important things like cleaning the blackboard, sharpening pencils or opening the window with the very long pole with a hook on the end, the teacher kept for her special pets and I was never asked to do them.

It wasn't until Junior School, I think, that there were class monitors. Monitors were not, like prefects, chosen by the pupils but nominated by the teacher. They did things like handing out the text books, rulers, etc. I think there was one for each section, the class being divided up into four sections.

In Junior School on Monday mornings we always had Assembly at which we sang:

> All things bright and beautiful
> All creatures great and small
> All things wise and wonderful
> The Lord God made them all.

And so on, and so on, in the same monotonous vein. At the end of the term we were again herded into Assembly to sing, but this time the song was one which I liked very much:

> Now the day is over
> Night is drawing nigh
> Shadows of the evening
> Drift across the sky.

On patriotic occasions we sang 'Land of Hope and Glory', except a number of us sang instead:

Land of Soap and Water
Mother wash my feet
Father cut my toenails
For my brother to eat.

Assembly was also the time for the headmistress or any of the teachers to bring matters to the schools notice. On one occasion we were told never to run with knitting needles, one of the pupils running with them had tripped and one of the needles had pierced her eye. This message was not wasted on me, I still put corks on my knitting needles when carrying them. Another time, a couple of girls who had been stealing from their class teacher, had to appear on the platform. The teacher had found out who the culprits were by marking the coins in her purse and then getting all the pupils to put their money on their desks. We were told the whole story as they stood there. Their parents had been asked to come to the school, though they didn't appear at Assembly.

Sometimes our class would be taken into the hall to do folk dancing. I presume they would have been from all over the British Isles but if the dances were explained to us I couldn't have been listening because they have left only a vague memory. Once we had to march around the hall singing 'Men of Harlech' but what the occasion was, I now don't know - I probably didn't then either as it didn't seem important to tell us these things.

We also had some sort of music lesson. There was a band with a few musical instruments, such as tambourines, but the bulk of the music came from triangles which you hit with a little metal stick. I only once got to do even this lowly task, otherwise I just had to stand with all the other unimportant pupils and watch the more privileged ones.

We learnt to sew; once we even had to make a dress for ourselves, taking turns at the sewing machine. Mine was white cotton. I had to hand-sew all the hems with blue blanket stitch. I thought it was fabulous. We also learnt chain stitch and running fell stitch. Or were they two different stitches, running stitch and fell stitch? Time has blurred the memory. There was the usual needle case which pupils seem to have been doing since time immemorial and will be for ages to come. It had a tapestry cover on which I did cross-stitch. Mother kept it for years. When it came time for my granddaughter, Emily, to do hers, she was about six then, it came already complete except for her school photograph which she had to put in. Such is educational advancement. As Mother with mine, I still have Emily's.

In Junior School one of my class teachers was Miss Owen who tried to teach us Welsh. I learnt one to ten in Welsh from her. She always wore a 'jigger' coat (which is what we called a smock) with deep pockets and would bring her cup of tea in after break and finish it off. She had a certain presence and I found the manner in which she walked and moved, even drinking her tea, interesting.

We graduated to learning English grammar in Junior School but the lesson which had a lasting impact was the one in which we were told of the man who was rescued when he jumped into the river after saying, "I will jump into the river and no-one shall save me." Whereas, another man who also jumped into the river but declaimed as he did so, "I shall jump into the river and no-one will save me," was left to drown. I was left amazed that people could be so particular that they would leave someone to drown because they used the wrong form of verb.

We never learnt what it was like for Ferg in his part of the school. He never spoke about it. Later on Mother would relate that the teacher he had during his first year at the school said that he couldn't get a word out of him.

The headmaster in the Boys' Junior School was a Mr Bradshaw. One Christmas the Boys' School put on a play and we all went. I can't recall whether Ferg was in the play or not, but Mother couldn't afford to buy a seat for Kath and me as well as herself, so Mr Bradshaw let me sit between them and Mother put a scarf or something down to make it more comfortable as I was sitting on the edges of two seats. We sat in the front row and the carol they sang during this play was 'In the Deep Mid-winter'. I've never been able to listen to it since without getting a lump in my throat. On the way home - it was winter and very cold - I saw a child, with a scarf wrapped crossways across his chest because he was so poor and didn't have a coat, being set upon by some bullies who stole the comics he was carrying. I was about seven at the time and I cried myself to sleep every night for days because I couldn't get this child out of my mind - he was so poor and had so little and yet someone had stolen from him. Mother would comfort me and say that Jesus would look after him. I grew up knowing Jesus very much as someone personal to whom I could talk. Mother told us that we could talk to him any time at all, when we were walking along the road, anywhere, and that we could tell him everything. We were well aware of our circumstances and Mother would say that Jesus would get us out of this. We always said our prayers before we went to sleep, if we happened to fall asleep before doing so because we were so tired, we would wake again shortly afterwards and say them. One of the prayers we said was:

Gentle Jesus meek and mild,
Look upon a little child,
Pity my simplicity,
Suffer me to come to thee.
Fain I would to thee be brought,
Gracious Lord forbid it not,
In the kingdom of thy grace,
Give a little child a place.

* * * * * * * * * * *

CHAPTER TWO

All the houses in the road were joined together, broken halfway by two semi-detached houses. The front door of each house was painted a deep green - the top third of which was fitted with glass panes. Just below the panes there was a brass letterbox slot. The green of the front door was the identical green of the cupboards in the classroom so there must have been co-operation between the Liverpool Corporation and the Education Department. The joined-together houses had a common roof and loft. Whether you could walk each half of the road from one end to the other via the loft, I don't know, but we used to think you could. The loft had a trapdoor to each house on the small landing to the bedrooms at the top of the stairs. I was scared of this trapdoor and every time I went up the stairs to the bedroom, I would stare at the panel which covered this, ready to run, expecting to see a face peer down at me. It was worse in winter when the trapdoor was left partly open to allow the heat from the house to rise into the loft to keep the pipes from freezing. I hated going upstairs at night-time. Kath was also scared but her way of coping with it was to walk up with her eyes closed and her arms stretched out in front of her. I could never understand that as I thought how terrible it would be if your outstretched hands were to touch someone. After I saw a picture starring Sydney Greenstreet and Peter Lorre, I expected someone like them to be waiting in the bedroom for me. I was scared stiff of the dark. Fortunately the picture 'Gaslight' with Ingrid Bergman and Charles Boyer I only saw later, otherwise I don't know what effect that would have had on me as it all had to do with someone walking in the loft and meddling with the gaslights.

The wall on either side of the stairs was a mottled brown. The corporation painted the houses at regular intervals and the tenant was allowed a limited choice of colour. I remember when they did the stair well; after the paint was applied, it was rubbed over with a stocking to give it a mottled effect, making it look like bakelite. I was most impressed. The stairs were carpeted and had removable brass rods to hold the carpet in place; we had to polish the rods with brasso on a regular basis. Along with the others, I would have to help with housework at home and Mother would say if we weren't doing any job vigorously enough, "Put some elbow grease into it."

Each house had three bedrooms and a cock-loft which was a small room off the main bedroom. Mother preferred to call it the box room. This had shelves at one end, where we kept what books we had, and a window at the other end. The bedrooms came off the landing which was square and just wide enough for the doors to the three bedrooms. Mother's room was to the right, the door to our room was directly opposite the stairs, and the door to the back bedroom was to the left. This was a single bedroom and its window overlooked the back garden with a playground beyond the back wooden fence.

The bedroom opposite the top of the stairs was the one that Ferg, Kath and I used when we were still children - when Ferg was older he moved to the cock-loft. Or, if Pauline and Pat were away, he slept in the single bedroom. The window of our room also looked out on the backyard. It had a double bed and a single bed, the double bed having iron bed ends with brass knobs on top of each of the four corner posts. Each bed had a bolster as well as feather pillows and feather eiderdown. There was a large black wardrobe with a full length drawer along the bottom and two doors either side of the mirror on the centre panel. My Father, who had been a carpenter and joiner, had made this wardrobe. There was also a washstand with a marble top. This room had a gas fire but this was never used. Running up the centre of the wall which backed on to the neighbour's house were three brown pipes which led up into the loft. A shelf ran the full length high up on this wall. On the mantelpiece above the fireplace was a carved lion made from the lava of Vesuvius, which my Father, who was in the Royal Navy during the First World War, had brought back from Pompeii. I still have this lion today, the only relic of my childhood. There was also a papier-maché policeman on the mantelpiece. Pauline had bought this for me and it had been full of sweets at that time. Later on it served the purpose of 'protecting' me from all the terrifying things that lurked in the dark. So Pauline said, and I believed her after she had come one night when I had called out, having imagined I had seen something in the dark. It was not even contemplated that the light be kept on to allay fear of the dark - budgets in those days didn't run to that sort of indulgence. There was also a yellow vase on the mantelpiece. I know this because we would sometimes pee in it if we had forgotten to bring the po upstairs. To save going downstairs to the lavatory, we would use the chamber-pot (known as a 'po') a common piece of bedroom furniture in those days. A standard joke was, "He fell through the bed into Poland." The chamber-pot was also known as a 'jerry'. Granny Elliott had a 'commode' - a chair with a flap which concealed the chamber-pot underneath. Like all the furniture in Granny and Granddad Elliott's house, this was an elegant piece.

Mother's room had a double bed with a feather eiderdown. There were small air-holes at the corners of the eiderdown from which the feathers would sometimes protrude and we would pick them out. Every now and then Mother would 'plump' up the eiderdown. The beds had bolsters as well as pillows. The pillows were always filled with feathers, some of which would occasionally find their way through the ticking. Mother's room had an open fire grate but it was never used. There was also a wardrobe in the room, a chest of drawers and, in front of the window, a wot-not. In those days there was a song - 'Oh, the wot-not's not, what the wot-not used to be'. I can't remember now what ornaments were on the wot-not, but either on there or on the mantelpiece above the fireplace in that bedroom there would have been the two Wedgwood candlesticks which Bert Large, the man to whom Mother was first engaged, had given her. There was a piece broken out of the rim of one of the candlesticks. The window was directly above the bay window of the kitchen so you could climb out and onto the roof of the bay window. Pauline's friend from high school, Marjorie Neville, who once came to stay during the school vacation, amused us younger children by climbing out onto this roof and jumping to the ground below. We thought this was very daring.

Downstairs there was the kitchen and scullery and outside the back door, off a small porch, was the lavatory. The knobs of the scullery and lavatory doors were so placed that we could grip each one and then walk with our feet up the corner where the doors were hinged and do a somersault.

The living room was always referred to as the kitchen and the scullery was in actual fact the kitchen. The bathroom was off the scullery, the red tiled floor of which continued through to the bathroom which had double doors. The bathroom had a bath but no hand-basin, all other ablutions having to be done in the scullery sink. Mother absolutely forbade hair being combed in the scullery, this had to be done either upstairs in the bedroom or in the bathroom where there was a mirror. There was a boiler perched in the corner over the bath. This huge boiler was heated by the fire in the kitchen - I don't know what we did in summer for hot water when the fire wasn't lit, I only know that the weekly bath was never foregone and we certainly didn't bathe in cold water. Kath and I always bathed together for our weekly bath. This generated disputes as we had two fears in common - one was of being sucked down the plug hole, the other was sitting under the boiler in case it fell on us. At either end of the bath, you were going to strike one or other of these problems. Our fear of being sucked down the plug hole we soon outgrew; the boiler was a different matter. However, we did later come to the conclusion that if the boiler did fall, it would fall forward to the one sitting at the plug end at the other end of the bath, so we then preferred sitting under the boiler. We had unconsciously grown in spatial recognition.

In the corner of the bathroom there was also a gas-heated copper in which some of the laundry was boiled every Monday. When we returned from school for lunch on Mondays the house would smell of soapsuds and steam from the copper and Mother's face would be flushed with the heat and moisture. We didn't like Mondays as she was too busy to have lunch with us and would just serve us our meal which was always left-over roast and vegetables from Sunday lunchtime. In the bathroom there was also a big round, fluted metal tub - known as a dolly tub - in which Mother would place the dirty wash, having filled it with hot water, and using the dolly pegs, a kind of milkmaid stool with a long handle, she would manually move the handle in a backwards and forwards motion, causing the water to swirl; the forerunner of washing machines. Mother would grate soap for use in the copper and dolly tub. Extra dirty clothes were put in the copper to boil and Mother used a thick wooden pole to lift them steaming from the copper, dropping them in the bath for rinsing. The mangle was a huge iron thing with wooden rollers which folded down to form a table. However, when not in use, this was pushed under the draining board, only half of it protruding into the scullery to provide a level top for food preparation, otherwise it would have taken up too much space. Monday was washday for all the ladies in the road and sometimes, after a long day of doing the wash, Mrs Davies who lived next door, would bring in a cup of tea to Mother and offer her a cigarette, saying, "We deserve this." Mother would take the cigarette just to be sociable, puffing at it awkwardly, and privately expressing her relief when it was over.

Mother said that my Father believed a person should only own three sets of clothing, one on, one off and one in the wash. Nothing to do with this belief of my Father's but more that necessity dictated it, we did not have a lot of clothes. When we came home from school in the afternoon, the first thing we had to do was go upstairs and change out of the clothes we only wore to school and into something not so good. If we had visitors, however, Mother would meet us at the front door and tell us to go straight into the kitchen.

For drying clothes on wet days there was a pulley-operated clothes rack in the scullery which stayed up near the ceiling when not in use. Otherwise the wash was hung out on the line and there was a clothes prop with which the line was sent aloft. Mother always hung the sheets by first folding them in two and then pegging them by their two ends to the line, which meant they captured the wind and billowed like sails. When the wash was brought in Mother would get one of us three younger ones to help fold the sheets. We would have to hold one end whilst Mother held the other and then, in tune with Mother, would fold and pull every which-way to stretch the sheet into shape.

Tuesday was ironing day and Mother would heat the 'sad irons' either on the wood and coal stove in the kitchen or on the gas stove in the scullery. There were always two sad irons on the go, one in use whilst the other was heating. I can recall the singeing smell of the hot iron as it was swiped across a damp cloth to clean it before putting on the clothes.

Above the gas stove in the scullery were shelves for crockery and other kitchen utensils. On the wall opposite the bathroom and just inside the back door, there was a cupboard where the coal was kept - we called it the coal-hole. The coal was delivered on a horse-drawn cart in hundred-weight sacks. An entry divided each set of two houses and was used by both. At the end of this entry a gate on either side led to each house. The coalman would come down this entry bearing a hundred-weight sack on his back, coming through the back door into the scullery and depositing the coal in the coal-hole. The coal dust flaked the coalmen's faces and hung about their nostrils. When the coalmen came, they would first come down the road calling out to see if anyone wanted coal, there was no such thing as pre-ordering.

The dustbin men came weekly and also came down the entry to the backyard where the dustbin was kept. They carried the bins on one shoulder which was protected by a piece of leather and they wore leather mitts. The dustbin cart was also horse-drawn. This was an enormous hopper on wheels with two or three openings on either side which had covers which could be slid down when the hopper was full. When this happened, a lorry would arrive with a fresh hopper which would be winched down a ramp from the tray of the lorry and the full one winched up and taken away, the horses being changed from one to the other. Keen gardeners kept on the lookout for the horses' droppings.

The postman came twice a day, putting the letters through each letterbox slot on the front doors, giving a little rap of the knocker.

Off the kitchen was the 'glory-hole' - this was the space beneath the stairs. The larder was inside the glory-hole - it was at the highest end and had shelves - the lower shelf being a stone slab for keeping things cool, this was where Mother would set jellies. Otherwise the rest of the area was used generally to store things and was where the gas and the electricity meters were. The gas meter took one penny at a time and the electricity meter, one shilling. On one occasion someone stole the coins from the gas meter and Mother had to make good the loss. The culprit had entered by way of the window which was off the entry. When anyone walked down this entry, you could hear the echo of their footsteps if this window was open.

In the kitchen was a big iron stove - cooking was not only done on the gas stove in the scullery, but also on the kitchen stove which had cooking plates and an oven, all heated by the open fire. We made our toast in front of this fire when it was lit, which was most of the year but not in summer. We would place the bread on a long, three-pronged fork, turning it when one side had been done. When summer came we had to do our toast under the grill in the gas stove in the scullery, not nearly as cosy. Above the cooking plates were also racks for drying things when the hot-plates were not in use. This stove was kept blackened and shiny and every week the brass fender of the hearth was polished. There was a plate-lifter to lift the plates off for cleaning; we would brush off the soot which had gathered underneath with a wire brush. Once a year the chimney sweep would come and clean the chimney. He had a very long pole with a round brush on the end which he pushed both up and down the chimney, the housewife making sure she had her floor in front of the grate well-covered. One of the duties we had as children was to make 'fire-lighters'. This was done by rolling up a few sheets of newspaper diagonally and then bending them in two and plaiting together the two pieces. Coal or coke was used on the fire and these 'fire-lighters' were a substitute, or an addition, to the small pieces of firewood known as 'chips', to start it. We would create a draught to start the fire by putting a sheet of newspaper over the front of the grate, leaving just a small gap underneath. Often the suction whipped the paper out of one's hand and up the chimney. Mother would damp down the fire by adjusting the flue vents.

The first hint of summer was not actually welcomed by us as we would come home from school to find that Mother had done the spring cleaning and the fire was out of action until the cool weather came again. Sometimes she would put a bowl of flowers in the empty grate. The windows would be open and the freshly washed lace-curtains would be wafting in the breeze. It is not that we didn't like summer and fresh air, but it took time to adjust to the absence of the intimacy of an open fire.

On the mantelpiece, set at either end, were two bas-relief, chocolate brown, papier-maché vases with Grecian scenes. In between was a row of plaster-of-paris black elephant ornaments, going from large to small. There was a cupboard on one side of the fireplace, known as the 'airing' cupboard, and it was here that sheets, towels, blankets, etc., were stored. The pipes leading from the hot-water system would have gone through the back of this cupboard providing the warmth to keep it dry.

Also in the kitchen was the dining-room table. This had leaves, one at either end, which were extended when the table was in use and then retracted when we had finished our meal. There was a chair at each end of the table, three more down one side and, opposite, a couch for people to sit on when at the table. There was a long mirror on the wall above the couch. On the wall which backed onto the scullery there was a sideboard with a Philco wireless - this was the first wireless we had ever owned and came to us in 1932 when Mother's brother, Hugh, who had bought a new one, gave us his old one. On the sideboard there was also a fluted, shell-shaped, silver dish with a rounded handle. Either side of the fireplace there was an armchair. Around the room was a picture rail from which pictures were hung on removable triangular-shaped metal hooks. This picture rail was also useful when at Christmas we received a monkey which ran up the wall by means of a cord which we hooked on to the picture rail and operated through a pulley system.

In front of the bay window was a sofa. Kath and I liked to sit on the back of this sofa and bang on the window when anyone passed in the road. Before they had time to turn around we would throw ourselves backwards, our legs still hooked over the back, but the rest of us lying across the seat where we couldn't be seen, leaving the passer-by looking around, wondering where the knocking was coming from. I can remember when this sofa and the two armchairs were delivered. It was brown leatherette with removable cushioning in fawn-coloured velvet. Ferg and Kath had been invited to some children's function at the church but I was too young to go. Mother, to console me, said that I would be the first one to sit in all the chairs, but when Ferg and Kath came home they were not a bit impressed with that, they were too busy saying what a good time they had had.

Kath and I invariably did the washing up, though we didn't have to do the breakfast and lunch dishes on schooldays. When we had fish, the forks we used were taken outside and thrust into the garden till the soil covered the prongs and left there for half an hour or so. I don't know at all why this was done. I do know why our bone-handled knives were not allowed to be put in the sink when we washed-up. There were two reasons, firstly, hot water was not good for the bone handles and, secondly, Mother was afraid that we might take hold of the cutting edge of the knife and hurt ourselves, so they had to be left on the draining board and washed individually. Our knives were sharpened on a knife-sharpener consisting of two rows of interlinking hardened steel disks. We would draw the blade of the knife firmly through this. Kath and I squabbled as to who would wash and who would dry. We took it in turns but there was often a dispute as to whose turn it was. At first we preferred to be the one who washed, but later it occurred to us that that was the worst job as the washer also had the pans to do. Sometimes an item would be put, by mistake, into the sink again and if it was recognised as having been already dried, the dryer-up would take umbrage and refuse to dry it a second time. Cutlery and other items of silver were polished on a regular basis, usually by Kath and me.

Mother had special sets of china and glassware which only came out when we had visitors - when these were used Kath and I didn't have to do the washing up. There was the set of fruit bowls which were green and fluted - the flutes alternating, one clear and one opaque. My favourite was the fruit set which was reddish-bronze and shimmered like shot-silk. Our milk jug was a deep blue with 'DUMBARTON' etched in white on the side and the sugar bowl was made of bubble glass with a silver band around the rim.

It was Mother's boast that only one of her children ever had an accident in the house and that was Deryk who had caught his fingers in the mangle, fortunately not too seriously. Mother was always at pains to see that when pans were on the stove, the handles were turned inwards so that the 'exploring fingers of little children' would not grab the handle and tip cooking food onto themselves. Long after we had grown up it stayed a rule of the household as she felt that it should be a habit to do this, not knowing when there would be young children around. For the same reason she always insisted that cups or hot food not be placed on the edge of a table. She was also insistent that cold water be put in the bath first, before the hot water, to prevent scalding.

There was a small garden front and back. All the houses in the road had a privet hedge along the front of the garden and a white, wooden front gate. There was also a hedge of privet dividing the gardens between neighbours. These were all in place when the houses were rented. The rest of the garden was the occupiers' own to do with what they liked. In our garden amongst the plants which stood out was the lilac bush, this was next to the window near the dividing hedge with our neighbours, the Finnegans. I never saw a single flower on it. It was a good place to hide when playing hide-and-seek, and also if one was in trouble and wanted to keep out of the way. To the left of the path leading to the house and in front of the privet hedge separating our garden from that of our neighbours on the other side, the Davies', there was a clump of gypsy grass, some white-flowered rock plants and a few pinks. The back garden had a small rock garden where there were also some pinks and rock plants as well as dog daisies and, along the fence at the side, wallflowers. Nasturtiums grew here and there and we liked to nip off the tip from the flower's trumpet and suck it, thinking it was honey. Amongst the grass of course there were buttercups, daisies and clover. We made chains of the daisies and wore them around our necks. On occasion we would go looking for a four-leaf clover, said to be lucky. Sometimes there would be a clump of rhubarb along the fence which Mother would fertilise from the slop bucket. Apart from rhubarb, the only other edible things Mother grew were mustard and cress, these in a washbowl. Along the fence with the Finnegans there was an elderberry tree, this wove itself into a tangle and we could hide there too. The berries were very pithy. Mr Finnegan had put up a high trellis on his side over which he grew rambler roses, just to smell them brings back memories of my childhood. The perfume of wallflowers does that too and to this day I find their perfume achingly evocative. Another smell from my childhood which comes to mind is of hot tar on a summer's day and how it formed bubbles on the road. Mr Finnegan had a greenhouse and once managed to grow grapes - he gave us one each.

We watered the garden with a large tin watering can with a spray nozzle, we didn't have a hose, and we kept the hedge in trim with garden shears. For keeping the grass cut there was a hand mower.

In the garden were earwigs, spiders, bumble-bees, butterflies and ladybirds. We loved ladybirds and when we caught one would say to it as we gently held it before seeing it on its way,

"Ladybird, Ladybird, fly away home,
Your house is on fire, and your children all gone."

The butterflies were just the white cabbage butterfly, we seldom saw others.

When very young, Kath had a fascination for bumble-bees and would catch them with her hand until one day she was stung and didn't do it after that. Earwigs we didn't really mind, though we thought 'ear' meant that they got into your ear. Spiders were only the 'daddy-long-legs' kind and we liked them. We occasionally saw 'bluebottles', fat flies with a bluish sheen; if they bit you, the bite sometimes went a little septic. Ordinary house flies were kept down by a sticky fly paper which hung above the dining-room table and we also had a fly-swatter for the occasional pesky one. They were not really a problem.

We had a swing in the garden which Mother had got someone from Southdene Road to erect. Mother took me with her when she went there to discuss this with him. One of his children happened to be sitting at the table drinking tea and when she had finished, she licked the cup all over. Even drinking out of a saucer was frowned on in our house so I was quite amazed.

We liked this swing but one day, whilst Kath and I were on it, it broke. Kath had been standing, I was seated and she was 'jerking me up' as we called it, when Ferg called out that one of the hooks holding the swing was straightening. He often teased us so we just laughed and didn't believe him. He called out again but we still took no notice. Then I went flying through the air and landed flat on my face. Kath clung on to the one chain which hadn't left its mooring. I couldn't open my mouth for a week and Mother took me to the doctor. This had been at the insistence of Auntie May, one of Mother's oldest friends who lived in Dovecot, who had looked in concern at my face when I had been sent to her with a message. The doctor found that the inside of my mouth was deeply imprinted with tooth marks. He didn't recommend anything more than what Mother had already been doing. In later years a dentist asked me if I had been in an accident as the top part of my jaw was out of alignment with the bottom. I assumed that it dated from this time.

When I look back on my childhood, the supposedly awful weather of Liverpool is not a part of my memories. A lot of people when they go there remark how drear the weather is. What I remember is basking summer days and the wallflowers growing along the fences and the smell of rambler roses after the rain. Fogs and crisp frosty evenings when we played outside and our breath formed ectoplasm under the street lamp. Coming home in the rain in the dark and the glow from the lights in the houses and how comforting they looked. Frost which caused icicles to form from the drainpipe and the ice on the flagstone pavements which made them hazardous to walk on, made more so by us kids making slides. How beautiful the twilight was as it played on the walls and bathed us in its mellow light. Twilight and wallflowers are my Liverpool childhood.

* * * * * * * * * *

CHAPTER THREE

Mother was on a widows pension which, I think, was 4s. 6d. per week for herself and 3s. 6d. for each of us children. She also received something from the Parish each week but I don't know how much that was. The rent was 10 shillings a week. Mother never admitted to the neighbours that she was on a pension but would say that she was "off to the bank." A couple of times when she had to go to the Parish she took me with her. On one particular occasion we went before a group of people sitting around a table and one of the women was wearing a fur coat. They addressed Mother by her surname, "Jackson," not even saying, "Mrs." When Mother said, "I am entitled to... ," one of these awful women said, "Entitled to! Entitled to! You are entitled to nothing." On the way home Mother's distress was palpable. I can still picture the buildings around as we walked through Dovecot on that cold and cheerless day. Later on Mother saw the British Legion and told them what had happened. The man she spoke to there got in touch with the Parish and told them off - later he told Mother that he had reminded them that they were dealing with a lady. She didn't have any trouble with the Parish after that.

My Father was in the Royal Navy during the First World War and maybe that is why she contacted the British Legion - not that she received any pension from the military despite my Father having contracted malaria during his war service. Mother said that when he had a bout of malaria he would go from shivering to sweating and sometimes became incoherent with the fever. Later on he got T.B. and that is what he died of. She said that the doctor had told her that the malaria had complicated his T.B. My Father had what was then described as 'galloping consumption'. Mother said that before he died he had lost so much weight that you could see through him. Otherwise, I learnt very little about my Father when I was growing up; Mother seldom spoke about him. The same applied to Deryk, my brother, who had died six weeks before my Father, she rarely spoke of him either. Pauline was very fond of my Father, but Pat was indifferent to him - in fact she said that the night he died she happened to be standing in front of a shop window with a friend and the light had suddenly gone out. She had turned to the friend and said, "I bet you my Father's dead."

 Though Mother didn't talk about my Father much, it was plain that it had been a marriage with a lot of difficulties. However, she always gave him credit for being a good father. She said he would help her put us children to bed and would look at us and say, "We might not have any money, but look at the treasure we have in these children." She said that she could only once remember him getting angry with one of us children and that was when Pat had given me a gob-stopper when I was still in my pram and I almost choked. It appears that, like Mother, he was fond of quotes and homilies. She said that he would quote the man who said to another regarding that person's child who had misbehaved, "If that were my child, I'd give it a good hiding;" receiving in return the response, "If it were your child, I'd do the same." Mother said that he was not averse to bringing home people who were down on their luck or had been paid off from their jobs and had nowhere to go. Mother had to find the means to feed them as well, so she wasn't always too happy about this. His response was, "Cast thy bread upon the waters and it will return to you a thousandfold." Having little, he believed, was no hindrance to giving - in fact he believed that the opposite more often than not applied and one of his other quotes was, "Where little is wanted, little is given."

 He once brought home someone who was down on his luck and also had a club foot. At that time Mother was fed up with my Father for his untidiness. He would come home from work and empty his pockets of all the nails and screws and other bits and pieces that carpenters use and didn't care where he put them down. This frustrated Mother who kept a clean and tidy house so she decided to teach him a lesson. As my Father always went around the house in his stocking feet, she put the nails on the stairs, but instead of him walking on them, it was the friend with the club foot whom he had brought home. Both she and my Father had found this hilarious. From what Mother has said, she and my Father had a similar sense of humour and it would seem that even when the marriage was under a lot of strain, they could find something to laugh about. Mother said that once when my Father complained that she no longer kissed him, she said, "Oh, Cyril, look what kissing's done for me," and counted off all her children one by one. They had both laughed at this, she said.

Occasionally Mother would talk of the Depression years and how they had had to move from one house to the other just to save a few pence on the rent. One time they flitted in the night to avoid paying the rent. For a period they also ended up living in a caravan. Pauline and Pat told us that often chips were the staple of their diet.

It seems that my Father during the Depression was out of work more often than in. The only relief from the government, apart from the dole, was 30/- when each child was born - but not double for twins as my parents found out. However, there was a real community spirit of helping each other and when my Father died, Mother said that for a couple of weeks she received coal free from the men who delivered it - from what I can gather, this is something the coal workers themselves organised to help out widows. In those days some people didn't even own an alarm clock and if anyone didn't have one, they depended on a neighbour who did, to knock them up - and they in turn would knock someone else up. It seems there was a song which went something like this:

> We have a knocker up
> But our knocker up
> Didn't knock us up
> So we couldn't knock up
> Our to knock up (?)

Mother told us about how she and other women would go along the railway tracks, picking up the coal which had fallen off the trucks.

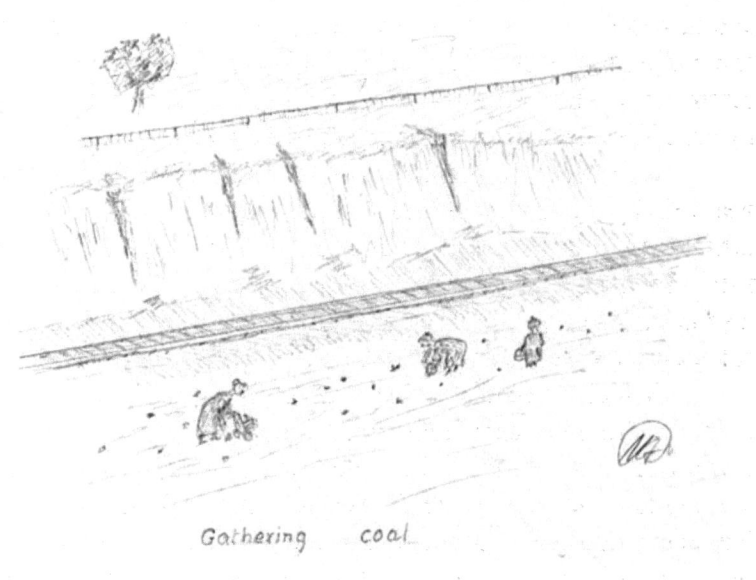

Gathering coal

Mother also said that she and the other women used to raid an orchard and, on one occasion, Mother was caught up in a tree when the farmer arrived, the other women having fled when they saw him.

The Orchard Robbers

Mother couldn't afford a doctor when I was born and I was delivered by a midwife with a friend helping. We were then living in Beeston and our neighbours were mainly miners. My Father, she said, had little time for them, feeling that they remained miners because they didn't have the ambition not to be. Though his father had only been a brickyard labourer, he had seen to it that all his sons had a trade and his two daughters were trained as teachers.

There were moments when I had some insights on the ups and downs of their marriage and had financial circumstances been better, so perhaps might have been their marriage. One of my Father's sayings had been, "When poverty flies in at the window, love flies out the door." Mother said that when my Father was dying, he took her hands into his and said, "You still have beautiful hands, in spite of all the hard work you've had to do."

In recent years I have wondered what it must have been like for him knowing he was dying and leaving his wife to raise 5 children alone and with no money. Mother said that one of the last things my Father said to her before he died was that she was to keep us children together and not separate us. Granny Jackson had wrung her hands in despair when he died, wondering what was going to happen to his children, but Granddad said to her, "You mustn't worry, Alice, they are in good hands." Meaning we would be all right with Mother; which we were.

Very many years later, when Mother was over ninety, she was dozing off when she suddenly woke and said, "Your Father was a good man." On another occasion, a few years before, she told me that after my Father died he appeared to her in a dream and said, "You'll be all right."

Mother was never stumped - she found a solution for everything. An example of this was when she was visiting her parents in Liverpool when the twins were just babes in arms. Ferg, who was seventeen months old when they were born and not walking at that stage, went with her. My Father, who saw her off on the train, was concerned as to how she would manage. "I'll manage," she said. The journey required that she change trains en route. When she reached the station where she had to do so, she got off the train with the twins in her arms and, seeing two women sitting on a bench on the platform, went over to them and placed a twin in each of their arms saying, "Here's one for you and one for you!" The startled ladies laughed delightedly. She was then able to collect Ferg and her luggage from the carriage.

Mother wasn't perfect and in later years, on rare occasions, she could go into a self-pitying mood and speak of her "hard life." We inwardly groaned when this happened. We had to listen then to how she even had to pawn her wedding ring. In those days there were people who would go door to door offering to buy gold - amongst the poverty stricken they could depend on there being someone who was in dire straits, willing to sell what gold they had. Mother then bought herself a cheap ring - a respectable woman with children could not be without a wedding ring. On days of particular martyrdom, Mother would add "But I never earned my daily bread by night."

Mother supplemented her income by making cakes for a few people. Once she tried working as a cleaner at the Royal Infirmary but one day was enough as she had to scrub down their endless miles of tiled walls. When she told them she wouldn't be back, they were understanding and said they didn't think it was the sort of job for her. For a while she looked after the mother of Mrs Naylor, a neighbour, who lived independently of her daughter in a nearby close - Mother cleaned her house and tended to her. During this period I would go there after school and Mother would tell me to go upstairs and say hello to her. She was very, very old and I was a bit scared of her but Mother thought she was sweet - she always had a particular penchant for old people. Mother used to say, "As long as I have these two hands I will be able to earn my living."

The cakes which Mother sold and which were so popular were eccles cakes, maids-of-honour, vanilla slices, and coconut macaroons which Mother shaped by moulding in an egg cup. For vanilla custard slices she made puff pastry - the dough for this had to be rolled so many times in one direction and so many times in another. She was an excellent cook but we could never help ourselves freely of the things she made. If we had visitors and she had baked cakes, we were always spoken to in the scullery beforehand and told what we could have and what we could not have, and that we were to wait until the visitors had gone when we could have what was left over. The visitors would be amazed that we didn't just tuck in but would politely refuse when offered. All we could ever just help ourselves to were things like carrots and turnips which we liked to eat raw, or bread and dripping, or bread and lard. Mother deplored how most women in the road kept the bread on the table which she never did, and she would never allow us to do what the other children did, and that was cut themselves a 'door-step' as they were known (a very thick slice of bread) and eat it outside. Mother insisted that the bread be cut properly and it had to be eaten inside the house. Mother also insisted that there was always a cloth on the table at mealtimes, unlike in quite a few of the houses.

There were times when Mother was not able to pay a bill and on a couple of occasions she told us to duck down so as not to be seen when there was a knock on the door - once someone actually peered through the window to see if we were in. It was probably the rent man. Or it could have been Mr Roberts the insurance man. He rode a motor bike and came every week and always had dolly mixtures in the pocket of his leather jacket which he would distribute to the kiddies in any house he called on. I went off him when I once saw him blow his nose by sliding his fingers down it and shaking the resultant mucus off onto the garden. Mother said my Father hadn't believed in insurance, called them "body-snatchers," but she did. I don't know what sort of policy it was that she carried but she paid something like sixpence a week for it. She told us that when my Father was alive, she had had some sort of endowment policy which paid out after a certain time. She had struggled to keep up the few pence a week this cost, scrimping from her housekeeping money and was annoyed that when it matured, my Father expected to have half of it.

Mother coped valiantly with seven years of widowhood. There was precious little help in those days. Her family had been comfortably off so she hadn't been schooled to a life in which one didn't know where the next penny was coming from. When my Father died it was during the Depression and there wasn't even the money to bury him - his mother had to pay for that. The fact that Mother rose above all that shows her amazing character. Mother never cried - she said she cried all her tears away when Deryk died. Mother once described his last moments. She said the doctor passed his hand in front of Deryk's face, and Deryk's eyes were unseeing. He said, "He's going now" and Mother threw herself across Deryk, saying, "Don't leave me." Hoping in some way to comfort her, the doctor said that had he lived, Deryk would have been blind, but Mother's response was, why did he have to get meningitis in the first place. She said that when he died, she thought she would never stop crying and then one night he appeared to her in a dream and said, "Mum, it is such a lovely place." After that she felt at peace about him. She had a photograph of him taken when he was about eight, on the back of which she had written, 'Till the dawn breaks and the shadows flee away'. That and one of his school exercise books, were two of the few items she kept for the rest of her life.

It is hard to imagine what it must have been like for her, visiting my Father in the Sanatorium and not able to tell him that Deryk was sick. He wondered why he wasn't coming to see him and she would have to make up some excuse. When Deryk died, Mother asked the nurse to tell my Father. She said he cried like a baby and she would hear him calling out to Deryk in the night. There had been a very strong bond between them - Deryk would meet my Father every evening when he left work and when it was pay day, the men would sometimes put a halfpenny or so in a wage envelope for him. Mother once left my Father but didn't take either Deryk or

Pauline with her as they were so attached to him. I gather this was before I was even born. The separation didn't last, people had to stay in marriages in those days, there not being enough money to run two homes.

Many, many years later, when we were all grown up and had families of our own, Mother returned to Nottingham and wanted to visit Deryk's grave. As it was unmarked by any headstone, she did not know how she was going to find it. Then a woman walking towards her said, "Mrs Jackson." She was the wife of the minister who had performed his funeral service and she was able to take Mother to where the church records were so she was able to locate his grave. Mother said that as she stood by Deryk's grave, she thought how strange life was, one of her children was lying there and the rest of her family were scattered.

My memories of Mother when I was a young child are very warm. Amongst my earliest memories is the time we were at the pictures and it was an MGM film which always had a roaring lion in cameo at the head of its introduction. The lion appears to wink after he has roared and Mother would say to me, "He's winking at you." I was not aware then, of course, that this was MGM's introduction and after that I always looked for the lion winking. Once when Mother and I were at the pictures, she sent me out for something or other, perhaps an ice-cream. When I came back I couldn't find her and walked up and down the aisle sobbing until Mother managed to attract my attention from out of the darkness.

Another very early memory is also about a time when I thought I had lost her. We were catching a tram and Mother had put me on the step when the tram started to move off without her. I bellowed in terror - the tram stopped, and she got on. Mother said that when we all went out, I never left her side. I had a recurring dream as a child in which Mother was being beaten and I would put myself between her and the attacker. I have no idea who the attacker was.

Mother was very patient with us young children. I can recall when out shopping with her and she had moved on ahead, I would refuse to move until she came back for me. On those occasions, having been obliged to do so, she would say, "I'll give you what for, young lady." That was as far as it went when she was exasperated. Other times she might address me as "madam," but it was a rare occasion when she actually smacked us, and then it was more of a 'go-along'. She never disciplined us when she was really furious with us, but would say grimly, "Get out of my sight." We knew then, we had better do so. She used to say that a child should never be hit when a parent was really angry as it might receive an 'unlucky' blow, as she called it. Along with being called "young lady" or "madam," if Mother was displeased with one of us girls (I don't know if she had a term for Ferg) she would also say if she thought we were being 'hoity-toity', "Who are you when you are not at home?" She was very good at taking a joke against herself. When we were laughing at some idiosyncrasy of hers or when we were looking at photographs of her when she was young, she would respond good-naturedly, "You'll be struck comical yourself one day." One of the things Kath and I teased her about in later years was what she used to say to us when we were children, "From now on I'm going to look after No.1." We would remind Mother of this and say, "What number are you now, Mother? Five, six, seven, eight?" She always took it in good part, laughing as much as we did.

Mother never disciplined us in company, believing that a child shouldn't be humiliated. When she herself was a child, her own mother had slapped her across the face in front of one of her friends and she never forgot it (her misdemeanour had been speaking sloppily, saying something like "I wanna"). Also her mother would force them to eat whatever she had put in front of them, even when they 'gagged', which is why Mother would never force us to eat what we didn't want.

Another thing that Mother told us of her own childhood was that her mother would send her to the bakers for bread and she had to ask for "A fresh, oven bottom loaf, with a dent in the middle, not crusty but smooth on the top." Sometimes she was sent with their own dough to have it baked. Their Grandmother Houston lived with them and Mother talked more of her than she did of her own mother, it was obvious she was very close to her. She said that if she went to her grandmother for sympathy when she had been disciplined by her mother, her grandmother would comfort her but would also say, "Your mother has a lot of work to do so we must try and understand." Her grandmother believed a little dab of whisky on the scalp was very good for the hair and she would sometimes put a dab on Mother's head. Mother's sister, Georgie, told me in later years that her grandmother would sometimes get her to go to the Public House for threepence worth of whisky. Auntie Georgie was very prudish and was strict temperance all her life but she said that she would do that for Grandmother Houston but no-one else. She, too, loved her. Mother said that her Grandmother Houston would sometimes go over to the chiffonier whilst she was with her and would take a drink of something. When Mother asked her what it was, she would reply "It is 'Bite the meddler' my dear". Mother when she got older, realised of course that she was having a drink of whisky.

Mother was fourteen when her grandmother died. Knowing how close she was to her, I once asked her how she had felt at her grandmother's funeral and she said, "I didn't go to her funeral, I was raised strict Presbyterian and ladies didn't go to funerals." When Mother spoke of her Grandmother Houston, she invariably added, "She was eighty-eight when she died and still had all her faculties."

Mother used to talk of 'Cabbage Hall', just a name to me and I can't remember in what context. Granny and Granddad were living at 100 Stanfield Road, Everton, when Mother was born. They seemed to move around quite a bit, she also mentioned Lother Road, but it was Cathedral Road, Anfield, Mother mainly reminisced about. She would have been a teenager when she lived there. Also her mother's brother, Dave (known to us as Old Uncle Dave), lived opposite them for a while in Cathedral Road and he was Mother's favourite relative.

As a child Mother went to Anfield Road School which cost her parents one shilling per week. Mother said that the child who sat next to her was Bessie Braddock, later to become a well known member of the British Parliament. It must have been a school with a very high standard because Mother was well educated and her knowledge of poetry and history, in particular, was extensive. She was an excellent speller and put this down to the fact that at school they had Spelling Bees. She said that she didn't learn as much as she might have done because the discipline at home was so strict that when she was at school, all she wanted to do was play.

When she was growing up, Mother and her siblings had to sit upright in their chairs, not lolling against the back. Mother had erect posture to the end of her days. They were also never permitted to be idle and had always to be doing something, for the girls this meant some sort of handicraft. Her mother was a great believer in the fact that "Satan finds work for idle hands to do." This was a lesson well learnt by Mother who was always busy doing something. Mother also never raised her voice or spoke incorrectly, her parents being sticklers about this. When she was a teenager and was going out, she had to appear before her father to see that the neck of the dress wasn't too low and the hem of the dress wasn't too high. She said that the minute she was out of the house, the neck was pulled down and the hem was pulled up.

After she left school, Mother had a variety of jobs. One was in the office of a yeast factory and she said she would bring slabs of yeast home and the family would nibble on them. She also worked in the showrooms of Frisby Dyke's, this on a commission basis. Another job was as a governess to a little girl called Pauline, the name she would one day choose for her first born daughter.

* * * * * * * * * * *

CHAPTER FOUR

Kath was one of twins, her twin sister, Maureen, having died aged thirteen months of enteritis on 19th October 1929. Kath had also been seriously ill with it and the doctor told Mother that she too would die, but Kath began to get better after Maureen died. Mother always said that Maureen left her strength behind for Kath.

My Father was buried on Kath's birthday, September 17th. It's odd, that on her birthday something always seemed to happen so that she couldn't have a party, and I suppose that year she missed out on her fourth. I missed out too in a way because, though my brother Ferg was three years older than me, our birth dates were within three days of each other and so our birthdays were always celebrated together. One birthday Mother's friend, Mrs Burns, gave me a threepenny box of Milk Tray chocolates and I was overjoyed until she said that I had to share it with my brother.

Like most siblings we each felt that our positions in the family put us at a disadvantage. Ferg and Kath felt that, as the middle children, no notice was taken of them, whereas I, as the youngest, received all the attention. I thought otherwise, feeling that as the youngest I had no say at all. Ferg, having two sisters older and two sisters younger, probably had reason to complain.

We all had a name that came from an older generation, Ferg, Pauline and I had two. Pauline, born 31st May 1920, was Margaret Pauline Ida; Margaret and Ida were, respectively, Mother and Father's eldest sisters. Pat, born 8th February 1922, was Marion Patricia, Marion after Mother. Deryk, born 22nd October 1923, was Deryk Elliott, Elliott being Mother's maiden name. Ferg, born 17th April 1927, was Cyril Ferguson, Cyril being after my Father and Ferguson was a name which had come down through a number of generations from when the first Ferguson had migrated from Scotland to Ireland. The twins, Kathleen Mary and Maureen Alicia, born 17th September 1928, were called after the two grandmothers; Mary, Kath's second name, after Granny Elliott, and Alicia, Maureen's second name, after Granny Jackson. Granny Jackson was actually called Alice but Mother didn't like that so changed it to Alicia. I, born 14th April 1930, was Lena Jean, Lena being Granny Jackson's sister who was actually called Milena and what Mother intended but my Father registered me as Lena, a name Mother disliked so much she made sure I was never called it. In later years she was still telling me to get it changed. Jean was after Mother's sister. Of the surviving siblings, only Kath was known by her first name.

    Pauline and Pat called Kath 'Petal' because she was very dainty and had exquisitely soft skin. I was known by them as 'Yennie'. Mother called me 'Jane' more often than she called me Jean. She sometimes called Pauline 'Tawdy' and Pat 'Our Little Dats'. Ferg often called me 'sparrow-legs' because my legs were so thin. Ferg didn't have a nickname, though at school he was known by some of his classmates as 'Jacko' and by others as 'The Judge'. Mother said that my Father's pet name for me was 'Ruby' because I had ruby-red lips. Pat called Mother, 'Ma-ma', Pauline said 'Mother' and Ferg, Kath and I referred to her as 'Mum'.

    We were quite different in looks, Kath was the only one with brown eyes, Pauline and Ferg had blue, Pat hazel, and myself, grey. Pauline, Ferg and I were tall, Pat medium height and, until she caught up in her teen years, Kath was very short. Pauline, Ferg and Pat were dark haired while Kath and I were fair haired. Ferg was the only one of us who was left-handed. Mother was fair haired with blue eyes, whilst my Father had been dark haired with hazel eyes, so their offspring were a variety of this combination. Mother was about 5' 4" and my Father 6' - this also expressed itself in the varying heights of their children.

Pauline, Kath and I were Monday's children, Pat was Wednesday's child, Ferg was Sunday's and Mother, Saturday's; Mother felt this very aptly summed up her role in life. ("Monday's child is fair of face; Tuesday's child is full of grace; Wednesday's child is full of woe; Thursday's child has far to go; Friday's child is loving and willing; Saturday's child works hard for its living; but the child who is born on the Sabbath Day is Bonnie, Blithe, Good and Gay"). Ferg was actually born on Easter Sunday and Mother told us that she had found him in an Easter egg.

We likened ourselves to the characters in Louisa M. Alcott's, 'Little Women'. Pauline was Meg, Kath was Beth and they couldn't make up their minds whether I was Amy or Jo. The latter because she was a tomboy and the former because, like Amy, I liked to use big words but didn't always know what they meant or how to spell them.

Pauline did a lot of things for us, made our clothes, took us out and generally took an interest in us. However, she was a strict disciplinarian and very domineering. Despite the complex relationship she had with Mother, she must have been a great support to her when we younger ones were growing up. She was highly intelligent, very capable and mature and never ducked a difficult situation - or confrontation! In fact, one could say, she was a 'confronting' sort of person. She was also very liberated and not in the least modest. If she were having a bath she would sometimes take me in with her. To undeveloped me this was embarrassing and I didn't know which way to look.

When Kath and I were small and were walking along the road with Pauline she would play 'Windy Weather' with us. She would hold each of us by our hand on either side of her and as we walked along she would sing "Windy weather, frosty weather, When the wind blows, we all blow together," and on "blow together" she would swing us at each other.

It was Pauline who brought Snowball home from Queen Mary High School one day. She told me to go and fetch the box which was in the basket on her bicycle. And there was Snowball. I loved cats to distraction. I used to steal cats. I would bring a cat home and Mother would tell me that I had to go and give it back, at which I would protest that they didn't want it because it was just sitting outside. Pauline then decided I had better have a cat.

The Cat Burglar

I would dress Snowball up in dolls' clothes and he would lie placidly in my dolls' pram. Mother said she had never known a cat who would allow that to be done to it. But one day I took him to show my friend, Blanche Andrews, and their dog Spike leapt at Snowball who shot from the pram. I quickly picked him up and in his terror he scratched me down the side of my face. I took him home for Mother to tend to him, but Mother was more concerned about my face, so I protested that she had to look after Snowball first. Sometimes Mother put camphorated oil on our chests if we had a cold and Snowball would lick my singlet where the camphorated oil had soaked through. I would sit for hours, never moving, not wanting to disturb Snowball if he were on my lap.

SnowBall

Mother housetrained Snowball by rubbing his nose in it when he dirtied in the house and then putting him out in the garden so that he would understand where he was to go. I didn't like this at all. I also used to protest vehemently when Mother held him by the loose skin on the back of the neck and she would say that that was how the cat's mother carries her kittens.

Kath didn't like cats, didn't even like the feel of them, and first thing in the morning when Snowball would be in a frisky mood, I had to enter the room before she did and get hold of him as she was scared he would grab at her feet. She had a memory of when she had been very young, waking up to find a cat lying across her face.

Later, when Snowball became very ill and kept getting worse, Mother decided to have him put down and called on Mr Hemming, a neighbour, to do it. Mr Hemming came and filled Mother's washtub with water and then put Snowball in to drown. Mother had tried to prepare me by saying that Snowball had looked up at her that morning begging to be put out of his misery. It was hard to believe because I could hear Snowball leaping up at the lid put on the washtub to stop him jumping out. There was no such thing in those days of being able to take an animal to a vet to be put down. Much later, when Smuts, another cat we had (all black this time) got sick a van came and took him away.

Kath was very shy and when visitors came would hide under the table, whereas I would entertain them if Mother happened to be out, offering to get them tea. Mother told me in later years that the visitors were charmed by the way I would sit talking to them in an adult fashion. Kath would sometimes say, "No-one knows what I am thinking." (A secret wish we both shared was that Mother would take us aside one day and tell us we were adopted!). At times Kath would wistfully regret that she hadn't been born a boy. She had a lot of talents, was excellent at English and liked organising plays. She also had a melodious singing voice and it is a pity that her shyness might have prevented her from fulfilling that talent. If Pauline and Pat wanted to save their money, they gave it to Kath to mind as they knew that no amount of beseeching on their behalf would soften her to hand it back before the time agreed at the start - she was very strong-willed. She was also very responsible and was therefore the one chosen to mind the front door key if she, Ferg and I were out together.

Though Kath was shy, she was very brave when it came to things like having loose milk teeth pulled or having injections, whereas I would have to be bribed before I would allow either. On one occasion we were both leaning over the fender when a lump of coal exploded, a piece striking Kath on the face and another piece striking me on the neck. I squawked so loudly that everyone came running to me, whereas Kath had to remove the piece from her cheek by herself. Kath also kept much fitter than Ferg and I. Whereas we went through the usual routine of measles and chicken-pox, Kath remained immune. However, she did have to have her tonsils out. Before she did so, she had a slight stutter but afterwards this disappeared. I don't know why the memory persists, but when I went with Mother to collect her after the operation to bring her home, I seem to recall it was to St George's Hall we went and she was waiting there for us in a red dressing gown.

I even had whooping cough when I was six weeks old and, later, scarlet fever. When we had measles and chicken-pox, Kath slept with us hoping she would get them so she could stay off school too, but to no avail. Ferg also had chronic bronchitis. Mother regularly applied camphorated oil to his chest, over which she placed a flannel pad. If he had a particularly bad bout, she would give him a mustard bath. She told of the time that he was so sick that he wasn't able to go to school and she had arranged to go with Old Uncle Dave on one of his charabanc trips for the poor in the parish in which he worked. She decided to go anyway and took Ferg with her, adopting the attitude 'Kill or Cure'. Later, when she related this tale to others she would say that it did Ferg the world of good. But Ferg was a very stoical person and never complained, no matter what. Pauline and Pat had diphtheria when they were young and were admitted to Fazakerley Hospital. For a short while I suffered from occasional bouts of aching legs which I was told were growing pains.

Despite the fact that we three younger ones had no say at all in the running of the household, it was Ferg, being the only male in the house, who was called upon to do all the jobs that Mother believed men should do - such as minor household repairs, lifting heavy things and digging the garden, etc. Mother had strict demarcation guidelines when it came to women and men's household tasks - she didn't believe that men should do things like washing dishes, cooking and making beds, etc., and by the same token, she felt that women shouldn't lift heavy things or dig the garden and do household repairs not needing a tradesman - those were men's jobs. In this she was at odds with her mother-in-law who, being country-raised, could put her hand to anything. Once when Mother was staying with her and a heavy suitcase needed lifting, Mother said, "We'll wait for Cyril to do that." "Why?" said Granny Jackson, "We can do it ourselves." Mother was also at odds with Pauline who didn't see why men shouldn't help with domestic work and, like Granny, was quite capable of supposedly male-only work. Mother was caught between two generations for different reasons. As for us disenfranchised three younger ones, we just lived with what the Titans decided.

Ferg was very good at making things and looked for every opportunity to do so, particularly for us three younger ones. Where Ferg found the materials for these enterprises, I don't know, but he was always resourceful. Some of the things he made had startling results, such as the gun which shattered the light. It was a gun without bullets, of course, and I don't really know how it worked except that the projectile which he fired from it hit the lamp above the kitchen table and smashed it. He once used a bunsen burner in the scullery and scorched the bottom shelf. One of the few times I remember Mother being angry at an escapade of ours.

On one occasion when it had been raining so heavily that the gutters became blocked, the road was flooded to kerb height, which we, along with all the other kids in the road, thought was marvellous. Ferg made a raft of sorts and though the water wasn't deep enough for it to float, we used the oars to propel ourselves to the other side.

During one winter when it snowed and was very cold, someone cut down trees in the woods and gave firewood to anyone who went there. This news spread like wildfire. Ferg, Kath and I went and took a sledge which Ferg had made. I was wearing a little white fur tippet, I don't know how I came to have it but I treasured it. I lost my tippet somewhere either going or returning and we tried looking for it but couldn't find it because it was white like the snow. We piled the sledge with firewood and brought it home but the whole episode was spoiled because I'd lost my fur tippet.

Then there was the two-storey structure Ferg built inside the posts of the swing, but the upper floor was so perilous that it wasn't safe for anyone to be downstairs if someone was moving around upstairs. Once I was upstairs when Ferg and his best friend, Eric, came in down below, unaware of my presence. Keeping perfectly still, I heard some illuminating 'boy talk'.

For a brief period Ferg kept rabbits, building a hutch for them at the bottom of the garden. One of the rabbits, a chinchilla, was so savage that if our fingers came too near when feeding it, we got a sharp bite. We thought we would share this task and invited Freddie Davies who lived next door and was about my age, to feed the rabbits - he was delighted to do so until he got bitten for his pains.

The Cat and the Chicken

At one stage Ferg wanted to keep a rat but Mother put her foot down. However, the chicken that he got from somewhere was welcomed by all. It was only a few days old and Ferg kept it in the backyard in a cage he had made. One day the Davies' cat managed to open the door of this cage, the chicken escaped and the cat then stalked it. I saw this and came to the rescue with a big stick, bringing it down with a great swoosh on what I thought was the cat, but it turned out that it was the chicken which I killed in one fell swoop. I wasn't allowed to forget it and was called chicken-killer for some time after that.

Ferg played tricks, particularly on me. On one occasion he called to me from the bottom of the garden. When I went towards him I fell down a hole which had been covered in such a way that I didn't know it was there.

The Booby Trap

We three younger children were very high-spirited. One of the things we did was let our friends into the house when Mother went out. When we were older she would sometimes lock us out of the house, but Ferg would hide in the copper or the washtub and then, when she had gone, open the door and let us in, including the neighbourhood kids. If he were forestalled and not able to do that, we would sometimes climb in through the bathroom window. This required a contortionist act as only the top pane opened and you had to go in head first. We would keep an eye out at the time we expected Mother to return and when we saw her in the distance, would shoo everyone out and would be innocently waiting for her in the road. Once, when we had a group of children in, we were playing a riotous game of chasey through the house and one child pushed the back door closed to stop another catching him. The pursuer couldn't stop in time and his fist went through the glass pane half-way up the door. We hoped Mother wouldn't notice as it had a lace curtain over it. Mother, later, shut the door by just pushing on what she thought was the pane but it was all jagged under there and she gave her hand a nasty gash. She told a neighbour, "I lost a pint of blood", and I had an image of her catching the blood in an empty pint milk bottle (our milk was always delivered by the pint and in bottles). Mother wasn't a bit mad with us, just said that we should have told her. Another time we made some pastry - what we thought of as pastry anyway, it was just flour mixed with water - when Mother came home unexpectedly. In our panic we threw it out of the back-door and onto the cat which happened to be sitting there. Mother never got too excited on these occasions.

Mother was like that, she never told us off for anything we had done, but only if she were in a bad mood. I have to say that this was not often - she really was very tolerant and we must have driven her patience to the limit many times. We never came in when called of an evening if we were out in the road playing with the other children - she would have to call half a dozen times and then, when we decided to come in, she would wait the other side of the door to give us a go-along, but we were very quick and merely received a flick across our bottoms. Mother never raised her voice but always spoke in a lady-like manner. She would try at times to be really angry but it never worked.

If Mother was going out of an evening and wanted to leave before our usual bedtime, she would move the clock forward. We would be mystified why it was still light when we were sent to bed and it wasn't until many years later that we found out the reason. Kath, Ferg and I got up to all sorts of things after we had gone to bed and when Mother went out, we made hay. We did things like rowing around the room on the eiderdown - once we broke off the towel rails on the washstand and used them as oars. We had pillow fights, and would nibble at the pink block of Gibbs toothpaste or the candles, something you could do then without fear of poisoning yourself. We would bring the brush (our name for the long-handled broom, the short-handled one being known as 'hand-brush') upstairs and use it to put the light on and off from our bed, we did this so vigorously that the switch would sometimes go on or off if anyone walked near it. Eileen Finnegan lived on the other side of us and was about a year or two younger than I. Her bedroom was next to ours and we would pass things to her by tying them on a rope which we strung between the two bedrooms. Once Ferg made a tube with a funnel-like mouthpiece at each end and we spoke to Eileen down it. Sometimes we would also go downstairs and raid the larder - not that there was ever much to raid.

At one stage, after we'd gone to bed, we went through a period of taking it in turns to tell stories - these stories were so long that sometimes they would extend over a few nights. I never knew what to do with my characters when I wanted to end my story, so always had them die off one by one. We thought that the last thing we had to do after saying our prayers and before we went to sleep, was say to each other, "Goodnight, God Bless," so if we wanted to talk after that we went through the ritual of saying, "If we go to sleep, we go to sleep; if we don't go to sleep, we don't go to sleep. If we talk, we talk; if we don't talk, we don't talk." And then we could say, "Goodnight, God Bless," to each other and go on talking after that, falling asleep when we wanted to.

If Mother brought us a piece of fruit, or some such thing when we were in bed, she always cautioned us not to eat it when we were lying down. We couldn't understand why not, and the minute she left the room, would lie down to eat whatever she had given us.

Kath, when she was very young, went through the stage of shoving paper up her nostrils, once having to be taken to the doctor to have a piece removed. Also as an infant her arm had been pulled out of its socket by a child pulling her along too vigorously and again had to go to the doctor who gave her a sound punch on the shoulder to push it back in. Mother was always fearful after that if someone pulled us along too vigorously by our arms. On rare occasions Kath would sleepwalk. One night Mother woke to find Kath standing on the sill in her bedroom, the window wide open. She was able to gently lead her back to bed. Another time Kath took the eiderdown off our bed and took it downstairs. I woke up complaining that I was cold and then it was discovered what had happened. Sometimes Kath would also talk in her sleep.

On many mornings we would get into Mother's bed and she would tell us stories, or recite a poem or sing a song to us. They were never the familiar nursery rhymes or fairy-tales, but dramatic poetry and heart-rending stories which brought Kath and me to tears. There was the one of the poor little girl who was always being told she was in the way. One day she was dying and was told that she would be going to heaven. She asked sadly, "Will I be in the way there too?"

She told Pauline and Pat these same stories when they were small. It was always the same repertoire but we could never get enough of stories like 'The Little Match Girl' and 'Little Nellie'. In these the children were always desperately poor. Little Nellie and her brother were orphans and had no home; one day Little Nellie became very ill and was dying and her brother, who had never prayed before but had heard about God, prayed to him in desperation saying, "If you were me and I were you, I wouldn't take your Little Nellie off you."

Amongst the poems she recited, she knew them all off by heart, were 'Lord Ullin's Daughter' by Thomas Campbell, 'The Wreck of the Hesperus' by Henry Wadsworth Longfellow and 'The Inchcape Rock' by Robert Southey. Mother could really get the drama into these. One of our favourite poems - she sang this one - was 'The Golden Vanity'. (See at end of 'Twilight and Wallflowers' for all these poems).

Another she sang to us, but only at Christmastime, was 'The Little Boy that Santa Claus Forgot'.

Mother was superb at recitation and had a number of party pieces. One of them was a parody of the 23rd Psalm which went something like this:

> The Ford is my car,
> I shall not want another,
> It maketh me to lie down in wet places,
> It leadeth me into deep waters,
> It annointeth my head with oil,
> It's tank runneth over,
> Surely if this car follows me all the days of my life,
> I shall dwell in the house of the insane forever.

And the 'Irish Landlady':

> You three are a fine pair if ever there was one,

You didn't get home last night till early morning,
If you want to stop here and do that,
You'd better pack up and leave at once.

There were others, one a very clever riddle piece, but I've forgotten it now. Mother was also fond of witticisms like - "All the world's queer except thee and me, and even thee's a little odd." She had her standard jokes, "Look over there," she would say, "There's a man with two hands in front and one behind." Or, "What odd legs that person has, the bottom is at the top."

One of the poems Mother recited was Solomon Grundy, which went like this:

Solomon Grundy born on Monday,
Christened on Tuesday,
Married on Wednesday,
Very ill on Thursday,
Worse on Friday,
Died on Saturday,
Buried on Sunday,
That was the end of Solomon Grundy.

* * * * * * * * * *

CHAPTER FIVE

Even though Mother was a superb cook she had trouble getting Kath, Ferg and me to eat as we were picky eaters. In an effort to get us to eat she would sometimes tell us the tale of Augustus:

> Augustus was a chubby lad,
> Fat ruddy cheeks Augustus had,
> And everybody saw with joy,
> The plump and hearty healthy boy,
> Who ate and drank as he was told,
> And never let his soup grow cold.
> But one day,
> One cold winter's day,
> He screamed out,
> "Take the nasty soup away,
> I won't have any soup today."
> The third day came,
> Oh! what a sin,
> To let himself grow pale and thin.
> Yet when the soup is put on table,
> He screams as loud as he is able,
> "Take the nasty soup away,
> I won't have any soup today."
> The fourth day comes,
> He scarcely weighs a sugar plum,
> And on the fifth day,
> He was Dead!

Most of the times she would just take our uneaten food away, but every now and again she would become exasperated and say, "You are going to eat that" - one time endeavouring to reinforce this by putting a ruler on the table. It never worked. She would then say, "All right then, you'll eat it for tea," and would put it in the larder to bring it out at tea-time, with the same result. Mother had to also contend with the fact that Ferg, Kath and I had different dislikes. Kath couldn't bear to have any fat on her meat at all, whereas Ferg and I liked it. Kath liked her meat cooked to a crisp, Ferg liked his just right and I liked mine rare. I loved the juices which poured from still-rare cooked beef and would sneak into the larder and drink them straight from the meat dish. Ferg liked bread-pudding, Kath and I didn't. I liked mustard, Ferg was indifferent to it and Kath couldn't even stand the mustard pot in front of her.

We all liked 'dip' however, this was a favourite with us. Dip was simply heated up fat, whether dripping or lard. We would pour some on our plate and dip our bread in piece by piece. Kath and I were fond of drinking vinegar and if sent to the shops to buy some, would sip it on the way home. Kath drank it to the degree that her lips would temporarily turn white.

We three younger ones loved dried peas which had been soaked overnight and then, when they were cooked, were nice and mushy. We also loved dried haricot beans which were soaked overnight in the same way. When we had fresh peas we liked to shell them and eat the pods when they were young and succulent. We would eat cooked carrots and turnips only if they were mashed together, though we liked both of them when they were raw. We also liked raw cabbage even though we were told by Auntie Lizzie, Old Uncle Dave's housekeeper, Mrs Wade, that we would go mad if we ate it.

For breakfast we would accept a small serve of oatmeal porridge but with sugar only and no milk. We also wouldn't have milk on our cornflakes, only tea. We didn't like milk or cheese. Mother sometimes made Welsh rarebit; we didn't like that at all. We liked dripping on bread, lard on bread, condensed milk on bread, sugar on bread, treacle on bread, and banana on bread. We probably would have preferred to eat our banana 'as is' but Mother would say we had to eat some bread with it, so we would peel the banana long-ways, just removing one strip and then scrape our knives along and put it on the bread. Our bread was always sliced by standing it on end and then cutting it cross-wise. Many years later, Maurice, my husband, was taken aback to see this, thinking that the danger of slicing oneself instead was very high, but we must have had the knack for I don't remember this ever happening.

Buttered bread was always referred to as a 'buttie' and we particularly liked chip butties, but we were only allowed to put our chips on bread when we were at home and there were no visitors. Also dunking a biscuit in tea was only permitted in the privacy of the home.

Some of the desserts we had were blancmange, always set in a pottery mould shaped like a rabbit and we liked to get either the tail or ears when it was served. We also had tapioca, rice pudding and semolina (which we called ground rice). We liked semolina and would sweeten it with jam; the jam Mother bought had a gollywog sticker on the lid. We tolerated tapioca but called it 'frog spawn'. As for rice pudding, Ferg liked it but Kath and I were not struck, though all three of us liked the thick brown skin on top. Sometimes we had custard with dates in. Mother made beautiful pies, mainly apple, but occasionally plum. When she baked a plum pie she always put a china egg-cup upside down in the centre. An added pleasure when we had plums was lining up the stones on the rim of the dish and counting out "Tinker, Tailor, Soldier, Sailor, Rich Man, Poor Man, Beggarman, Thief." In the case of Kath and me it was a foretelling of who we would one day marry, in the case of Ferg, it was what he was going to become. Pies were usually served with custard and occasionally with evaporated milk, never cream. Other tarts she baked were egg custard, which she sprinkled with nutmeg, and lemon-curd tarts, always making the lemon-curd herself. If she made jam, it was always with plums. She would put a coin in the bottom of the pan whilst it was cooking, to prevent the jam from 'catching' - that is, sticking to the base. Trifle was for special occasions only, though we might sometimes have jelly with custard. The gelatine for making the jelly came in flavoured cubes, six to a block. How we would have liked just to have had one of these cubes just to eat by itself. On rare occasions Mother would try to get us to eat 'pobs', pieces of bread in warm milk and sprinkled with sugar. We were not interested.

We often had 'scouse', which we liked very much, though would pick out the pieces of onion in it and line the rim of our plate. It is interesting that many years later when I went with Maurice to Norway, we had lap-scouse at a restaurant. It showed the Nordic connection to Britain. Also there was the ginger wine Mother made at Christmas. Maurice and I were served ginger wine by friends in Sweden during one Christmas season we spent there, it was just like that which Mother made and they too had a tradition of serving it at Christmas.

Mother's Scotch broths were much less popular, though Ferg liked the dumplings she put in them, Kath and I wouldn't touch them. We also didn't like the barley in the broth and would pick it out to join the onion on the rim of the plate. Mother's Scotch/Irish background was very evident in her potato cakes and soda scones, both of which we loved. Mother cooked the latter on the top of the stove on a large black iron griddle. We always had a roast on Sunday and if it was beef, we would have Yorkshire pudding with it, and if it was lamb, we would have mint sauce. Only on rare occasions did we have chicken and then we all wanted to have the wishbone. The chicken was always served with sage and onion stuffing. Occasionally, as a special treat on a Sunday, we would have a large bottle of sarsaparilla between the three of us and Mother would have a glass of Guinness. We would be sent off to Bloomers to buy the sarsaparilla.

Bloomers was mainly a sweet shop which also sold soft drinks. I once went in there with the unheard of fortune of twopence and asked for Rowntrees fruit pastilles because behind the counter on the wall there was this enormous tube of them. The assistant handed me a normal size tube and I said, "No, I want that one," pointing to the one on the wall. Of course she told me that that was not real.

Near to Bloomers was Dougherty's which also sold sweets. Dougherty's was an ancient shop that you stepped down into and there was a little bell poised above the door which tinkled when you entered. It must have been one of the original buildings in the whole area and pre-dated the whole development of corporation rental housing. The couple who owned the shop were just as ancient.

The Co-op was also near there - it sold every sort of grocery and was clinical looking, white tiles everywhere, not very interesting to go into. Every customer had a number and when buying anything, gave this number, receiving points according to the amount of the purchase. A slip recording this was then given. These points could be used as cash to purchase something at their department store downtown, the number of points, of course, dictating what we could buy. Mother once had accumulated enough to get me a grey, woollen coat with high, built-up shoulder pads, in fashion at that time, with a tie belt, and red and blue inserts on each lapel. I can still reel off our Co-op number to this day.

These shops were around the corner from our main shopping centre, a crescent row of shops, amongst which was Bertie's that sold bread and cakes as well as sweets. We only rarely received any money but when we did, we loved to buy the 'wet nellies' which Bertie's sold; a lovely soggy concoction of dried fruits between two wedges of pastry which had pink icing. Mother referred to wet nellies as rubbish. Rubbish, in her eyes, was also the toffee that an Indian hawker, who wore a turban, peddled on very rare occasions down our road - we were forbidden to buy it but still did so if we happened to have any money, which was seldom, and if Mother wasn't looking, which was often. We would look at the hawker warily though as we never saw anyone foreign in our road.

Berties also sold sticky lice, as did all the sweet shops, and sherbet which we sucked out of the corner of a triangular-shaped packet through a hollow liquorice straw. We particularly liked both of those. Then there were gob-stoppers, lollipops, very hard liquorice sticks shaped like a paddle and which you had to suck, and Pontefract cakes which were also liquorice but were soft and round. We could also buy sweets shaped to look like cigarettes and kali lumps which were chunky. When we bought aniseed balls we would say as we sucked them:

Yum, Yum, Pig's Bum,
Aniseed Balls and Chewing Gum.

We bought lemonade powder, though didn't make it up into a drink but had it straight, licking it out of the packet. If we bought chewing gum, we shared it around, all having a chew. I thought Aero chocolate was marvellous, but it was too expensive to buy so I only ever had a piece if an adult had a bar of it. Another item out of our price range was the small, threepenny box of Milk Tray chocolates. One year Ferg, Kath and I pooled our resources and bought Mother one for her birthday. One of my dreams as a child was that one day I would look after Mother and would sit her in the garden giving her all the chocolates she could eat. Ferg also had his dreams for Mother and would say to her in those struggling days, "Never mind, when I grow up I'll bring you in £5 per week." "I'm sure," Mother would reply, "Five pounds of potatoes."

Mother, as was common with women then, had one of those envelope-style change purses, which opened out like a fan to reveal a number of sections, each being held together by a small metal clip. I promised myself one of those when I grew up. Mother always carefully checked her change. Apparently Ida, my Father's sister, didn't, saying, "When it's gone, it's gone," but Mother could not afford to say that. When Mother emptied the tea into the caddy she opened out the packet to make sure she got every leaf; the same with the packet of sugar, it was opened out so as not to miss a grain and the butter or lard wrappings were scraped clean. Every penny, leaf, grain and morsel of fat counted in our house. If we were given a bad egg by the shop, Mother returned it in a bowl to show them and either got her money back or a fresh egg.

The comics available were 'Beano', 'Dandy' and 'Film Fun'. One girl in our class received one shilling a week pocket money, unheard of wealth to me, and she would take me with her on a Friday to watch her spend it. She would buy a couple of comics and the rest she spent on sweets which she ate in front of me, never ever giving me one. Once, when I went to walk back to school with her after lunch, her mother asked me what I had had for lunch. I had actually only had bread and dripping as Mother had been out and her brother

John had come and, seeing lunch laid out and not realising it was for us, ate it, so we had had to resort to bread and dripping. I told her this and she said to her daughter, offering her some food, "Here you are, darling, you eat up - I wouldn't want people to think that you would only have bread and dripping for lunch." We children 'swopped' whatever comics we had with other children so you got to read a lot more than you could afford to buy. Of the many characters in the comics, one of my favourites was Billy Bunter, I think because he was invariably depicted in front of delectable food - iced cakes with a cherry on top for instance - which I would have loved to have had.

Lunt's was a white-walled, tile-lined shop with stone slab counter tops and the assistants were clinically dressed in white. They sold bread, including Sally Lunns and Hovis, eggs, cheese and butter, the latter coming in a large block from which the assistant would deftly take off a wedge and pat it into shape with a flat wooden paddle in either hand. I liked going in there just to watch them do this. The cheese also came in blocks and the assistant used a razor sharp wire to slice it. There was a hand-operated cold meat slicer for slicing the bacon and ham. They also sold black puddings, ham knuckles and brawn (Mother never bought this). For some reason or other, they also sold slab chocolate.

Then there were the two vegetable shops, Waterworth's and Atkinson's. They sold every sort of local fruit and vegetables and different types of potatoes. Mother always wanted King Edwards. They kept these different types of potatoes in large bins which were the full height of the wall at one end of the shop and would replenish the bins by emptying the sacks in at the top end, the potatoes feeding into a tray at the bottom. The bananas we bought had the brand name Fyffe printed in white on a crescent-shaped bright blue label which was stuck onto each hand of bananas. We children always took off the tip at each end of our banana as we felt we would catch leprosy from them if we didn't. To this day, I still nip off the ends of my banana - no longer afraid of leprosy but can't bring myself not to. It's like the 'crossed knives' superstition that supposedly foretells a death. I know it is ridiculous, but I don't like to see crossed knives and have to resist the temptation to un-cross them, not always successfully. I don't have the same problem with spilt salt, not having the same fears of being turned into a block of salt like Lot's wife if I don't throw a pinch of it over the left shoulder.

There were a couple of butcher shops but the shop I liked best was the chandlers - this always smelt of mothballs and Aunt Sally. Aunt Sally was a thick, reddish liquid which was used to wash the scullery floor and had a lovely clean smell. It was sold loose so we had to take along a container. The chandlers sold all sorts of things - candles, buckets, mops, pegs, ropes, etc.

At one end of the crescent there was a fish and chip shop, though we seldom had fish and chips, no doubt too expensive. For different reasons we never had sausages - Mother said you didn't know what went into them. The fish and chip shop also sold cooked peas (lovely mushy ones) and fishcakes. It also sold tripe - not that we ever bought any of that. If my memory serves me right, it also sold 'fin and haddie'. One lunchtime I was sent to buy fish and chips and an alsatian dog came after me. I ran in terror and the dog's owner kept shouting, "Don't run." In the end I threw the fish and chips at the dog. On the rare occasions we had fish and chips, it was chips for the kids, only the adults had fish. Not that we minded, we loved to make chip butties.

From the chemist shop Mother bought Scott's Emulsion, Parish's Food, and malt, which she dosed us up on to make us strong. We loved all of these, except when she tried to sneak cod liver oil into the malt and then we wouldn't touch it. Parish's Food had a nice, pithy tang to it and was red and rich in iron. Once every spring Mother gave us sulphur mixed in treacle to clean us out. Mother provided her own recipe to the chemist for cough medicine and he would make it up for her. Two of the ingredients were paregoric and tincture of myrrh, but I've forgotten what else it had in it. Mother used kaolin for making poultices when we had an infected wound and gave me Phillips' Milk of Magnesia when I had hives - thought to be caused by overheated blood. We had iodine for putting on cuts and abrasions and this stung so much it brought spontaneous tears to the eyes. Then there was Fryer's Balsam with its pungent, pleasant smell. Aspro was sold by the strip at the chemist and you could get just six or so. This would have been a very infrequent purchase by Mother as she never gave us aspirin, it was a vinegar bandage on the forehead for us when we had a headache and I can't imagine that she would ever have had reason to take one - Mother never had headaches, nor did she ever have colds. I just know that there was a strip of Aspro in the house with a few tablets and it was there forever. Occasionally she would take a Beecham's pill. Sties on the eyelids were treated with Golden Eye Ointment. Mother would sometimes bathe her eyes in Optrex and she had a little blue eye bath with which she did this. The Optrex bottle was also blue. Warts were treated with a caustic stick. For a while during my growing up years I had five small warts on my right hand but these just disappeared of their own accord. When we had a cold Mother rubbed our chests with camphorated oil. When we had toothache a dab of clove oil was administered to the tooth. Constipation was treated with California Syrup of Figs but if there wasn't any in the house, a piece of soap was formed into a smooth pessary and this was put in your rectum. A ghastly procedure. Chemists were held in high regard and people would consult them for minor ailments rather than go to the doctor. Otherwise the only other chemist-bought thing was Witch Hazel. This was to keep your complexion nice but would not have been used by us three younger ones and probably not by Mother either. Mother used make-up very sparingly, lipstick being the only thing she used apart from a dab of powder on her nose. She had an exquisite complexion but was conscious of the fact that her lips were so pale they were practically colourless. At the age of three, Mother had been seriously ill with pneumonia and part of the treatment she received at that time (this would have been about 1903-4) was that a leech was put on her lips. This, she thought, explained why she had exceptionally pale lips. For Pauline and Pat there were Pond's Vanishing Cream and Pond's Cold Cream.

Our shops were closed on Wednesday afternoons and open all day Saturday. On Wednesdays if we needed anything we would go to the shops at Huyton. This meant a walk up Kings Drive to Prescott Road. When Pauline was at Teachers' Training College, two or three times during her holidays she took Ferg, Kath and me up to Huyton to a very nice bakery there and we were allowed to buy a cake each. We usually chose a meringue or angel cake. Mother never baked either. I remember angel cake as having a dark brown skin on top and baking paper on the underside which you had to peel off. During one college vacation Pauline got a temporary job, I think in one of the shops, and I heard her arguing with Mother in the scullery as Mother felt she should hand over some of her earnings to her. I was devastated as I loved them both.

In some shops I went into, but not in our area, the cashier sat in a cubicle in a corner perched above the level of the counters and the shop assistants, after placing the money they had received in small metal containers, would shoot them across to her, catapulting them on a pulley system. The cashier would return the docket and change via a snake-like vacuum tube. The tall mother of one of Pauline's friends was knocked out by one of these metal containers as it hurtled across the shop and when she came to, was given a bag of groceries as compensation. It was the sort of thing that happened to this person - we thought of her as somewhat like Old Mother Riley, a character always full of woe and to whom everything happened. She was played by Arthur Lucan whose wife, Kitty McShane, played his daughter, Kitty, in the show. I went to see them once on stage at the Empire Theatre.

Caught Unawares

When we went shopping we usually took the black shopping bag which we had. It was oval shaped and made of heavy leather. Shops remained open till late in the evening then and I sometimes went when it was dark. I might have been afraid of going upstairs in the dark at night but wasn't afraid of going to the shops after it was dark. I suppose I intuitively knew that ghosts were more indoor types.

Our milk was always delivered in pint bottles with a cardboard cap which fitted inside the inner rim. Occasionally Mother would order calves' foot jelly or buttermilk. We loved both of these. We were only given one spoonful at a time of the calves' foot jelly. I was probably the only one of the younger children who liked the buttermilk and wasn't a bit put off by the globules of fat floating on the top which it did in the pre-homogenising days. I've liked buttermilk ever since. When the milk went sour (often it would be a thunderstorm which had caused the milk 'to turn') Mother would put the curds in a muslin cloth and hang it on the line to strain off the whey. We liked the resulting cream cheese. Salt was delivered in huge blocks on the open flat tray of a horse-drawn cart. The salt man would hook a big hook into the block of salt to lift it. This salt was used for cooking only. Sometimes the 'rag & bone' man would come down our road. He also had a horse-drawn cart with an open flat tray. Once when Mother was out, Kath and I sold him our coats. When Mother came home and found out she went after him and got our coats back. The bread cart was enclosed and was a far more dignified affair. Painted on the side was 'Hovis'. One day the horse ran amok and bolted down the road. The bread-man caught up with it and flung himself around the horse's neck to calm him. These horses were all fed at intervals via a hessian feed bag looped around their necks; the horse

Twilight & Wallflowers

throwing back its head every now and then to get another mouth-full.

Our vehicular traffic was usually horse-drawn except for the man who sold small goods, he came in a van and sold things like black puddings (blood sausage) which we loved. He also sold ham hocks and such like.

Every so often the Walls' ice-cream man would come down our road. He rode a tricycle with, over the back axle, a large container holding the ice-cream. This came in long blocks about 1" square and 6" long, encased in cardboard. A full length cost twopence but you could have a half block for a penny. He also sold ice sticks. Walls' slogan was 'Stop Me and Buy One' - but we seldom were able to do that and the rare occasions we did were treasured.

Other commercial slogans were 'Out of the Blue Comes the Whitest Wash', for Reckitt's blue, and 'Ah Bisto', showing a young lad with a cap, breathing in the aroma of the gravy. Capstan 'Cut' Tobacco showed a fisherman in a sou'wester smoking a pipe while at the wheel of his fishing vessel in a storm. The De Reszke Minor slogan was 'Ten minutes to wait so mine's a Minor'. Players was 'Players Please'. But the one which caught the eye of us children was on Tate and Lyle's Golden Syrup tins. A picture showing a lion lying down with bees buzzing about its face was accompanied by the words 'Out of the strong comes forth sweetness'. Whether it was based on Judges 14:14 ('Out of the eater, something to eat, Out of the strong, something sweet') I couldn't say, but if it was, I don't remember it being acknowledged on the tin.

Sunlight Soap had a cherub etched on each block. Mother and a friend once went on visiting day to the Lever factory at Port Sunlight where they were given soap and a slab of chocolate.

Not a commercial slogan, but the newspaper boys always called out "Last city Echo." There never seemed to be an edition of 'First city Echo'.

The main activities in our area took place along Prescott Road. To catch the tram downtown (trams were always spoken of as 'car', from tram-car, never just as tram) we had to go to Prescott Road. We could either walk up Kings Drive or take the bus. Needless to say, taking the bus was for adults only. The trams we took from downtown to our area were either labelled 'Knotty Ash', 'Prescott' or 'Wavertree'. For the Kings Drive stop you alighted at the 'Eagle & Child'. This pub had quite a reputation and the 'black maria' was frequently stationed outside - later on they built a lock-up nearby. Not only the 'Eagle & Child' had a reputation, but in later years this spread to the whole area and when Ferg started his apprenticeship at Charles Birchall & Sons, his boss would joke, "I believe they are sending missionaries out your way, Ferg." We found this very funny but Mother didn't and told us not to say we lived at Huyton but say we lived at the district further on, whose name I've forgotten now but which I think was St. Helens.

It was along Prescott Road that we were taken to see the King and Queen after their Coronation in 1937. We school children were lined up alongside the kerb and were each given a little paper flag to wave. The car drove by so quickly that I couldn't make out who was in it. All schoolchildren were given a coronation cup to mark the occasion. I presume we were given them as I couldn't imagine Mother buying them for us. We were raised on 'They're no different to you and me'.

Along Prescott Road, between where Kings Drive and Fincham Road joined it, there were two groups of shops - one at Huyton and another further along near Fincham Road at

Dovecot. In between were the swimming baths - a very modern building in those days. There was a full length pool for general swimming, a diving pool and a smaller pool for little children. After putting on our swimming costumes, we were then required to go under the showers before being allowed in and there was an assistant to see that we did this. Also, on the way to the pools, we walked through water which assured that our feet were clean. Some girls only had knickers and a singlet as a swimming costume, and some boys only underpants.

There was also a library on Prescott Road - this, like the swimming pool, had been part of the original development. Near the library was a hall for concerts. Kath and I once went to a concert there which was taking place in an upstairs hall. There was a long queue to get in and in the crush on the stairs, one of Kath's legs was forced against a scalding hot pipe and she developed a terrible blister.

The Granada picture-house was close to Dovecot. Cinemas were known then as picture-houses and we didn't talk of going to the cinema, movies, or films, but always as going to the 'pictures', or going to the 'flicks'. On occasions we went to the Granada for children's Saturday afternoon matinees. These were invariably cowboy films and I hated them and hated the loud noise and almost always came away with a headache, which I was prone to as a child. I can't stand cowboy films to this day. At the Granada children in the balcony would chew sticky lice and spit the cud over the end which would land on the people sitting underneath. I would look at that balcony and could not understand how it stuck out in mid-air with no posts holding it up.

This was also the era of Shirley Temple and 'The Good Ship Lollipop' and all that. How remote Shirley's life was from ours. The film which most stands out is 'The

Wizard of Oz' with Judy Garland. By the time it found its way to our area, Pauline was at Teachers' Training College and one unforgettable evening, after she had received her grant, we all went to see it.

Later on I liked the Nelson Eddy and Jeannette MacDonald films, such as 'Rosemarie', in which Nelson Eddy was a Canadian Mountie. They sang 'The Indian Love Call', with lots of "Yoo ah hoos" sung across a valley, of course. They also starred in 'New Moon' and, once again, their yearning love waxed and waned in a landscape which was a far cry from that I lived in at Knotty Ash. Nelson Eddy remained my favourite male start for many years.

I also liked Sabu, the elephant boy, though I don't remember the names of the pictures he was in. Nor do I remember the name of the film in which there was an invisible man, but I remember how he wrapped bandages around himself if he wanted to 'materialise'. I thought of all the things you could do if only you could be invisible when you wanted to be.

We always went to Sunday school but at first we had gone to St. David's, the Church of England at the top of Kings Drive and it was awful. Sunday school was taken by the minister's wife who would berate us if we didn't bring any collection. She was from some African country and had three, very handsome sons. Mother said the sons had wonderful manners and would always stand when their mother entered the room. One of them ended up marrying a doctor. The minister himself was a very open-minded person and would join his parishioners in the 'Eagle & Child' after the service. The minister said, that as a good many of his parishioners went there, it was his duty to be amongst them. For a while Ferg had been in the Church of England choir and Mother bought him the outfit, but he didn't stay long. It was the same with the Boy Scouts, he was in it just long enough for Mother to buy the uniform.

Ferg, Kath and I decided we would go to the Methodist Church on Prescott Road instead and, without asking Mother, we changed over - at least Kath and I did, Ferg decided to skip it altogether and just walked around till it was time for us to go home when we would meet up with him. Later I was overcome with guilt and confessed to Mother that we had changed to the Methodist Church and that Ferg wasn't going at all. Ferg and Kath gave me blazes afterwards but Mother wasn't at all upset and we continued as before. Toward her self-willed three younger children, Mother often adopted the line of least resistance.

The Methodist Church was very much better, two young men, twins, took the Sunday School and they were just wonderful. We had to join with the adults for the first fifteen minutes of the service before we went to the Sunday School. The minister had a prominent Adam's apple which would go up and down as he spoke; this had the effect of holding my attention. I remember one of the sermons he gave about a little girl who had a relative who scorned her belief in God. One day the little girl prayed for something and when the desired thing didn't happen, the relative said, "You see, where is your God now? Your prayer hasn't been answered." "Oh yes, it has," said the little girl, "God said 'No'."

It was at this church that Kath put on a play during their church concert. She chose 'Sleeping Beauty' and I was the wicked witch whilst Kath was 'Sleeping Beauty'. Kath kept to the original story but changed the dialogue considerably to give it a new slant. Mrs Morrisey, one of our neighbours, lent us a veil and I had a fight with another girl for it and in the process we tore it in two. Mrs Morrisey was a bit upset. As the wicked witch, I had to shriek at one stage

"You shall die, die, die" whilst letting out a diabolical laugh. I was killed at the end and Ferg said it was the only time that he knew of a dead person smiling broadly at everyone - I was in my 'dead' state facing the audience.

For 'Harvest Sunday' at the Methodist Church we were asked to bring something in the way of fruit, vegetables or flowers - these were to be displayed in front of the altar. But instead of something one would usually gather at Harvest time, Mother gave us a framed picture to take and I felt very ashamed. However, the saintly twins who took the Sunday School thought the picture was lovely and hung it at the side of the altar. The hymn we always sang on Harvest Sunday was, "We plough the fields and scatter the good seed on the land." Like our school text book, 'Milly Molly Mandy', it bore no relationship at all to our environment.

Mother continued her involvement with St David's Church. Ronnie was a parishioner who became a good friend of the family. He kept hens and it was said in the family that he looked like one because he had the lumpy, red neck of a rooster. He also kept pigeons. He often came to visit and in later years he fell in love with Pauline and once went down on his knees begging her to marry him. One year he won an Easter egg, a wonderful thing, large and with iced flowers all over it. He gave it to me because I was the youngest. Kath used to get fed up that if there was only one of anything, I got it because I was the youngest. We found Ronnie very good company. He said once that he had told the minister that, "If ministers wore their trousers the same way they wore their collars, there would be fewer waifs and strays." We thought this was hilarious.

Other friends from the church were Mr and Mrs Friend who had a daughter a little younger than me, and Mr Friend's mother who lived a couple of doors away from them. I liked going to their house. The daughter, rather plump, was very indulged by her parents and grandmother. The grandmother described fondly one day her granddaughter's bath time and what a cute, plump little bottom she had. Once when we visited, the younger Mrs Friend had been crying, she had fallen out with her husband. I was so surprised to think that they ever quarrelled.

St David's Church had an annual May Day parade and a couple of times Kath and I were in it but we only walked behind the float which carried the May Queen. We wore white dresses with paper flowers sewn on. I longed to be the May Queen. There was always a fête after the May Day Parade and Mother would run one of the stalls. Sometimes the people had to name all the items on a tray after having only glanced at it briefly, or try to blow out all of a large number of candles with one breath - the same sort of games Mother arranged at home for her guests when we had a party. Only this time they had to pay a penny or so to compete. There would of course be a prize for the winner.

I was shocked as a child that one family along Kings Drive had 'Jesus Christ' written on their front door mat - which meant people wiped their feet on this mat before entering the house.

We often went walking with the other children in the road and one of the most popular walks was down Mab Lane. When the hawthorn was in bloom it smelled lovely but we would never collect it because we called it 'Mother Die' and thought that if we took it home our mothers would die. I lived in dread of Mother dying and would pray to God every night that if Mother were to die, that He would let me die too. Sometimes, along with other children, we would try not to walk on the cracks between the flagstones of the pavement and would say, "Step on a crack and you'll break your mother's back." When we walked with a particular friend, we were careful not to let any object come between us, such as a lamp-post, as we thought this would break the friendship. Another childhood ritual was to hook little fingers together and make a wish. This would be done if a black cat crossed our path, thought to be lucky, or on other occasions thought to be omens of good fortune, such as a bird dropping landing on one from the sky.

Somewhere in the area there was also a farm with a pond in front of it - I think it was on the way to Mab Lane but I couldn't be sure of that. I have forgotten the name of this farm or where Mab Lane was in relation to Yew Tree Lane. I have always had a hopeless sense of direction. The bus to Barn Hey Green where Mother's brother, Arthur, and his wife, Eve, lived went along Yew Tree Lane and the same bus continued on to Tuebrook where Granny and Granddad Elliott lived on Millbank. It has taken me all these years to appreciate what beautiful names the streets had. At the top of Millbank there was a gazebo, in the centre of which was a four-sided fountain - the spouts of the fountain being lions' heads, the water coming from their mouths and tipping into bowls underneath. On the other side of the road was the public house, the Jolly Miller.

On one of our walks when I was very young I was grabbed by a boy who pulled me away from the other children. They ran to fetch someone who came and rescued me. Mother took me to the police station where I was taken into a room full of people who questioned me. Then I was taken into another room and physically examined; I felt awfully humiliated. Everyone bent over to have a look and I could have died. It happened again when I was ten but I refused to tell Mother anything despite her pleadings as I couldn't again face the thought of another physical examination and questioning in front of a pile of people. I also managed to get away that time but it was still a nightmare experience.

Once a year the lord of the estate near to us let the locals walk through - this was when the rhododendrons were in bloom. I have never forgotten how beautiful I found the rhododendrons and they have continued to be one of my favourite flowers. I have also never forgotten the deep resentment I felt towards rich people on one occasion when, from the other side of the hedge, I heard a couple of lads being beaten by the gamekeepers for poaching. I had the same feeling of resentment when one of the priests from St Dominic's drove down our road and when little Ronnie, one of the neighbour's children, threw mud at his car (it was the only car ever seen in our district) he got out and grabbed the rest of the mud Ronnie was holding and shoved it down Ronnie's shirt. Ronnie was about four at the time.

The doctor's surgery was on Kings Drive. Near the surgery there was a large tree, the only one on Kings Drive which just had grass verges. I don't know at all what sort of tree it was but it was a marker of my childhood and I was sorry that it was no longer there when I returned many years later.

The Eagle & Child was not the only pub in the area, there was also another in the vicinity of the Co-op but I've forgotten its name. All I recall about it was they would have 'Smokers' Night' on a regular basis.

* * * * * * * * * *

CHAPTER SIX

We had a lot to do with relatives. Mother's parents and four of her five brothers lived in Liverpool. In order of age her brothers were - David, Billie, John, Arthur and Hugh. David was the only one not in Liverpool - he lived in Barton-upon-Humber and was married to my Father's sister, Ida.

Arthur had three names, Arthur James Balfour, after the British Prime Minister whom Granddad admired - I don't know the reason why. Arthur had been born with a drooping eyelid. His parents had tried to have it corrected when he was a child and he remembers being taken for treatment with the surgeon popping his eye out whilst he worked on the lid. It hadn't done much good.

Hugh's other names were Reid Houston. Billie (short for William) I don't think had a second name and John certainly didn't. David's second name was Ferguson and sometimes Mother would address him as Fergie instead of David.

The brothers were all different in personality. David was witty and entertaining, a great raconteur. He worked in the office of a bicycle company in Barton. Billie, my favourite, easy-going and warm-hearted, was a rent collector for the Liverpool Corporation. Arthur had followed his father into the printing trade and worked at Charles Birchall & Sons, a shipping paper at 17 James Street. Billie and Arthur had no children. Billie was married to Jessie (née Birchall) and Arthur was married to Eve (née Thompson). Arthur was pleasant but I can't say that I ever really got to know him, though Mother had a lot to do with him when we were growing up. When he came he would slip us younger children a penny each. Hugh was in the office of a flour company - Lions, I think. He was a very stiff and starched person. He was married to Winnie (née Newton) and had two daughters, Dorothy and Lorna.

All Mother's brothers loved playing cards, as did Mother, though she was more of a social player, whereas Dave and Billie in particular were skilful players.

Along with Mother's brother, Arthur, John had also started an apprenticeship at Birchall's. This was during the Depression years and when Birchall's couldn't keep them both on they gave the parents the chance to say which one should go. They decided on John. John always had a job but they were ones without any particular future. He was unmarried and a couple of times stayed with us for brief periods when I was a child. He was born with what was known as 'water on the brain'. This in no way affected his intelligence but his larger-than-normal head had obviously led to difficulties in relationships with others. Mother was not only very fond of John but also very defensive towards him and would brook no criticism of him. During the times he stayed with us he would have had a falling out with his parents. He got on well with all of us. It was during one period that John was staying with us that I asked Mother if he had 'smoker's fur'. John was a smoker and one day I had seen that he had bits of fluff on his face. Advertisements in the newspaper talked about 'smoker's fur' and I thought that was what these bits of fluff were. It turned out they came from rubbing his unshaven face on a towel. How they laughed. When John came to visit or to stay, he would relieve us of our job of making fire-lighters. I can recall him telling Mother that a woman they both knew had lockjaw and her mouth had locked open.

Mother had been one of four daughters. They were, in order, Margaret Reid, Sarah Georgina (always known as Georgie), Mother (Marion Morton), then the youngest, Jean

Reid. Granny Elliott gave three of her children the second name of Reid, which was her mother's maiden name. Granny's Christian names were Mary-Ann Morton; Marion was probably Mary-Ann in a new form and therefore, in a way, Mother was named after her.

In the family hierarchy, Mother came between Billie and John. Mother said that she remembers one night there being much activity in the house and Billie saying to her, "I bet you mother's having another baby."

Margaret had died in childbirth giving birth to twin girls. She had gone to South Africa as a bride with her husband, Sam Preece. Mother used to say that Margaret was married, confined, and died within eleven months. One of the twins had died with her, the other had been returned to Liverpool and was being raised by Sam's sister, Lottie. Granny Elliott had written to Margaret before her confinement suggesting that she return to Liverpool for the birth, but Margaret had written, "I don't want to leave my beloved." Mother had obviously been enormously fond of Margaret. She gave an image of her as someone very dignified and correct and would say, when referring to her, "We all looked up to her." She said Margaret did beautiful embroidery and had made the vestments for the church.

Mother's youngest sister, Jean, had died in a diabetic coma at the age of twenty-one. Mother, Granny Elliott and I were in Barton-upon-Humber, staying with Auntie Ida and Uncle Dave, when news was received that Jean had died. She had gone with her fiancé on a bicycle ride from Liverpool to Manchester, during which she had fallen into a coma. We took a taxi all the way from Barton to Liverpool and my only memory of the journey is being car sick. I was invariably sick on buses and had even been known to be sick on the tram journey downtown. The coffin was in the parlour and I sneaked in one day and tried to peer in but it was too high up – I was three and a half at the time. I was taken to the cemetery in which there was a summer house where people got water for the flowers that they had brought. I thought it was where God lived and when Mother and Granny went off, I called out to God, expecting him to answer.

Margaret had been twenty-one when Jean was born and had been very embarrassed that her mother was pregnant, but when she was born was overjoyed. Of the four sisters, there were only Georgie and Mother left. Georgie lived in South Africa and was this same Sam Preece's second wife. Mother thought it a great honour that he had chosen two sisters from the same family. Though most people called Georgina, 'Georgie', Sam often called her 'Dodo', as did Mother and one or two of Georgie's close friends. When Pauline was a toddler, this had been her best pronunciation of Georgie and the name had stuck.

Apart from Mother's immediate family there were also heaps of uncles and aunts and cousins. Mother could reel off family lineage with no problem at all, she would have made a fantastic genealogist.

I didn't like Mother's parents at all - Granny Elliott was a very cold person. She tried to stop us calling her Granny and to say Grandmother instead, but it was a losing battle, we kept forgetting. Two of her favourite sayings were 'Oh, go to grass' and 'You little hairpin', said good-naturedly, but she lacked any sort of warmth. She was formal to the extreme, never 'harum scarum' as she, on rare occasions, described us. She was small and dainty and even in old age was still attractive - she had no doubt been very beautiful as a young woman.

Once she became very ill with blood-poisoning and her fingers became so swollen they had to cut off her wedding ring. I visited her whilst she was ill and Dorothy and Lorna were also there. Granny had some chocolates by her bedside and offered them to us. Dorothy and Lorna took one and I thought they were awful to do so, that they should have left them for Granny. I was really upset that she was sick.

It was probably shortly after this that I was sent to stay with Granny and Granddad over the school holidays to help out with the housework. It was awful. I was nine at the time. When I had to clean around Granddad's spittoon I would hold my breath. Granny would ask me sometimes to comb her hair, something I often did for Mother who also liked it, but I never tried out different hair styles on Granny as I did with Mother. On occasion she would send me to the shops for some boiled sweets, and sometimes she would get me to make blackcurrant tea which I did by putting a spoonful of blackcurrant jam in a cup of hot water. She was an awful cook and as I was a picky eater at the best of times, I found her food almost inedible. She made a ghastly dish for tea sometimes, soused herrings, and I had to eat them - not like at home when Mother never really forced us to eat anything we didn't like. Granny was also very correct and exacting and she would suddenly snap at me to "Stop that!" Without knowing it, I would sometimes let my head lean to one side and this was not allowed. She said it looked as if I had a 'wry-neck'. What with Mother telling me I had flat feet ("Just like your Father") I was deficient at both ends it would seem. I became friendly with the boy from next door, Peter his name might have been, who was about my age, and he asked me to marry him. I went in and seriously told Granny that Peter and I would be getting married when we grew up. I think it must have been the only time I made her laugh and I certainly hadn't intended to.

As a child I loved Granny because you were supposed to love relatives and I wept buckets when she died. I was eleven years old then. I had grown up by the time Granddad died and had discovered that you didn't have to love them just because you were related and so I didn't cry at all. In fact I told Mother just what I had thought of him and she said, "Now, now, let him rest in peace - he was never the same after Granny died." Which wasn't true, of course, but Mother was particularly fond of her father. Once she asked her mother for some money and was refused, but in the scullery later Granddad gave her some saying, referring to his wife, "She's very hard." Mother did Granny Elliott's washing and ironing, getting half a crown for each.

Mother told us in later years that Granny had a fear of being buried alive and would say that she wanted a knife thrust through her heart whilst she was in her coffin to make sure she was dead. She would have been even more concerned had she heard the tale that Ferg had been told by someone he worked with in Birchall's who had woken to find himself in a coffin; he had some sort of affliction which gave the appearance of his being dead. From then on he carried with him a document which said in medical terms that he might not be dead even if he appeared to be.

At the start of each day, Granny Elliott would read the Bible, as would Granny Jackson. On the wall of Granny and Granddad's house there was a green baize plaque with letters in gold which said - 'Christ is the Head of this House; the Unseen Guest at every meal; the Silent Listener to every conversation'. When I was bored out of my mind, which I often was when staying there, I would mentally read this forwards and then backwards time and again. John made elaborate kites and one Sunday morning took me with him to Newisham Park to fly them; this was a nice change from the tedium. It seemed Sunday morning was kite-flying time in Newisham Park as there were quite a few other people there.

Granny liked to play cards and it must have been from her that the Elliotts got their love of playing cards because I never saw Granddad play. However, she would never play on a Sunday. Mother, knowing how her mother felt about this, couldn't bring herself to play cards on a Sunday either and would say that she had promised her Mother that she wouldn't. In later years she relaxed this rule after much badgering from her children.

There is one thing about Granddad Elliott which stands out and that is, he knew how to tell a tale. He was born in Belfast and came to Liverpool in his early twenties but had never lost that lovely Irish accent, or the Irish ability to tell a story. He could make even the weather sound interesting. He had come to Liverpool with his mother and his brother, William; his eldest brother, Robert, having gone ahead of them. The three brothers were known as 'The Three Gentlemen'. Granddad was tall, at his prime he would have been about six foot and, as Mother would put it, "a fine figure of a man." He, Robert and William opened a dancing school to generate some extra money, though they were printers by trade. Granddad was a compositor and worked at Charles Birchall & Sons. At Birchall's he was also responsible for putting together the 'African Review' (Journal of Commerce). Ferg later did his apprenticeship at Birchall's - he became a stereotype operator. Robert also worked at Birchall's. William opened his own printing firm in Liverpool, the Horton Press.

Granddad Elliott's father had died when he was three and his mother, Mary Ann (née Brannigan) must have been a remarkable woman as, apart from three sons, she also had three daughters (Margaret, Sophie and Elizabeth) and had to raise them herself when her husband died. He had been head gardener on a lord's estate in County Sligo. Mary Ann saw to it that her three sons all had a trade. One of the daughters, Margaret, became a midwife. All the children did well. The Brannigans had a grocery shop in Ballymena. Mother never spoke of her paternal grandmother. If asked, she would just reply that she had died before she was born and she hadn't known her. Mother could be suitably vague when she wanted to be. However, Robert's wife, Isabella, didn't like her mother-in-law, according to their daughter, Edie.

When the National Anthem was being played on the wireless, Granddad Elliott would make us stand. He never spoke to us about Ireland but Mother said that when she was young he tried to talk to her about the Ireland of his youth and the 'Troubles', but at that stage of her life she hadn't been interested and later regretted that she hadn't listened. Behind his chair there was a picture frame with three photographs in it. I presume these were of his family but I didn't even bother to take a closer look. Now I regret I know so little about him. He was obviously a very talented person; according to Ferg, when Granddad was a young man in Ireland he and a cousin (a Vipond) published their own newspaper. Granddad Elliott's family motto was 'Perseverance'.

Granddad had a big, red, bulbous nose, which fascinated me when I was very small so I would stare and then be told off for doing so. He also had a spittoon next to his chair which he would expertly spit into from the corner of his mouth. He smoked a pipe and had a row of pipes in a rack on the wall alongside his chair. Occasionally he would clean out his pipe with a pipe cleaner. At times he would take his teeth out and wrap them in one of his very large handkerchiefs and put them on the table. One of his handkerchiefs was red with polka dots, another blue, also with polka dots. In the hallway of their house there was a stand for walking sticks. Granddad always used a walking stick when going out, it was part of his dress long before he ever had genuine need of one. When he went for a walk he referred to it as 'taking a constitutional'. These constitutionals were usually just around where they lived but there are photographs of him in the countryside, fully dressed as if for the city, complete with starched collar, bow tie, and, of course, his walking stick. A place he liked to go to was Skifiog, in Flint, North Wales. Why this particular place was chosen, I have no idea. Mother said that when he went to the country he used to remark how wonderful farming life was, having no idea at all of all the hard work it required. It was the same with lovely gardens, he was a great admirer of them but thought they just happened. He certainly didn't take after his gardener father. I imagine it was John who kept the garden at Millbank so neat and tidy.

Their living-room, known to us as the kitchen, had a dining-room table with chairs around. Either side of the fireplace were Granny and Granddad's armchairs. Granddad's armchair was wing-backed and upholstered in a nondescript grey moquette. Granny's chair was much smaller but had a high back. There was also a sofa in the room and one or two occasional chairs. Against the wall to the left of the room as you came in, and directly across from the window, was a very large dresser with mirror. This was carved on top and the drawers and doors were curved. On this dresser there were a pair of crystal decanters in a silver stand which could be locked, a crystal cruet set also in a silver stand, a brown, polished, round wooden biscuit barrel with a silver lid and some sort of medallion on the side. Granny had a lot of antique furniture and ornaments. These all came from her side of the family who had been fairly well off. On her twenty-first she had been given a beautiful ring studded with pearls and rubies. After Granny died and Mother had left England,

Granddad was taken in by some second-hand dealers who got a lot of this for a song. In the centre of the mantelpiece there was a clock which was wound up by a key in the centre of the face. Granddad would open the glass door of the clock at nine o'clock sharp every evening and would wind it. Both Granny and Granddad lived by the clock; I have been allergic to people who do things at exactly the same time ever since. When I return in memory to Millbank, I can hear the "tick, tick, tick" of that clock and also smell the tobacco smoke.

The kitchen overlooked the back garden. Every morning Granny would cut off her bacon rind, chop it up, and put it out for the birds. In winter the bird getting the rind would always be the robin redbreast. He would be there when the other birds had migrated. A jingle we said was: "The North wind doth blow and we shall have snow, and what will poor robin do then, poor thing." When I think of the garden I think of the lupins and delphiniums growing there. Otherwise the most pressing memory of that garden is that Granny sent Ferg, Kath and me to eat at a table there whilst she sat our cousins, Lorna and Dorothy, at the table inside with them. Mother was very upset about that, feeling that we were being treated as the poor relations. But it was possibly because Hugh was a particular favourite of Granny's and hence so were his children.

In the scullery there was a large, brown, wooden chest, this is where the wood and fire-lighters for the kitchen fire were kept. There was a coal shed in the back garden from which the scuttle was filled. The scuttle was kept next to the hearth along with the stand for the pokers.

Granny and Granddad had a parlour, which all the better homes had. This overlooked the front of the house and had a gas fire. During the years I was growing up, it was seldom used. Only after Granny died and we went to live with Granddad was the parlour brought into everyday use.

Granddad was surprisingly liberated for his era - he didn't believe that a woman should have to get up and cook her husband's breakfast - he made his own so his wife could have a lie-in. He began most days with a glass of Andrew's Liver Salts and would always stand up to drink it. He would then make himself a pot of tea, putting it on the hob to brew for a while, after which he would pour himself a cup, pour it back in the pot, and then pour it out again. He was methodical in everything he did.

A particularly close friend of theirs was a Mrs Roberts, who by the time I was aware of her, was then a widow. Granddad once told me that when he had first invited Mr and Mrs Roberts to his house many, many years before, he had offered Mr Roberts a drink. Mr Roberts had declined and Granddad had then offered Mrs Roberts a drink. Mr Roberts said, "I do not allow my wife to drink." When Granddad told me this, he added that a man has no right to tell his wife what to do.

Granny and Granddad had a number of life-long friends - one I particularly liked was Mrs Kingham. She was very autocratic-looking and dressed in an old world manner, wearing long grey serge skirts and high-necked blouses with lots of lace. Her hats were a confection of ribbons and stood high on her head. Her manner was regal. She had had a breast off with cancer and the arm on that side was enormous. We thought it was because the blood which now couldn't go into the breast, flowed into the arm instead. She was the only one I ever heard of who had cancer, but talk of people having T.B. was commonplace. Mrs Kingham also came to our house to visit us. Mother, in referring to Mrs Kingham would often add, "She had seven sons and they all turned out well." Her eighth and last child was a daughter and she was called Marion. Mother told us that Mrs Kingham, when she was raising her children, would say, "If you won't do this because you love me, you will do it because you fear me."

Another friend that Granny and Granddad had was stone deaf and had an enormous trumpet which she used as a hearing aid, you had to put your head in this and shout at the top of your voice.

Granny and Granddad liked a glass of Guinness now and then. On one occasion they were taking the chill off a bottle by placing it near the fire and the top blew off. The pair of them couldn't stop laughing. They obviously had fun together.

In recent years my opinion of Granddad has mellowed. I can now think of him with some degree of warmth and appreciate that he was an interesting person. I have not yet been reconciled in my mind with Granny Elliott. Granny and Granddad had first met when she was working in the office at Birchall's and one day had noticed this very handsome young man who was then working there as a compositor. She had obviously fallen in love with him and remained so to the end. Once when I was staying with them, Granddad hadn't come home at the usual time and Granny was anxious and took me with her to walk down Millbank to the tram stop to wait expectantly for him. But when one tram after the other came and he wasn't on it, we went back home and Granny was crying. She said, "It's always been like this." I didn't know what to say. I remember once Mother saying to Old Uncle Dave when her father was being difficult, "I don't know how mother puts up with it." He replied, "There are some women who love like that." One, however, wonders what she was feeling on her deathbed - Pat later recalled that she had then said that she was sorry that she had married him.

Dr Bogle was the Elliott family doctor - he had delivered Mother and later on delivered one of her children. Mother said that when she was moaning in pain whilst giving birth he said, "I bet you didn't make this much fuss when you were making the baby." He was still attending Granddad in later years, in fact he told him once, "Give up the whisky, man, you're pickled in the bloody stuff." It's interesting that Granddad, who couldn't stand swearing, didn't mind Dr Bogle doing so.

After Granny died Granddad would sometimes come down to the house and Mother would get Mrs Gates over who could play the piano, and Granddad would sing Irish songs. He particularly liked 'And her name was Mary, Mary, Sweet as any name can be', because his wife was named Mary Ann. He could get quite emotional and his eyes would fill with tears. This piano had belonged to Mother's late sister, Jean, and had only come to us after Granny died. For a while both Pat and I took piano lessons but the piano teacher came into some money and gave up her pupils. I came along quite well in the brief time I was taking lessons. After a short while I was able to play, 'Drink to me only with thine eyes', 'Annie Laurie' and 'Merry Bells'. During this latter piece I had to cross my hands over as I played. Mother could play a little, she had taken lessons as a child but had only been allowed to play hymns so that was all she could play.

Our favourite relative was Old Uncle Dave. He was Granny's brother and different altogether from her. He was known as 'Old' Uncle Dave to distinguish him from Mother's brother, Dave, though we never added the 'Old' when we were talking to him. At the time I was aware of him, he was Superintendent of the Christian Street Presbyterian Mission in downtown Liverpool. In earlier years he had worked as a Corn Porter. That was in 1901 when he was unmarried and living with Granny and Granddad and his mother, Margaret Houston, in 18 St Domingo Vale. Also staying there was Edward Vipond, Granddad's 21 year old cousin from Ireland. Like Granddad he too was a compositor. Later Old Uncle Dave worked in the office of the Cotton Exchange but his brother, Hugh, on his deathbed, had implored him to enter the church. Old Uncle Dave had gone to see him for the last time and had asked "Are you prepared?" Hugh had responded with "Are you prepared?" It was from then that Old Uncle Dave began to work for the church. The Cotton Exchange still occasionally called on him to do some work for them, according to Mother.

Old Uncle Dave lived in Fell Street near the downtown area. It was a terrace house and built right up to the pavement. There was only a small, bricked-in yard at the back and this is what their living room looked out on - a very depressing view - not a flower, not a blade of grass. A gate led from this yard into a back alley. Auntie Lizzie was his housekeeper and she and her son, Clifford, lived with him. Auntie Lizzie had a dog which, when she returned home, would go upstairs to get her slippers for her. Also he would go each morning to the shop to fetch the newspaper.

During the period when I stayed with Granny and Granddad, Old Uncle Dave would visit. In an effort to encourage me to read the Bible, he offered to pay me a few pennies for verses he selected if I could say them by heart by the next time he came. That way I memorised quite a few verses and one day he gave me a Bible.

Old Uncle Dave was very religious and would often just start singing a hymn - one of his favourites to us children was 'What a friend we have in Jesus' and I can never hear it today without thinking of him and my eyes becoming moist. At the time, however, we were just a little embarrassed but wouldn't have hurt him for the world by showing it. He also used to sing these songs to us when we were very young:

> Jesus bids us shine with a pure clear light,
> Like a little candle burning in the night,
> In this world of darkness so we must shine,
> You in your small corner
> And I in mine.

And:

> Jesus loves me this I know,
> For the Bible tells me so,
> Little ones to him belong,
> They are weak but he is strong.
> Yes Jesus loves me,
> Yes Jesus loves me,
> Yes Jesus loves me,
> The Bible tells me so.

He was such a lovely person and sometimes when he came to visit and Mother happened to be out, the neighbours would vie to have him in for a cup of tea. He was the greatest comfort and help to Mother when she was a widow and Mother said that she only ever knew two saints in her lifetime, one was Old Uncle Dave and the other was her father-in-law, Granddad Jackson. When Mother reminisced about Old Uncle Dave she would invariably add, "He was a fine orator."

We only ever said grace if Old Uncle Dave was having a meal with us and then it was invariably:

> Be present at our table Lord,
> Be here and everywhere adored.
> Thy kingdom come and grant that we,
> May live in Paradise with thee.

Cousin Douglas in later years related how, when they came to Liverpool from Barton-upon-Humber, Old Uncle Dave always took them to a restaurant and before the meal would say grace out loud for all the patrons to hear. As a young boy he found this embarrassing.

During World War II when Pauline had met and married Leon who was at the time serving in the Merchant Navy, Old Uncle Dave asked him if he said his prayers. Leon told him that he went down at night on his knees to say them and, it turned out, in the cabin with all his shipmates there. Later still when Ray joined the family as Pat's husband, Old Uncle Dave asked him if he went to church. Ray was serving in the Royal Air Force and he replied that Sunday was the day lectures were held at the base on what to do if your plane was in trouble and that these lectures might one day save his life. Old Uncle Dave replied, "Isn't it better to save your soul?"

I was with Mother on one occasion when she went to visit either a friend or relative, I don't know which, but he obviously knew Old Uncle Dave for he said that he had been to see him, saying that he wanted to give a donation to his work at the Mission. Old Uncle Dave had been very pleased until this person had added, "Yes, I've been lucky on the horses lately." Old Uncle Dave had then said, "Then I don't want your money." He would never accept what he would regard as ill-gotten gains. Pat once received a letter when Old Uncle Dave happened to be there and said, "The stamp hasn't been franked. I'll be able to use it again." She was chided with, "The stamp has done its duty, Pat, you mustn't use it again."

Every year Old Uncle Dave would hire a charabanc and take the poor people of his parish for a day out. Mother would also go and, on one occasion, took me along with her. I was once with him on a tram when a fish-wife came up and warmly greeted him. She was obviously from his parish.

Old Uncle Dave often visited us and sometimes would be there for a meal. Some of our dinner plates had a picture of a bright red sun and Old Uncle Dave would pretend he thought it was a tomato. He kept up this joke for a long time and we still laughed at it, even after we had realised that he was just having a joke; we wouldn't have wanted to hurt his feelings. When Ferg was in his teens he happened to meet up with Old Uncle Dave in the street - at the time Ferg was smoking a cigarette which he quickly thrust in his pocket, trying to hide it. Old Uncle Dave just said, rather sadly, "You can take it out Ferg." That was how it was with Old Uncle Dave, you didn't want him to think badly of you.

When Old Uncle Dave visited he would sometimes look on the scullery shelf to see what left-over tonics were there - things like the Scott's Emulsion and Parishes Food that Mother dosed us up on, and he would take those home with him. He was something of a health buff and took a cold bath every day. We said it was why he later got lumbago.

Old Uncle Dave had been married but his wife, Maggie, had died. Before they had married, she had become very ill with arthritis and he had had to wheel her to the altar in a wheelchair. When people wondered why he went ahead and married her, he said that he had loved her before, why should he not still love her. One of the pleasures of her life was cats and she would hold tea parties for them. All this is what Mother said as I never knew her.

Every so often we would visit Auntie Lottie, Uncle Sam's sister. It was Auntie Lottie who raised the surviving twin of Mother's late sister, Margaret. The house Auntie Lottie lived in was referred to as a bungalow which raised it above that of the hoi polloi and was indicative of high class. I can't remember whether it was pebble-dashed or not, which was my idea of a dream home. Her house was very luxurious - or so it seemed to me - and she had a telephone. I was once agog at seeing a dish of fruit on the table and went to ask her if I could have some. I was told to help myself, but couldn't find my way back to the room where I'd seen it. Mother and Auntie Lottie sparked off each other in a very genteel fashion; on one occasion Mother had a ladder in her stocking which, of course, Auntie Lottie had to notice. Mother, out of her hearing, referred to her as Pottie Leece - a play on her name, Lottie Preece. Margaret (who had been called after her mother) went to Hull Teachers' Training College at the same time as Pat and later became a magistrate in Liverpool. She married a doctor and Auntie Lottie would introduce him to people by his full title, even to Mother when she first met him despite the fact that Margaret was her niece. So later on when Pat became engaged to a pharmaceutical chemist, that was how Mother introduced him to Auntie Lottie, but it was something of a mouthful to say "Pharmaceutical Chemist Raymond Taylor" and therefore had run out of steam by the time she got it all out. We all liked Auntie Lottie, she was always nice to us, but we could sympathise with Mother as she did put on all sorts of airs and graces.

A favourite relative was Auntie Cissie. She was a descendant of a half-sister of Granny Elliott. Granny Elliott's mother, Margaret, was the second wife of James Houston. Auntie Cissie lived with her husband, Dick Kennett, in a very large, gloomy terrace house with a cellar. Her position near the top of my list of favourites teetered a little when she said she would put me in the cellar if I didn't behave.

On a couple of occasions Great-Aunt Nellie Morton visited us. Her parents were Mary Ann Reid and Tom Morton, sister and brother-in-law of Margaret, Mother's grandmother.

According to Mother, the family thought very highly of Tom Morton which is why her mother, and she herself, came to have Morton as a second Christian name. Great-Aunt Nellie Morton lived in London and was headmistress of an exclusive Girls' School. She was quite awesome in a nice sort of way and we liked her - we always had to address her as "Great-Aunt Nellie." Later on Kath and Pat went to visit her and she referred to them as "Big One" and "Small One."

Mother kept in contact with a lot of our relatives in Ireland. She told of visiting one of them who lived in a manse and also had a farm. The wife cooked for all the farm workers and Mother described how she made batch after batch of soda scones. One time when she was staying with her brother, Dave, in Barton-upon-Humber and was 'phoning one of the relatives in 'Ballymena', Dave heard her say, "But you've got me Ballymoney" and thought she was swearing at the operator when in fact the operator had merely connected her to the wrong place. I am sorry now I don't know where all these relatives lived as, on Granny and Granddad Elliott's side of the family, our ancestry is in Ireland.

Mother told us that Annie Reid, the daughter of her maternal grandmother's brother, had written a book on Liverpool entitled, 'A Little Book About Liverpool'. I found out later that this had been published in 1911 by Henry Frowde, Oxford University Press, Hodder & Stoughton. On the frontispiece of the book is this, 'Deus nobis haec otia fecit' ('God has made this rest for us') which is the motto of Liverpool. Annie's brother, Hugh, had a Teamona business in Old Hall Street in Liverpool. Apparently 'Teamona' is another word for Horse Contractors.

Apart from relatives, Mother had lots and lots of friends who visited often and we in turn visited them. They were all very nice but one who stands out in particular is

Auntie Kitty. She lived with her two sisters in a flat over a shop in Tuebrook and their living room was cluttered Victorian gloom - heavy drapes, lace-covered round tables, overstuffed furniture, brown woodwork and dark wall-paper. I don't remember seeing an aspidistra there, but it was the sort of room you expected to find one. None of the sisters was married and they bore the gentility of a bygone era. Mother always referred to them as 'maiden' ladies - she did not like the term 'old maid'. Their father had been a jeweller. Auntie Kitty would sometimes bring one of the sisters with her when she came to visit. This sister had lost all her hair and wore a wig. The other sister never socialised.

 Uncle Alf came sometimes. He had been my Father's friend and would tell us stories of the First World War - both he and my Father were in the war. He told us of how he once came on a trench, dead tired and thirsty, and found there a soldier who had been shot dead whilst he held a bottle to his mouth. He took the bottle from him and said, "I know you would have given me a drink if you'd been alive." We lapped this story up but Mother said when we repeated what Uncle Alf had said, "You can't believe everything Uncle Alf tells you." Sometimes we couldn't understand Mother. Uncle Alf gave Ferg a magic lantern which had only one film; this we played over and over again even though it was just a Red Indian running round and round in circles.

 It wasn't unusual at all for us to share our bedroom with the many friends and relatives of Mother who came to stay from time to time. Auntie Flo and her children, Bunty and Derek (the latter known to his mother as 'My Little Drummer Boy') came every year and stayed for a week or so. They ate separately from us and far more lavishly - a small table being set aside for them in the bay window. Bunty slept with me and did naughty things in bed. She wore rings on her plump little fingers and was obviously much better off than we were; I thought she was so lucky. 'Little Drummer Boy' is a line from a lullaby with a plaintive tune which goes like this:

> Now go to sleep my little Drummer Boy,
> The sun has gone down long ago,
> So close your eyes my little Drummer Boy
> And say goodnight to all your friends and foes.

Auntie Flo's 'Little Drummer Boy' was foe to me, he was a very spoilt little hellion who had scabs all over his legs. I once kicked him on his scabacious legs because I had had enough of him, whereupon Auntie Flo told me off. I retorted that if Derek hit me, I was going to hit him back - I wasn't averse to answering back. Her husband, who was a captain on one of the ferries to the Isle of Man, came that afternoon for a few days and he and Auntie Flo took me along with Bunty and Derek to Blackpool the next day. They gave me a wonderful time. I was even given a handbag made of Blackpool rock! It is a day in my childhood that was simply magical.

A great friend of Mother's and sister-in-law to Auntie Flo, was Olive. We liked her. She would tell us fantastic stories about what we did when we were very small, like running down the road without our clothes on. We thought it very funny but Mother didn't at all. Later on she had a falling out with her and we never saw her again.

Relatives from Manchester who came to stay for a while (I think they were the Viponds) had a car and they provided another special moment in my childhood when they took us for a ride in it. They stopped the car at one stage and bought us some sweets. How much better could life get? Another couple who came brought their dog and it slept in the bedroom with them. Mother was very fastidious about animals and didn't like them in bedrooms, so I don't know how she felt about that. If she handled the cat, she always washed her hands afterwards, and she often implored me to stop kissing the cat.

* * * * * * * * * *

CHAPTER SEVEN

Pre-war Liverpool was a Dickensian world. There were undernourished children, children with rickets, children with so many vermin crawling in their hair that you could see them, people coughing their lungs out, chicken chests, chicken-bone fingers, pasty faces. One of the children in our road was hospitalised for a couple of years with T.B.; another died of it. When I was very young Mother sent me with some food to a neighbour whose husband had T.B. and told me not to go inside but just to hand it to her. When I got there I was invited in, so I went in, I didn't know how not to. I held my breath in case I breathed in the germs. Her husband was lying on a bed in the kitchen and Mrs Jones said, "They're coming to take him to the hospital, luv." He died a couple of days after he went into hospital. Some years later the daughter in the household died of T.B. As my Father had died of T.B., Mother kept an eye on any symptoms that we might show and I was taken to the T.B. clinic downtown. One of the women in the waiting room when she saw me said, "Oh, just look at the poor little thing, her eyes are so heavy they are coming out of her head." They gave me an injection in my forearm which swelled up. At the time I didn't know that this was called a Mantoux test. People spat in the streets in those days and a notice inside each tramcar warned 'Do not expectorate'.

On either side of No. 32, our immediate neighbours were the Davies and the Finnegans and we liked both these families very much. However, when we first went to No. 32, Kath and I looked out of the bedroom window and could see down into the next door neighbour's back garden where Mrs Davies happened to be bending over. We yelled out, "Wah, wah, big bum" so she came protesting to Mother who had a hard job keeping a straight face. Mr and Mrs Davies both smoked heavily; Mrs Davies told Mother that if she had to choose between a meal and a cigarette, she would choose the cigarette.

Wah! Wah! Big Bum

The Davies' had two children, Freddie and Jean. On the wall of their kitchen was a big picture of a Cavalier standing at the bottom of a grand staircase. Mrs Davies told me that he was Freddie's uncle. I thought Freddie was so lucky to have such an uncle. One day I asked Mrs Davies why she had those big pimples on her face, and I was surprised when she said that I was very rude to ask - I had just been curious. I liked to watch her clean Freddie's glasses, she was so meticulous about it, blowing on the lenses, rubbing with a clean cloth, then repeating the process, and finally holding them up to the light to see that they were absolutely clear. In those days we children would feel very at home in other people's houses. One night, having been left on my own, when it became late I was scared and so went and knocked on the Davies' door - they were already in bed but they told me to come on up and I sat in their bedroom till Mother came home.

We shared a common entry with the Davies and on many mornings I could hear the echo of Mr Davies' footsteps as he left very early for work - it was a familiar, comforting sound to hear him taking his bike up the entry as I snuggled down for a little longer in bed.

On the other side of the Finnegans were the Crossets. Mrs Crosset was a tall, very thin woman, who had a little baby and it was said that Jean Davies went to her one day and said "Mrs Crosset, can I wheel your baby up and down?" (In those days a new baby was welcomed by all the young girls in the neighbouring houses and a big treat was if they were allowed to wheel the baby up and down the road in its pram). However, Jean spoke very poorly indeed and couldn't say 's' and also only said the first couple of letters of a word so it came out something like, "Mi Cro ca I whe yo ba u a dow" and it was some time before Mrs Crosset could understand what it was she was saying. Jean was two years younger than me but by coincidence we not only shared the same name, but also the same birth date.

Directly opposite to us was another family of Davis, but without the 'e'. Their daughter, Joan, would have been just a little younger than me. Joan had two thumbs on each hand. In a fight, I once threw something at Joan, leaving her with a not-too-serious cut. However, Mrs Davies from next door, made a great to-do and said, "You just wait till her mother gets to see that." To my relief, nothing happened.

To the right of Joan Davis' house lived Mr & Mrs Lott. Mrs Lott would sometimes call me to run an errand to the shops for her and when I returned, would offer me a piece of fruit. I would have preferred a halfpenny, but accepted it nicely - I thought she was lovely. Her house was not only spick and span, but also very nicely furnished. She and her husband never mingled with the neighbours - no-one saw them - they kept themselves to themselves. We never knocked at her door and ran away, all we kids liked her.

Mr Hemming who had put Snowball down, lived further up the road on our side. He was ruggedly handsome, with jet black hair and muscular arms. He and his wife had two sons but they were still too young to join in our games. A sweet old lady lived next door to the Hemmings and Mother, who supplemented her meagre pension by baking cakes, baked cakes for her. When I took them to her, her hands shook so badly she had trouble getting the money from her purse. Next to her lived the Naylors. They only had one daughter, Margaret, who was about my age, but she only occasionally played with us.

Near to the Hemmings and the Naylors lived the Andrews family. It was their dog, Spike, who had attacked Snowball. I thought Joan and Blanche Andrews were so lucky because their parents had a motor-bike with a side car and they would go out in this, the parents dressed in leather jackets and goggles. The Rimmers also had a motor-bike with a side car but somehow or other they weren't nearly so flash. Joan and Blanche took tap-dancing lessons which I would also liked to have done. But we tap-danced anyway in our un-tipped shoes, imitating the steps of the more experienced. One dance was called 'The Sailor's Hornpipe' and another, 'By the side of the Zuider Zee'. There was also the repetitious

> I am a little Dutch girl, a Dutch girl, a Dutch girl.
> I am a little Dutch girl from over the sea.
> And your friends are my friends and my friends are your
>   friends.

I am a little Dutch girl from over the sea.

The Gates family lived between the Andrews and the Hemmings and they had four boys and one girl. Eric, the eldest, was Ferg's age and they were close friends. When Mother ran out of money it was to Mrs Gates she would turn - sending me to ask if Mother could borrow a shilling until she went to the bank. Mrs Gates would do the same if she ran short. Mr Gates had a good job as a fitter and turner and must have earned good money but I don't think Mrs Gates saw a lot of that - he was a somewhat mysterious figure and the rest of the road seldom saw him.

Most of the women kept immaculately clean houses inside and outside. They whitened their doorstep with a compressed block of white powder - first of all scrubbing the step clean with sudsy water and then rubbing this block over it. Some even went so far as to scrub the front path on their hands and knees and whiten a two inch strip on either side. The letterboxes on the doors were of brass and they were always kept polished. There was a window-cleaner for the outside of the windows who would come every now and then on his bike, with his expandable ladder alongside him and his bucket and chamois leathers dangling from the handlebars. I don't know how much he charged but he did good business as most of the housewives would employ him. The inside of the windows the housewife did herself, also using a chamois leather. Mother was horrified one day to see Mrs Gates cleaning her windows when only a couple of days before she had given birth. Mother remonstrated with her but she said that she had been lying in bed and noticed that the windows needed cleaning, so had to get up and do them.

Mrs Morrisey who lived further up the road on the opposite side, I didn't like, though Rosie was my close friend. It seemed to me she always shouted. I would go there of a morning to walk to school with Rosie and her sister, Gertie, and when I knocked on the door she would scream at me to come into the house and then continue doing her daughters' hair. Both of them had luxurious heads of hair, though Gertie's was soft, silky, and a lovely golden auburn, Rosie's was flaming red, extremely thick and so curly you couldn't get a comb through it. Mrs Morrisey would thrust Rosie's head under the tap in the bath and then attack it with a wire brush, shouting all the while. Then she formed it into ringlets. Kath's hair and mine was so fine and silky that it couldn't be formed into anything, not even the plaits that some girls wore as the clips holding the plaits slipped out and they unravelled. Mother would sometimes try to put a ribbon in our hair on the top of our heads, fastening it down with a hair slide (which we called a 'barrette') but more often than not both ribbon and slide slipped down. Rosie and Gertie had a tandem bicycle and once or twice we were allowed a ride on it.

Mrs Morrisey was a great reader and would spend a lot of her time reading in front of the fire, causing that red mottling on her legs which people get when sitting in front of an open fire for too long. She read 'Gone with the Wind' practically in one sitting. Mrs Morrisey didn't waste her time by whitening her doorstep each week, but painted it white so that it didn't have to be done again; which was the only sensible thing to do, but this caused more surprise than praise in the road as, in those days, to step out of what was common practice, was not done. One day a week Mrs Morrisey went downtown, always very smartly dressed. I went with her once when I was off school for some reason. We went into a shop where I had never been before - it was a large shop which sold lots of delicious food and smelt of coffee beans. We children never drank coffee, always tea. On Sunday, after lunch, Mother would have her only cup of coffee, made with milk.

This was Camp coffee with chicory, an essence which came in a square-shaped bottle. It was all right in those days to have the trade name 'Camp'.

Mr Morrisey was a Catholic and Mrs Morrisey was a Jew. It was said that Mrs Morrisey was thrown 'out of the tribe' for marrying a Catholic. Mr Morrisey had no time for the Catholic Church and sent the priest packing when he tried calling on him. It was rumoured the church then 'put his name on the bridge'. I never understood these terms. Rosie and Gertie were being raised in the Jewish faith and at Passover would give us some unleavened bread. On the Morrisey's gate there was a notice which read: 'No Hawkers. No Canvassers. No Trespassers'. Mr Morrisey was a handsome man in a 'Heathcliffe' sort of way. He and Granddad met on the odd occasion and shared their memories of Ireland. Even though Granddad was Protestant Irish and Mr Morrisey was Catholic Irish - that sort of thing didn't matter in our road.

Another neighbour was a Mrs Holme, an enormously fat lady with a hen-pecked husband, Jim, and two children, Alec and Gladys. Mrs Holme, once on her way over to our place, tripped and fell on Gladys which we felt explained why she wasn't the world's brightest person. Mrs Holme was so fat that she couldn't fold her arms under her breasts, but folded them on top. Mrs Preston, Mrs Holme's mother, lived with them. She had gone senile and I would see her sometimes out walking and she'd say, "Ethel says I should go for a walk." Once at a birthday party for Alec, Mrs Preston sang to the children "All the birds of the air came a-sighing and a-sobbing when they heard of the death of poor cock robin." I remembered all the words of this song for many years.

There was a Mrs Wye who lived in a nearby road and who spoke beautifully (at least Mother said she did, I couldn't distinguish between adults' manner of speaking). Mother said she had come down in the world. Mrs Wye had three sons and a daughter and had trouble coping with all the woes that bound her. If one son wasn't in Borstal, the other was. You could smell Mrs Wye's house before you reached it. Mother helped her whenever she could; she felt very sorry indeed for Mrs Wye. Many years later when Pauline was teaching, Mrs Wye's daughter was in her class and Pauline once had to restrain Mrs Wye who had chased her all the way to the school and into the classroom.

Then there was the couple on the corner whose daughter was intellectually challenged and skipped endlessly. Every time any of us passed she would tell us that she had had a bath and asked when we had had ours. We always spoke nicely to her. We learnt at an early age from Mother that 'There, but for the grace of God, go you".

There was another family of Jacksons in the road, it consisted of the father and his two children, a son and daughter who were both a little younger than I was. An auntie lived with them and looked after the family. The son was hospitalised for a long time with T.B. They were a family who kept to themselves. It was said that Mr Jackson's wife had walked out on him. Mother, being somewhat of a feminist, automatically blamed him.

A nice old lady lived next door to the Jackson family. She was another customer of Mother's who ordered the cakes which Mother baked, but she wouldn't accept the cakes from anyone but me - Mother had always to send me. But there was another old lady who lived on Southdene Road and when I went down there I kept to the other side as I thought she was a witch - sometimes I would dream about her.

In a nearby road there was a family who had a daughter, Nellie. Nellie was kept shut in the bedroom all day and would look out the window at us children playing on the swings - their bedroom windows overlooked the playground. We felt so sorry for Nellie. Many years later when we had moved to Tuebrook, Nellie came to bring a message to Mother from her parents. Nellie at that stage was a maid in a big house; it was called 'going into service'. She always smiled and was as gentle as an angel and had no sense at all of self. Without meaning any lack of caring for Nellie, Kath and I would say if we thought we were being put-upon, "What do you think I am - a Nellie?" We were critical of the way Nellie's parents treated her but Mother would only say when we spoke about it, "You don't understand." Mother never gossiped about adults to children.

Nellie's mother ran a sweet shop of sorts from her scullery. If we had a halfpenny or penny to spend, which we seldom did, we would sometimes go there. She had a limited assortment of sweets but it was mainly the card that we wanted to punch that attracted us to her scullery instead of to the shops which sold sweets. This card was about 6" by 6" and you took a metal punch and punched out one of the circles - if green came up you got a bar of toffee, but green seldom did and it was invariably lesser colours and all you got was a sweet or two for those. I never once drew a green.

Amongst other families in the road were the Norris' - theirs was the end house of our row and was on the corner. I don't remember too much about them except that their son Raymond died in December 1943. He would have only been about twelve years of age.

As I look back I realise what a wonderful sense of community there was amongst the neighbours in the road; despite this closeness, however, it is interesting that very few referred to each other by their first names. Mother always said that she was very happy at No. 32. I don't recall any squabbles over fences or encroaching plants, or any of the other things neighbours seem to get upset about these days. Despite living cheek-by-jowl, an Englishman's home was still his castle and privacy was respected. To peer out of the window just to see what neighbours were doing was frowned upon and there was only one neighbour, to my memory, who did this. People felt free to tell other neighbours' children off, by the same token they also kept an eye on them when their parents were not there. One incident stands out of neighbours' tolerance in those days. I had been trying to light the fire and it just wouldn't light. I threw something on it, I've forgotten what, and there was an explosion. Mrs Finnegan, whose fireplace was back to back with ours, came running over, thinking something was wrong. When she found out what had happened, she said that she'd only just finished cleaning out the grate and blackening the hearth, when the explosion caused the soot to come down the chimney and messed everything up again. She thought this was very amusing. How special those people were amongst whom I grew up.

My childhood playmates in the road were - Freddie and Jean Davies, Eileen Finnegan, Rosie and Gertie Morrisey and Betty Heathcote. Ferg's special friend was Eric Gates. They were the main friends but we also played with Joan Davis, Brian Rimmer and his sister, Agnes, Joan and Blanche Andrews and Margaret Naylor. Teddy (Eric's brother) only played with us on rare occasions, we didn't like him much. He once sank his teeth into Ferg's leg, leaving deep indentations. They had had a fight and Ferg, in trying to get away, had clambered over the fence of the swings when Teddy grabbed him by the leg and bit him. Mother went to complain to Mrs Gates who called Teddy in and gave him a good hiding - Mother hadn't expected that and was horrified and asked her to stop. We never got more than just a go-along from Mother - she did not agree with children being hit. But good hidings were the order of the day in most of the homes - it was not uncommon for the father to take off his belt and hit the children with it - when they were particularly bad they got the buckle end. Pauline and Pat were by no means averse to spanking us when they were in charge.

Betty Heathcote only came to live in the road when Mr and Mrs Edge and their son, Raymond, moved out - Mrs Edge had won the Irish sweep. I liked Mrs Edge, I thought she was very pretty and she used make-up. I wished that my Mother would use make-up too. She was also a lot of fun - if you were there and she was sweeping the floor, she would just sweep the dust under the carpet and say things like "Why not?" - or "That's what everyone does." She smoked as well in a very sophisticated way. Sometimes Mother and Mrs Edge would have a little flutter on the horses. In later years Mother visited Mrs Edge and she had been keen to know how I was doing. She said to Mother that, cheeky as I was, people couldn't help but like me as I knew we were all poor and would refuse the halfpenny or penny given in return for running a message. When Betty came to live in that house we were all a bit shocked because her mother wore a shawl, had a rocking chair and her children often ran around without shoes. You only wore a shawl and went shoeless in the slums. She also said "Haitch" instead of "Aitch." But soon Mrs Heathcote was one of the most popular women in the road, her children were well-behaved and her house always immaculate and she got on well with everyone. Also her children started to wear shoes and she gave up the shawl and Rosie confided one day that she had taught Betty not to say "Haitch."

We enjoyed playing outdoors of an evening under the street lamp, playing games like hide and seek, and knocking on neighbours doors and running away. It was particularly wonderful on those crisp evenings when our faces would glow and our breath would form fog. One game was 'Oranges and Lemons' which we played to the tune of:

> Oranges and lemons say the Bells of St Clemens,
> I owe you five farthings, say the Bells of St Martins,
> When will you pay me, say the Bells of Old Bailey?
> When I am rich, say the Bells of Shoreditch.

In this game two children form an arch with their arms, clasping each other's hands and singing 'Oranges and Lemons' as one child at a time passes under the arch. The idea being to pass through before the last word 'Shoreditch', when the arch would come down, imprisoning the last one, who would then have to replace one of those forming the arch.

We also played 'Stamp, stamp, I want a match'. One person was chosen to be 'It', and had to stand facing away from the others who would creep up quietly behind, saying, "Stamp, stamp, I want a match." The reply from 'It' would be, "You can't have one," as they turned suddenly, trying to catch someone moving. If they did, that person became 'It'. The aim by the others was to reach the front and tap 'It' on the shoulder, at which 'It' would turn and try and catch one of them, who then became 'It'.

There was a Gypsy Field not far away and we were told never to walk through there, although we sometimes did. In those days the gypsy caravans were just like those in children's storybooks, they were wooden and gaily painted with a chimney, shuttered windows, and steps leading from the back door. They were also horse-drawn. The gypsies were not there all the time, but when they were they would sometimes come around to the houses offering to sharpen knives, mend pots, or tell your fortune. They also promised to bring you luck if you crossed their palms with a coin. A rhyme we said when we were choosing who was to be 'It' in any game we were playing, went something like this:

> My mother said, I never should
> Play with the gypsies in the wood,
> If I did, she would say,
> Naughty child to run away.
> One, two, three, you're It.

Another rhyme to determine who was to be 'It' was:

> Eeny-meany, mack-er-racka
> Rare-rye domin-acka
> Ala-packa, choor-a-packa,
> Rum-tum-tush.

Girls often played whizzy. In this two girls stand opposite each other, holding hands with arms crossed; feet, toes to toes. They both then lean back and twirl around going faster and faster.

We tested each other's endurance by Chinese burns. The skin on the wrist is twisted in two different directions at the same time, the tension being taken up by a thin sliver of skin on the innermost part of the wrist. We were all fairly good at yodelling, but generally it was only the boys who whistled.

There was a season for various games such as whip and top, marbles and yo-yos. For some reason each season would end as quickly as it had come and then it would be the season for something else. When it came to whips and tops, I didn't like the tops that were shaped like a cone, but preferred those shaped like a mushroom. Marbles we played along the gutter, which Mother disapproved of. The most important marble was the 'parrot' which was opaque white, large and with red stripes running through it. It had to be hit three times before you claimed it as your own. Sometimes one was unlucky enough to lose a marble down the heavy iron grid covering the drain below. When it was the time for yo-yo's, it didn't take us long at all before we became adept at them. Not so common were the large wooden hoops which were moved along with a stick.

Skipping was an all year round thing and Eileen had a very long skipping rope which stretched across the road. One of the rhymes we skipped to mentioned Knotty Ash, the area we lived in:

> Up and down, up and down, all the way to London Town.
> Swish-swash, swish-swash, all the way to Knotty Ash.
> Legs swing, legs swing, all the way to Ding-a-Ling.
> Heel toe, heel toe, all the way to Rotten Row.

Another action song - though not while we skipped - was,

> Here we go round the Mulberry bush, the Mulberry bush, the Mulberry bush,
> Here we go round the Mulberry bush on a cold and frosty morning.
> This is the way we wash our hands, wash our hands, wash our hands,
> This is the way we wash our hands, on a cold and frosty morning.
> This is the way we comb our hair, comb our hair, comb our hair,
> This is the way we comb our hair, on a cold and frosty morning.

After the first line about going around the mulberry bush, the other lines were made up spontaneously and in tune with the rhythm and always ending with "On a cold and frosty morning."

Other games we played were hopscotch, rounders, leap frog and donkey. The latter required a wall to hit a ball against, one throwing the ball at the wall and the next having to jump over it, the ball being caught by the person next in line, who would then throw the ball, and so on. We liked it when Mr Finnegan brought the lorry home from the glass factory where he worked. It had a big framework on the side where the sheets of glass were carried. He was very tolerant of us kids crawling all over his lorry. There would be Eileen, Rosie, Gertie, Betty, Joey, Brian, Jean and Freddie, Joan, Eric, Joan and Blanche, but never Margaret Naylor. Margaret Naylor's mother would call out "Time to come and have your cocoa, darling," as soon as it became dark. She never fitted in anyway - we were nobody's darlings.

Hide-and-seek was a favourite game indoors and outdoors and the seeker would often say, as he/she went looking, "Fe-fi-fo-fum, I smell the blood of an Englishman." Blind-man's-buff was only ever played indoors as was musical chairs. 'Pin the tail on the donkey' was only at children's parties.

Some of the indoor games we played were housey-housey, lexicon, tiddly-winks, noughts and crosses, snakes and ladders, ludo and 'dots'. For the latter we filled a page with rows of dots which ran vertically and parallel to each other and then would take turns joining up the dots, the one to complete the most squares being the winner. These games were usually just between Ferg, Kath and me and we played them only when it was raining or we'd been called in for the night. Day or evening, we were never encouraged to stay indoors - Mother would say, "Go outside and play." And most of the mothers preferred that you play in other children's houses rather than in theirs.

Later another boy came to live in the road, I have forgotten his name but he was very nice and fitted in from the start. Other late comers were the Mullins, they had two children, a boy and a girl. We didn't have much to do with them as we felt they were very rough. Mrs Mullin once shook her shoe in a neighbour's face because this neighbour's son had had a fight with her son. Another time she came to talk to Mother because Ferg had also had a fight with her son. Auntie Georgie (Mother's sister) happened to be visiting from South Africa at the time and, surprisingly, since this would have been a new experience for her, she sent Mrs Mullin packing with a flea in her ear. I was very disappointed when Auntie Georgie came as I'd been been telling all the children beforehand that I had a black auntie and they were very jealous. I was fed up to find that she was white.

It was 1938 when Auntie Georgie came with her three sons, Jimmy, Raymond and Stanley. She had been to England on a previous occasion - this I know because there is a photograph of Jimmy as a toddler with Granny Elliott. Also Mother was convinced I caught whooping cough from Jimmy when I was only 6 weeks of age. On this visit in 1938 we all went on a holiday to Wales. We stayed in a quaint cottage and one of the upstairs bedrooms had a door which led out to nowhere. Jimmy, Raymond, (Stanley being too young to join in), Ferg, Kath and I made a tent in a field where there were cows and one stuck its head through the opening. Apart from the door to nowhere and the cow sticking its head through the tent opening, the most pressing memory is that of Jimmy reciting a poem about a tiger, not because of the words, but because of the way he said it, his South African accent was new to us and it was that we wanted to hear. We would get him to say it over and over again. The poem went something like this:

I met a tiger in the grass
It made me so afraid to pass
It looked at me and wagged its tail
Till I felt quite sad and pale
But when I ran to get my gun,
The tiger too began to run…

I forget most of the rest but it ended with, "It was just my cat, you see."

The powers-that-be made a playground in our area. This playground had swings and when construction was finished there were plans for a big launching and the swings were kept chained awaiting this event. But the children had their own launching and broke the chains. They had the 'ocean waves', and the 'crown', and see-saws, and young children's swings, and older children's swings, and so forth.

One of the things Ferg and Eric Gates did was make their own cigarettes; this they did by stripping the veins from the fleshy leaves of a weed which grew low to the ground and which I think was dock-weed. They would then roll these veins in brown paper, forming a cigarette, which they would then smoke. Sometimes Kath and I smoked them too, though not very successfully because the brown paper would more often than not still be burning instead of just smouldering. We were ever resourceful. We made our own mouth organs by wrapping tissue paper around a comb.

Ferg and Eric were very good friends and Mother was pleased about this as she held Eric in high regard. But on one occasion they had a terrible fight - they fought with their bare fists and all the children in the road gathered around. Ferg, very handsome, was popular with the girls so they taunted Eric and cheered Ferg on. Eric got into such a rage that Mr Hemming came out, pulled him away and made him go home. It was like that in our road, there was a real sense of community and parents would feel an obligation to keep a general eye on each other's children. Apart from Mrs Mullin, all parents got on well with each other.

The neighbours were very tolerant of us children - only Mrs Wainwright wasn't. We thought that if a ball went into her garden she would cut it up, in fact Rosie and Gertie said she did and they lived next door so they would know. She called me into her house one day and I went with trepidation. I had been playing whip and top but all she wanted was to tell me I should plait the whip, that it would work better, and did this for me. It wasn't true, it didn't work better, but I hoped she wasn't looking when I un-plaited it.

Kath, Ferg, Eric Gates, Freddie and Jean Davies and I once ran a lemonade stall. It was successful in a minor way but Mother made us hand over our takings and gave us cakes in exchange. We were very embarrassed about this. Another time Ferg, Kath, Freddie and Jean Davies and I decided to leave home and see the world. Freddie took Jean's goat-chair along; we piled it with our home-made tent and some food that we had managed to scrounge and set off. After walking some way, we reached a field and set up camp for the night, but Jean Davies started to cry and Freddie took her home. Ferg, Kath and I stayed. After some time Pauline's boyfriend arrived, very angry that he had been sent to look for us and shouted at us all the way home.

Betty Heathcote and I one day decided to walk downtown - Betty took her young brother, Freddie, with her. We became hopelessly lost and by the time we arrived home it was very late. Mrs Heathcote was very angry with Betty and, in front of me, gave her a good hiding. When I went home Mother hadn't even realised that I hadn't been there. Sometimes Kath and I wished that Mother would say, "No you can't do such-and-such," as the other mothers said to their children. When we were much younger, Kath and I had got lost and Mother had the police out looking for us. We had tried to walk downtown on that occasion as well.

Childhood was not without it terrors and we shared these with each other - such as if you swallowed a pip a tree would grow inside you. And if you cut your hand between the index finger and thumb you would get lockjaw. We tried to out-repulse each other by thinking of the most revolting meal imaginable, such as snot sandwiches washed down with dog's pee. We had our own method of weather forecasting, which was simple, 'Red sky at night, sailors' delight; Red sky in the morning, sailors' warning'. If there were a ring around the moon, we said it would snow the next day. We parroted 'Don't cast a clout till May is out', but ignored the advice. The seed cloud of a dandelion enabled us to tell the time - we counted the number of puffs it took to blow it away. If a buttercup held against the neck reflected yellow, we knew that person liked butter. We knew how babies were born, they came out of their mother's belly buttons. We had no interest at all as to how they got there in the first place. Squabbles amongst children could be topped with one or other saying, "My father/uncle/grandfather is a policeman and he's going to get you." We had our jokes and witty comments - 'Two women were at the pictures and a yacht appeared on the screen; one said to the other, "A Yacht." "No," the other replied, "Are you?"' And, "What time was it when the Red Indian's tepee blew away?" Answer: "Ten-twenty." Anyone whose name was Isabel was asked "Isabel on a bike?" And the B.S.A. bicycle stood for 'Bits stuck anywhere'. Some of us had our special physical accomplishments - such as Ferg who could raise each eyebrow separately.

* * * * * * * * * *

CHAPTER EIGHT

It was seldom that we went downtown but they were exciting and special occasions when we did. We invariably went to both Blackler's and Lewis'. We liked Blackler's in particular because it had a huge parrot hanging from the centre dome and the wooden escalator felt good when it rippled under our feet. The Grotto at Christmas was just magical. We would go down a corridor with pageant-style displays of nursery stories and at the end hand in our ticket and choose what we wanted from a set range. Invariably I chose a sweet shop, but on one occasion chose a printer's set and was sorry later I hadn't stuck to the sweet shop. The sweet shop had miniature bottles of sweets, with a scoop for getting the sweets out of the bottles and weighing them on the tin set of scales, which left much to the imagination. There was also a cash register which left even more to the imagination but no child lacked what was required. Another shop was T J Hughes' known to some in our area and other like-minded ones as T J 'Yewses', the 'H' at the beginning of some words being regarded as superfluous. Other shops were Owen Owen's and George Henry Lee's, but they are now just names – it was the parrot at Blackler's and the Christmas Grotto both there and at Lewis' that loom large in memories of childhood.

The News of the World would send us three younger ones a present each at Christmas - one time I received a fountain pen, but was disappointed another time to get a skipping rope. Ferg once received a fairground which he had to assemble and the roundabouts actually revolved when he poured sand into a funnel-like arrangement. Every year we went to the Pantomime and sat in the front row and were given a bag of sweets each. Looking back I'm sure the News of the World gifts each Christmas and the Pantomime were for fatherless children like us.

Christmas in our house was wonderful. We had the same Christmas tree year after year - this was small and was folded away at the end of the season and brought out again the following year. We would decorate the kitchen and always had a bunch of mistletoe. Whenever someone walked under the mistletoe, they had to be kissed by someone of the opposite sex. When we were very young we wrote notes to Father Christmas telling him what we wanted and sent them up the stovepipe flue of the chimney. On Christmas Eve we each put a pillow-slip at the end of our beds and these were always filled to capacity. On top of that we also got one large present each that wouldn't fit into the pillow-slip. One year Kath and I received a pram and a doll's crib. Kath's pram was brown and mine was green. I always got the best colour because I was the youngest. My crib was draped with pink lace and Kath's with blue. Mother, I think, must have rallied all her relatives and friends to contribute as she couldn't possibly have afforded to buy us all those things but was obviously determined that, poor as we were, her children were going to have unforgettable Christmases. At the bottom of the pillow-slip there were always a few nuts, an apple, an orange, and a couple of new pennies. Another thing which never varied and which we looked for, was the selection box - these were boxes with a variety of chocolate bars in them. One year Kath and I received teddy bears. I couldn't reconcile the fact that the teddy-bear's body was half pink and half blue, though I liked the bag of sweets with which they came tied on their backs. It wasn't long before my teddy bear lost an eye but a button was stitched on to replace it. No doll or teddy of ours was fortunate enough to be taken to the dolls' hospital downtown.

One Christmas I received the most beautiful doll. Pauline had had to dress a doll when she was at Hull Teachers' Training College; all the items the doll wore had to be hand-sewn. This Pauline did with great expertise, she was an excellent seamstress and the doll was beautifully dressed. Those were the days of china dolls and it was a 'sleeping' doll which closed its eyes when it was laid down and had lovely long lashes. Kath once again missed out because when it came Pat's turn to dress a doll, she merely used the outfits Pauline had made. Dolls were also made of celluloid then and I was fascinated when I tore one apart and put the bits on the fire to see how they flared up.

A present which Kath and I often received was a book with cut-outs. The two dolls, boy and girl, were made up of the cardboard back of the book, but the thin, inner pages contained all sorts of outfits which you could cut out to dress them in. These books were special favourites of mine, I liked dressing the dolls in the various fashions. One thing I never received and always wanted was one of those cards which, when opened, the centre pops up to form an elaborate three dimensional picture. One year we received a kaleidoscope.

Ferg received, in our opinion, boring things like tool sets, fret saw with a jig, cap guns and toy soldiers and forts. These metal soldiers were made in various stances, some standing, some kneeling, and they could be arranged as in battle. One Christmas Granny Elliott gave him a flute but it wasn't long before it was broken into parts and being played as a whistle. Granny was not amused. Ferg occasionally received things that we were as interested in as he was, such as magic sets which invariably contained invisible ink. These magic sets also had tricks to play on people, for example, inkblots which you put on things like the tablecloth to make Mother think someone had spilled ink. And a buzzer which was placed under a cushion so that when people sat down, they made a rude noise as they did so.

Kath always carefully rationed out any sweets or chocolates that she received, whereas Ferg and I went on eating ours until we had finished, with the result that when ours ran out and we wanted a sweet, we had to barter with Kath for one of hers and she drove a hard bargain.

Every Christmas Mother made ginger wine. We had a huge brown, glazed earthenware crock which was kept beneath the sink and this was used to make the ginger wine. When we were a little older we were allowed a very small sip of this wine - otherwise it was for guests who called and were given a drink and a piece of cake. We always had goose with sage and onion stuffing, followed by Christmas pudding which had been boiled in a cloth. When the pudding was served, brandy was poured on and this was set alight. What we loved most about the pudding was the silver threepenny bit that we might find which Mother had put in. Mince pies were served at tea-time and no-one could make them like Mother.

One Christmas Mother played a joke on Pauline and Pat. When they each opened a parcel they found all the makings to start the fire - coal, wood chips and fire-lighters. The fire was always left to go out overnight and so someone had to clean the grate and light the fire each morning. Mother liked practical jokes and once a foot of the goose found its way into someone's bed. We children liked to take the foot of the goose and pull the sinew which moved the toes.

There was only one Christmas that wasn't a lot of fun and that was the one we spent with Granny and Granddad Elliott. When we tried to get up very early as we did at home, Granny shooed us back to bed. And then when we were allowed to get up, she disapproved of the noise we were making. In the end, in mid-afternoon, Mother took us home again. She could see that we were unhappy. Mother told us in later years that her mother would say when she brought us children to visit her, "I like to see you come and I like to see you go." Auntie Eve and Uncle Arthur had been there too and Auntie Eve had given both Kath and me a Father Christmas made of soap - Mother was furious at her meanness. I actually rather liked it. She offended Mother on another occasion when, after being at her house for tea, she parcelled up the left-over food to give Mother when we left. New Year is only memorable for the fact that the first person who stepped foot in the house after midnight on New Year's Eve had to be tall, dark and handsome.

One Easter Pauline bought Ferg, Kath and me a china egg-cup each, with a chocolate Easter egg in. The pelican was destined for Ferg, the swan for Kath and the teddy-bear for me, but when they were handed out they couldn't understand why I insisted on the swan; I didn't tell them that the reason was, I had discovered where these had been hidden before Easter and to me it seemed the swan had the bigger egg. Kath was only too happy to exchange. I regretted this later as the chocolate egg was soon consumed and I had to watch her enjoy the teddy-bear egg-cup every time we had boiled eggs.

Another time of the year that we enjoyed was 'Duck-apple Night' - apples were suspended on pieces of string and we had to eat them with our hands tied behind our backs. Afterwards nuts were scattered and we scrambled for them. And then there was Pancake Tuesday. Mother didn't actually toss the pancakes but there were always pancakes to eat that day. These were served with lemon and sugar. April Fools' Day never went by without someone being taken in - not invariably by Mother. Twelve noon was the cut-off point when you could say, "April Fool is dead and gone and you're the fool for letting on."

November 5th, Bonfire Night, or Guy Fawkes Night as it was sometimes known, was often celebrated by us kids. On a couple of occasion we made a 'Guy' and put him in a goat-chair and then knocked at various neighbours' doors asking "A penny for the Guy."

There were unforgettable days when we went to New Brighton. We managed to go a couple of times each summer, though other children in the road had never been to the seaside, as we called it. We had to take the ferry across the Mersey leaving from the floating landing stage. Mother would plan quite a time ahead and we dreaded that it would rain on that day – when it did we would beg Mother to go anyway, but she wouldn't. When we paddled in the water we would sometimes have rubbers on our feet, quite common in those days. We liked to find shells and would put them to our ears listening, as we thought, to the sound of the sea. It was a particular delight to stay until the tide came right in of an evening and we would keep on having to move further and further back. We were sometimes allowed to buy a bucket and spade to make castles on the sands, but only ever a wooden spade and a small bucket - I would have liked one of the larger metal spades but never got one. We never asked for these things and always just took what Mother offered us, we knew we didn't have much money. One of the things that Mother liked to do was to have a donkey ride, it was the closest she could come to a horse. She always had a yearning to ride a horse.

There was a fairground at New Brighton but as children we didn't go on any rides. I once tried to get something from one of those slot machines where one has to guide a clam-shell to pick up one of the toys in a certain time.

Needless to say it was like the colour green on the sweet card - a rare happening. Occasionally we would go to Seacombe, but we didn't like the sands there as they were all pebbly. Returning by ferry of an evening we would look for the birds on the top of the Liver Building.

On special occasions we went to Southport. I remember the walk down to the seafront and passing shops bursting with buckets, spades, large brightly-coloured beach balls, and other seaside paraphernalia hanging invitingly outside. Not for us, however. Once we went to Hoylake and another time to West Kirby, but they are remembered now only as names. One day we went to Morecambe and had to take the train, a family Mother knew was camping there. The names of Mother's friends have long since passed from my mind but not their tent or the wonderful sands. But how we shivered when we were warned of the quicksands. In those days, people being sucked down in bogs were part of scary films and the fear of them was well established in my memory. I don't know how I came to be so well off but I gave Kath a penny and would mention this a long time afterwards if I ever wanted a favour from her - "Remember the penny I gave you at Morecambe" I would say.

The passenger trains in those days had individual carriages and the window on the door was let down by a huge leather strap. Before the train pulled out of the station, the guard would come along and lock all the doors from the outside. Above the cushioned seats there were framed pictures of rural and sea-side scenes to entice the tripper. The station itself had penny slot machines from which one could get such things as bars of chocolate for a penny, or Wrigley's chewing gum. We never had a penny to spare so never got to use those. But we did get to use the slot machines for getting the penny platform tickets which were needed if you wanted to go onto the platform to see someone off. Another slot machine was for Woodbine cigarettes, five at a time. Earlier, according to Mother, there had been vendors selling sweets and chocolates on the station platforms. One of the few stories Mother related about Deryk was that when he was very small she had taken him onto a station platform and later he had said that when he grew up he wanted to work on the trains. Mother said, "You want to drive a train?" "No," he had replied, "I want to be the man who sells sweets and chocolates." By the time I came along, that type of vendor only still operated in the picture-houses - they would have a tray which was attached to their person by a strap around the neck. The tray displayed an assortment of sweets, chocolates and ice-creams.

An unforgettable time which involved going on a train was when we went with Auntie Nellie and Auntie Emily. They were so very gentle and sweet and we loved them. When Mother said, "Oh, Jean, look at your hair," which was a mess, Auntie Nellie said, "Unruly hair is beautiful hair." When we passed a field with potatoes and Kath called out, "Oh, look at those spuds," Mother chided, "You mustn't say that! You tell her, Jean, what they are called." I said "Spudiaters," at which Auntie Nellie and Auntie Emily laughed. We had winkles that day which we picked out of the shell with a pin.

Another thing we had to eat with a pin was our once a year pomegranate. How delectable we found them. A coconut was also a once a year thing – we shared one between us. What we liked most of all was the milk which we drank straight from the coconut. On very rare occasions we would be given a blood orange. Otherwise fruit was very limited in our house; occasionally we would have bananas, only ever one each. Mother would get huge green apples that she used for baking. They were very sour but we enjoyed eating them raw. When she peeled the apples for baking an apple pie, we would eat the peel and the cores.

Once we were taken to a zoo, where it was I have no idea - all I can recall is the ride that we children had on the back of an elephant which fed my childhood fancies - I dreamed of leading a parade and riding down the road dressed in a fairy costume on the back of an elephant.

* * * * * * * * * *

CHAPTER NINE

Every year we went to Barton-upon-Humber on holiday to stay with Auntie Ida and Uncle Dave. We always went by bus - Mother called it 'coach'. We would go by tram to downtown and it would still be dark when we left home. The bus left from a bus station in the centre of town (we never said 'city'). As we walked from the tram to the bus station, we would pass the tobacconists and sweet shops which would be open at that early hour and the brightly-lit windows of the sweet shops displayed all sorts of delectable things. Mother, who had a weak bladder, would invariably have to nip down a back alley for quick relief.

On the coach Mother would claim free fare for Kath and half fare each for Ferg and me. Because Kath was so small she was able to do this for some time after Kath was at the age when she should really have been paying a half fare. Mother would sit Kath on her lap and hold her head against her chest so the conductor was not able to see by her face what age she was. Kath said Mother clutched her so tightly once that she was scarcely able to breathe. However, those days came to an end when a conductor challenged Mother as to our ages and insisted that she pay a half fare for every one of us. Mother didn't have any money to pay the extra fare. A woman passenger on the bus offered to lend her the money, which Mother accepted gratefully. Later, when we returned to Liverpool from Barton and Mother had received her pension, she went to pay the money back to this person. The woman told her that she had been so impressed with how well-behaved we children were that she knew she could trust her. From then on, as we were now all paying half fare, on long journeys Mother didn't feel obliged to sit Kath on her lap when the bus filled up. However, she would sometimes say to someone who was standing, "It's a long journey and I don't want my children standing, but if you are prepared to sit one on your lap, you may have the seat." Of course, it had to be Kath as she was the only one small enough to sit on anyone's lap for a long distance. Kath used to get a bit fed-up at this. At times if we had to share a seat, it was Kath who had to sit on my lap.

Auntie Ida, Uncle Dave and their son, Douglas, who was Pat's age, lived in a beautiful house called 'Venita' on Caistor Road. It was very modern and all the woodwork was painted cream - in our house it was painted brown. The parlour was a bright and large room and its bay windows had leaded lights. The parlour was in daily use, it wasn't just for special occasions as it was in most homes I knew which had parlours. In the parlour there was a pianola and the favourite rolls I liked to play on it were Humoresque, Charmaine and Barcarolle. There was also a huge grandfather clock which had come from Granny Jackson's childhood home. The chime of this was so strong that they sometimes took the weights off. If my memory serves me right, the history of this clock was that Auntie Ida bid for it when Granny's childhood home effects were being auctioned off. Granny's father had married again after his first wife (her mother) had died and his second wife inherited everything. Granny did not believe in second marriages and especially as her father had remarried within eleven months of his first wife dying. Granny said that they could have contested the will, but she didn't believe in doing things like that.

'Venita' had a separate dining room which had French doors leading to the garden outside. Also in the dining room there was a hatch (known as 'the silent butler') through to the kitchen to save walking all the way around. They said 'kitchen' and not 'scullery' as we did. In the kitchen there was a table where breakfast was taken.

The staircase to the upstairs was open, unlike ours which was hemmed in on either side by walls. Not that we ever slid down the banister in 'Venita' but it would have been possible to do so. There were three bedrooms and a bathroom upstairs as well as an extra lavatory downstairs, which led off a small porch which came off the kitchen.

At the end of the back garden there was a row of pine trees. The back garden led to a lane and behind this there was a field where we would sometimes go. In this field there were poppies and nettles - we were often stung by the latter and would try to ease the sting with dockweed.

In Barton they spoke of 'yonder' for 'over there' and Auntie Ida called bread 'cake' and cakes 'sweet cake'. Their next door neighbour, a Mrs Dawson I think, was really nice and we were able to just go into her house when we wanted. Mrs Dawson used to tease me when she was vacuuming by bringing the Hoover close to me as if it was going to suck me up - I was a bit scared but confident that she wouldn't actually suck me up in it as she was such a nice person. We called all vacuums 'Hoovers', though we didn't have one at home, our carpets had to be done with a carpet-sweeper and the carpet on the stairs with a hand-brush.

Auntie Ida had a siphon for making soda water. There was also a cigarette lighter which was a knight in armour standing about 12" high with a visor that lifted and a serrated wheel which, when spun, struck a flint which ignited the wick with a spark. Uncle Dave smoked but I don't ever remember him using this lighter. They also had a gas poker for the quick lighting of the fire. Their house was full of things of which we could only dream.

Auntie Ida was a teacher and Uncle Dave worked in the office of the bicycle factory in Barton. I think it was Hoppers. Mother told us that Uncle Dave could rapidly total up three columns of figures, the £ s d, at the same time, not like most of us who total each column individually.

Uncle Dave was a true Elliott, very fair and blue-eyed. Auntie Ida, on the other hand, had a shock of thick, black frizzy hair, which seemed to drain the colour from her small, angular, very white face. She had bright, deep-set blue eyes and a soft, melodious voice. Like most of the Jacksons, she was fairly tall.

Barton is amongst my happiest memories as a child. The beautiful house, the sunshine, haunting country smells, fruit in abundance and delicious food (as Mother described it, "Ida kept a good table"). All this and gentle, warm-hearted Auntie Ida and visits to Granny Jackson.

Granny Jackson who also lived in Barton on Butts Road, was quite different to Granny Elliott. She never told us off and we could make as much noise as we liked. She would bring in a huge wash-bowl of strawberries from her garden and we could have as many as we wanted. Right into her old age she grew her own vegetables, only in later years getting someone to do the digging for her. Granny was the world's best cook and she said that when she grew up her family cured their own hams. Granny had taught Mother to cook and Mother always gave her the credit for that. She certainly would never have learnt how to cook from her own mother. Granny's family had been comparatively well off and had owned a farm. Granny said she remembered the child workers going to the factories - she believed that she had seen more changes in her lifetime than anyone was likely to see again.

Granny's maiden name was Ducker and her relatives still owned the greenhouses in Barton. They grew grapes in the greenhouses and these they exported to some place in Europe. I learnt later from my cousin Douglas that the son of the relatives who had inherited the greenhouses, had once, as a teenager, picked one grape from every bunch, thereby ruining the whole crop.

Before she was married, Granny and her sister, Lena, had run a tearoom in Hull for which they had done all the catering. The tearoom was near a theatre and was patronised by the theatre goers. On marriage Granny had given it up, but it was the money from this which enabled her to build the house she lived in and also the one next door. She named the houses 'Nisida' and 'Procida'. Though we were intrigued by these names, we never thought to ask why she chose them. Only recently I discovered that these are the names of two islands in the Bay of Naples and that 'Nisidas Procidas' means: 'Unless thou givest shalt thou fall'. Also I have since learnt that my Father visited these islands when he served in the Royal Navy during the First World War. Whether he or Granny knew the meaning of these names, I now will never know.

Lena, whom I was called after, was married to Arthur Grimwood. Had I been a boy I was to have been called Arthur, though I think this was probably more after Mother's brother, Arthur. Auntie Lena and Uncle Arthur had one son (Arthur Ernest Grey Grimwood, born 9 August 1892) who served in the army in the First World War and who was later reported missing, presumed killed. Auntie Lena never recovered and eventually committed suicide on 30th April 1939. I don't know whether she learned what had happened to her son before she died, but we have since discovered that he died in Basra, Iraq. This is how it is commemorated on the Commonwealth War Graves Commission monument:

In Memory of
Private ARTHUR ERNEST GREY GRIMWOOD
TF/290152, $1^{st}/10^{th}$ Bn., Middlesex Regiment,
who died age 25 on 31 August 1917.

Son of Arthur Edward and Melina Grimwood,
of 47 Bacheler St., Hull.
Remembered with honour.
BASRA MEMORIAL.
Their name liveth for Evermore.

Uncle Arthur died four years after Auntie Lena. Auntie Lena left an estate worth £24,000. By the terms of her will, each of Granny Jackson's children received £250; my Father's share being divided between his five children. However, we only received our £50 when we turned twenty-one and by the time I reached this age, my inheritance had deflated considerably in value. The rest of the estate went to charity, endowing a hospital bed.

Mother once wrote to Auntie Lena asking her for some money when she was in dire straits during her widowhood; Auntie Lena wrote back and said, "You've made your bed, lie on it."

Granny had two other sisters, Emily and Clara. Clara married an Allison and later died of T.B. Emily died in 1935 and I have no other information about her. There was one brother, George William. He was known as the black sheep of the family. The tale told in the family is that his parents locked him out one night and he took out the bricks from around the front door in his efforts to get in. The trouble with tales like this is, you never hear what happened in the end. Did he or did he not succeed in getting in? George William died in June 1921.

I once met George William's son and his wife when I was with Mother. We went to one of the public houses in Barton and joined them in the lounge there. Mother would no doubt have had a Guinness and I would have had a soft drink. George William's son said to Mother, "You were the most beautiful bride who ever came out of church." Granny might not have approved of that branch of the family, but Mother seemed to get on all right with them.

Mother had been married in Barton from Granny's house. In fact Deryk was born at 'Nisida', and Royce, Auntie Edna's son, had also been born there. Many people did their marrying, birthing and dying in Granny's house. One of those who died had pleaded on her deathbed to be cremated - something Granny totally disapproved of, but she agreed. She had to take the body over to Hull, paying double fare for the corpse, something which went against the grain. She vowed then that no matter how hard anyone begged, she would never again agree to arrange a cremation.

Granny was the family stalwart, everyone turned to her. Vera, the daughter of her sister, Clara, said that she couldn't imagine what her life would have been like without Granny. After her mother had died, her father had remarried and she had virtually been the drudge to a succession of children he had had by his second wife. She would go to Granny's house for a break now and then where she would find relief from the drudgery.

Granny spoke with a broad accent and used colloquial expressions like 'sup' for eat. In urging you to eat more she would say, "I wouldn't want your Mother to think I pined you." If Granny related a tale, she invariably ended it with, "That's where it 'cooms' in." And if she told you anything, would add, "Think on it." What she said became legendary in our house. When Granddad was dying and the doctor suggested that he be given a little brandy to relieve his breathing, Granny said, "Nay, he hasn't had a drop to drink all his life and he's not going to die drunk." She was strongly against drink, though did tolerate men smoking but never women. She had no time for 'fallen' women, those who had become pregnant out of wedlock, and placed the blame squarely on them, saying that men "couldn't help themselves." Her boast was that her husband had never even seen the tops of her arms. Church was always referred to as 'Chapel' and she went every Sunday. To Granny we were 'Towners' - people who came from the city and were therefore somewhat frivolous. She didn't like Mother - something we only really became conscious of when we were older - and only tolerated her because of us children.

Granny was very hospitable and generous, but also a careful housewife who had no time for wastrels, which she pronounced "werstrels." To be a wastrel was almost as bad as drinking, in fact a lot of the time one was synonymous with the other.

Her house was still lit by gas, though she had been obliged to have Procida, which she rented out, changed over to electricity. Granny didn't believe in 'new-fangled' ideas and electricity was one of them. This meant, of course, that she didn't have a wireless. In her kitchen (living-room) she had an organ which Royce, her grandson, would play. Who of Granny's own children played, I have no idea, but she said that they didn't go "gallivanting around of an evening like you Towners do today" but would all enjoy music together. There was also a parlour, but that was only ever used on special occasions.

When you went to Nisida, you went down the entry to the backyard which the kitchen window overlooked. If Granny was sitting in her rocking chair near the window, she was able to see you as you came around from the entry and would throw up her arms with delight and chuckle with glee, coming to meet you down the passage to the scullery as you came in the back door. She really was a special Granny.

The passage to the scullery - one step down from the kitchen - was long and the floor was made of stone which was well-worn with the passage of feet. First on the left was the bathroom, this had a bath and a hand-basin and also a geezer for heating the water. Next to it, also on the left, was the pantry. This was always full of good things, home-made jams, tarts, bottled fruits, etc. The scullery at the end of the passage was a rather cheerless room; it also had a stone floor on which were a few scatter rugs. To the right of the back door was a stone sink and draining board, and at the end of the draining board was a single gas plate. I think we had to heat up water every time we did the dishes, but this I am not sure of. But Granny, who wasted nothing, would leave a bucket of water out in the sun to heat up and use that. Along the end wall was the door leading to the lavatory and next to this was the laundry, which we called the wash-house. There was a copper in the wash-house. Alongside the wall opposite to the back door was a work counter. How Granny produced the delicious food she did in this rather barren scullery, I have no idea.

Granny did her laundry in the stone sink and would scrub away at the clothes as if she had been working down a mine all week. She once showed me a nightie that had been in her trousseau and it was still going strong, which was not surprising as the material was as substantial as tent fabric and as voluminous as a tent. It was also not surprising that Granddad had never seen the tops of her arms.

The kitchen was very cluttered. Besides the organ there was a horse-hair couch, Granny's rocking chair and another large armchair. Also a very large table with dining chairs around. The horse-hair couch, which prickled when you sat on it, was at one end of the table. Granny did most of her cooking on the stove in the kitchen, which was an oven, hot plates and open fire combined, just like ours at home. She would carry the steaming pots and pans and also things from the oven all the way down the passage to the scullery, as there was no sink in the kitchen and no work table. To the left of the fireplace was a cupboard. Granny's rocking chair was near the sash-window and, on the wall next to the window, there was a small mirror. Regretfully I can't recall what ornaments there were around the place but do remember the pictures. There were various inspirational sepia prints, usually of angelic women in diaphanous gowns, hands clasped in prayer, looking upwards with large doe-like eyes to an ethereal sky above, with shafts of heavenly light beaming down on them.

The front hall of Granny's house had a tiled floor; I think the tiles were fawn-coloured with a white pattern. On entering the front door, the stairs were directly opposite and there was a lace curtain at the bottom of them, held back in the middle to form a graceful fold. The top half of the front door had glazed panes. The first door on the left of the hallway led to the parlour and next to it was the door leading to the kitchen. On the right of the hallway was a hat and coat stand. The front door led off a vestibule, which is where we would deposit our galoshes, over-shoes, wellingtons, umbrellas and mackintoshes if the weather was bad. In the early days there was a wrought iron fence and gate along the front but during the Second World War these had been commandeered to help the war effort and then all that was left was a low stone wall and tall stone posts.

Upstairs there were four bedrooms. The house was split level and half-way up the stairs there was a landing, from which three stairs turned to the right leading to the two main bedrooms, the larger of which was at the end of the hallway and overlooked the front. This was Granny's bedroom. Above Granny's bed was a photograph of the grave of her first child who had been stillborn.

To the left of the landing, and one step up, a passage led to the two other bedrooms. The first on the left was something of a store-room, still very neat and tidy as it would be, but even though there was a bed in it, it was obviously only used as a last resort. There was a tin trunk in that room but I can't remember now what was in it. At the far end of the passage was the fourth bedroom.

Granny was practical to an extreme. When my Father was dying in Mansfield Sanatorium (near Nottingham) and my sister, Pauline, was taken to say goodbye to him, she leant down to kiss him and Granny was horrified, "You mustn't," she said, "The germs." My Father said, "Kiss me, sweetheart, I won't poison you." I understand that my Father is buried in Beeston graveyard, on the Presbyterian side. It is interesting seeing that he was raised Methodist. The Jacksons were originally Primitive Methodists.

One of Granny's neighbours was a young mother with a number of small children and Granny was nonplussed to see that she sometimes did her washing on a Sunday. One could see that this really bothered Granny but she would try and reconcile this with the fact that the neighbour was such a nice woman, and with all those children maybe she didn't have a choice, but it was easy to see she didn't feel a bit comfortable about it.

When we stayed with Granny, which I did later for a longer period, we could only read the Bible or the church newspaper on a Sunday. After Sunday lunch, which was the main roast meal of the week, a green, baize cloth would be put on the table and Granny would either read the church newspaper then or the Bible.

Granny loved to talk and I loved to hear her. Her tales were homely. She told me of a relative whom she had gone to visit and how this relative was always very careful with money - checking when she arrived home how much she had spent. Granny, on this occasion, looked through the window and saw her with her hand poised above her purse - when she went in she found she had dropped dead in that position. I am sure Granny would have approved of such careful housekeeping to the very end.

Cousin Douglas later told me, referring to Granny's penchant for talking, that she would, when needing to light the gas-lamp, first of all turn on the gas and then light a taper from the fire. However, she would continue to talk, holding the lighted taper in her hand whilst the gas hissed away filling the room. He said he would not have been surprised if one day he had heard that Granny had blown herself up.

Granny still dressed in the style that was probably in fashion when she married. She had button-up boots for which she used a button-hook to fasten. Her going-out dress was invariably black and came way down the calf. Her hats were a confection of velvet and ribbons on the crown which stood way up. Cousin Douglas said that when he was young he would watch Granny thrust the huge hat pins through this millinery confection, he thought she was actually driving them through her head and couldn't understand why she didn't wince.

Apart from visiting relatives and going to chapel, Granny's only other outing would have been to the Women's Bright Hour organised by the chapel. She didn't hold with picture-houses, art galleries, or any other such things. She told us that she did once visit an art gallery and there were paintings there of "nekkid" (naked) women which so shocked her, she got a funny feeling in the pit of her stomach. Pat said, "Poor Granny, the first thrill she'd ever had in her life and she didn't know it."

The bottom of her garden was a short distance from the railway line where the train ran from New Holland to Barton. When we were catching this train, Granny would stand at the bottom of her garden and wave goodbye to us as the train passed by. Sometimes, if we needed to catch the train and were late, we would run along the vacant land between Granny's garden and the railway line, and try to attract the driver's attention to tell him we were coming. He would wait for us whilst we headed down Butts Road to the station. In later years I learned to appreciate the sterling worth of Granny but, sad to say, I didn't then.

Granddad Jackson came from a different background to Granny. He was born at Keyingham, Yorkshire, in 1857, one of thirteen or fourteen children of which he was the eldest. He only had a few hours schooling each week (another source says that he went to school only during the summer) having to work in the brickfields at seven years of age for 7/- a week to help feed the family. He was mainly self-taught and was a devout Christian and taught Sunday School. Mother thought the world of him. He died in 1932, the same year that my Father and my brother, Deryk, died, and Mother said that it was interesting that the three, who had such a strong bond between them, should have all died within the same year. She said that it is wonderful when a father and a son have a strong and close relationship. If Granny Jackson took my Father to task over anything, he didn't take much notice, but if his father did, he was shattered.

Once, in the early days of their marriage, my parents were staying with Granny and Granddad Jackson in Barton and my Father had come in with a black eye from some fracas he and his friends had become involved with. With tongue in cheek he told his mother, when she told him off, that he had walked into a lamp-post. But he felt very ashamed when his father chided him. His father said that it was a terrible thing to do to his young bride. Mother said that she had actually found the episode very funny. But then I think that Mother, from the tales she told us, had been a bit of a handful to her parents as well.

We sometimes stayed with my Father's youngest sister, Edna, and her husband, Billy, in Scunthorpe. Their house was on the edge of a graveyard and one of the windows looked right out over the graves. Auntie Edna and Uncle Billy ran a shop which included the post office but they were also lay preachers in the Methodist Church. We liked Auntie Edna and Uncle Billy very much but their son, Royce, was a different matter, he was the same age as I and a proper little devil. He would, for instance, get under the table and pretend to be a dog and nip at our ankles. One day I was so fed up with him, I enticed him into the chicken run and then shut the door; his wails brought his mother who told me off. On one occasion when we had been staying there and were about to leave, Auntie Edna suggested to Mother that she leave Ferg behind for a few extra days, but Ferg didn't want to stay. My Father's family were always keen to have his children. Auntie Ida wanted to adopt Pat who stayed with her for long periods during her childhood, and Auntie Edna wanted to adopt Pauline. Mother didn't like this and would say to us, "But never you three younger ones. Oh, no, just Pauline and Pat who have reached a nice age." I didn't quite know how to feel about this. One time Auntie Ida and Uncle Dave refused to give Pat back after she'd stayed with them some time and when Mother insisted, Dave wrote to her angrily and said, "You can send her fare." Pat said years later how bitter she felt at having to leave Auntie Ida and Uncle Dave and go home. As she put it, "Who would want to go back to our house?"

* * * * * * * * * *

CHAPTER TEN

As a family we played cards a lot, amongst ourselves and with visitors. Some of the card games we played were: 'chase the ace', 'whist', 'old maid', 'switch', 'strip-Jack-naked', and 'Oh Hell'. The latter was a variation of whist in which the aim was not to take a trick. If you did, of course, the response was usually a spontaneous "Oh Hell!" A favourite game was 'grab-it'. This could get quite riotous and an old pack of cards was needed as a new pack would soon be in tatters. In grab-it four matching cards are selected from a pack for each of the players, the rest being discarded. This pack is then shuffled and dealt. In the centre of the table there are only sufficient buttons for all but one of the players. When the dealer calls out "pass" each player has to pass on one card to the person on their left, receiving one from the person on their right. The dealer must keep up the momentum of the game by calling "pass" in quick succession. As soon as anyone has a matching set of four, he or she grabs a button. Once one person has done that it is a free-for-all as everyone must then try to get a button. The player who misses out becomes the first letter of the word ASS. Those who lose three games are out of the game which continues until there are only two players left in. The first person to become an ASS is given a 'free life'. In other words, they can continue playing until they lose again and then they are out. When playing cards, if someone lost consistently, the comment was sometimes made, "Someone must have died in that chair." Or the person was advised to walk around the chair - widdershins - to 'break' their bad luck.

We also played other games such as 'tippit' in which we divided off into two teams. One team would put their hands under the table and pass a button, or some other small object, between them. Then they would put their clenched fists on the table and each member of the opposing team would take it in turn to guess which hand the object was in. They would tap various fists and say "Take that one away" and so on until they thought they had discovered where the object was and would say, "tippit." We also played blind man's buff and musical chairs. Sometimes we played what was a variation of a treasure hunt - an item was hidden and we had to look for it – the person who had hidden the item calling out if someone was 'warm' or 'cold' or 'hot', according to their distance from it.

Another game was consequences. In this game each person received a slip of paper and a pen or pencil. At the top of the piece of paper each player wrote the name of one of the males present, or someone personally known to everyone, and then folded down the paper to cover the name just written, passing it to the player on their left, receiving the folded down paper from the player on their right. The same was done for the name of one of the females present, or someone personally known to everyone, the folded down paper being passed on as before. This continued covering things like 'Where they met'; 'What he said to her'; 'What she said to him'; 'What the consequence was'; and finally, 'What the world said'. Each player in turn then unfolded his final strip of paper and read out what was on it.

Sometimes we would write a poem about someone in the room and the rest would have to guess who that person was. I recall two of the lines in one Pauline wrote about me, "Eyelashes that Heddy Lamarr would envy but legs that you couldn't give to asses."

When we had a party invariably there were party games. One which was played when there were adults was 'postman's knock'. I don't know how it was worked out but someone would go into the glory-hole and then someone of the opposite sex would be chosen and would go in and have to kiss that person. It was all very innocent and hilarious. In later years Mother and Pat once went to Ireland and met some of Granddad's relatives. Pat was disgusted that they played postman's knock, more for the fact that some poor young man had to go in and kiss some old woman who, Pat said, smelt because she smoked a clay pipe. But Pat was like that. Some of the games which Mother organised were competitive and there was a prize for the winner. Amongst the prizes which Mother gave there was invariably a bottle of smelling salts. These came in small fancy bottles. For these parties Mother prepared special treats. Sometimes she would make trifle in individual dishes which were shaped like ordinary dessert dishes, but were waxed and disposable and had fancy patterns on the rim. She also made jellies in smaller paper containers. These were also waxed and just a little larger than a paper cup-cake holder, but were firmer and the rounded sides were fluted.

Mother was raised strict Presbyterian and when she grew up she and her siblings were only allowed to read the Bible on a Sunday. Every Sunday afternoon they would sit in a circle and did what they called 'Turn-about', meaning each in turn had to read from the Bible. Mother's siblings, like her, all had a well-developed sense of humour, and they had to suppress their giggles when one or the other had to read out names like Beelzebub. As a consequence of this 'Turn-about', Mother knew the Bible from cover to cover and would often quote it. Judgment was ever at hand and we were never to tempt either Fate or Providence. Satan we were to banish with, "Get ye behind me, Satan." She never planned to do anything without saying "d.v. - God willing," and would caution, "Man proposes, God disposes." We learnt of Job's comforters long before fully understanding what that meant.

She would also say resignedly of anyone who seemed to bring her nothing but bad luck, "They are a real Jonah to me."

Mother was very well read and loved a turn of phrase. We were never sure where these quotes came from. One of her favourites was "The mills of God grind slowly, yet they grind exceedingly small." I particularly liked this one for the dramatic way in which she said it. Much later I learnt this was a line from Longfellow's translation of a 17th Century poem 'Retribution'. The retribution, as Mother saw it, was as likely to descend for some trivial matter as for some horrendous act. By the same token Mother could be philosophical about the loss of a material thing, or accept that she had been 'done down', and would say, "I'm none the poorer for it." "Needs must when the Devil drives," she would say when people commented that she coped with her situation so amazingly well.

Another saying of Mother's was - "He who takes from me my purse, takes but trash, but he who takes from me my good name takes everything I have." In later years we learnt that this was from Shakespeare but at the time she said it she would precede it with, "As my father used to say…" If she were feeling something of a mess, she would say that she felt like "The wreck of the Hesperus."

If we were overly pleased about something, we were cautioned "Don't tempt fate." And if we were having high-jinks and laughing a lot, she would say, "You'll be crying next." Her very sunny personality had this rather gloomy streak, she believed in a fate that waited to wipe the smile off your face if you were too happy. It was never explained to us what or who this 'fate' was and we never asked, though we knew instinctively that it wasn't something you could appease by touching wood. She was careful about what she said in jest, believing that a word said in jest might come true. One of her examples was of the time her eldest sister, Margaret, was getting married. After the ceremony she chided her new husband about something-or-other and he, Sam, jokingly, turned to her other sister and said, "I should have married you instead, Georgie." Eleven months later, Margaret died in childbirth and a few years after that, Sam married Georgie.

We three younger ones were not allowed to lie around in bed of a morning - Mother, an early riser, would admonish us with, "You are missing the shank of the day." If we were asked to do anything and we said, "We can't," Mother's immediate response was, "Can't means wont."

We never swore - not even 'damn' was permitted. When exasperated we would say either "drat" or "bother". Blaspheming was also not allowed. Mother, when we had driven her beyond her patience, would raise her eyes to heaven and say, "Gawd, why have I been given such children!" To say "God," except in prayer or reverence, was considered blasphemous. It was all right for Mother to say "Gawd," though we weren't permitted to do so. When exclaiming in surprise, she invariably said "Oh, Good Night!"

According to Mother's brother, Arthur, once when he was visiting and high-jinks were coming from upstairs where we three younger ones were up to our usual shenanigans, she went to the foot of the stairs and called out, "I shall come up there in a minute if you don't go to sleep if you dare." We did at times stretch her patience to the limit. When we were grown up and had caused her distress, she would reflect, "When children are little, they pull at your apron strings, but when they grow up, they pull at your heart strings." In later years when we criticised her for anything that had happened to us when we were younger and in which we felt she had fallen short, she would dismiss it with, "Yes, I'm the worst Mother you ever had."

I don't think Mother could get through a conversation without a saying of one sort or another - she was a veritable fount of them. She would caution us never to tell others our business, "Keep your own counsel," she would say, or, "Say nothing and saw wood." Some of her sayings were contradictory. She might say of someone who was not robust "He/she won't make old bones," and then would say when someone was very thin, "The slender willow bends with the wind, it is the oak which snaps in a gale." Or, "You can't fatten a thoroughbred." Some of her sayings could be irritating; if anyone were to say you were pretty and you passed this on to her, she would say, "Handsome is as handsome does." Some of them were incomprehensible: "The more things change, the more they stay the same." This was somewhat along the lines of the saying of my Father's which she would sometimes quote, "If things don't change, they'll stay as they are." Mother was never flustered. If something she had cooked didn't turn out like expected, she would say, "The proof of the pudding is in the eating."

Mother was very understanding of the young being young and didn't expect a maturity from them beyond their years, her belief being, "You can't put an old head on young shoulders." When unmarried women criticised the way children were being brought up, her response was, "Old maid's children are always the best raised."

"Look after the pennies and the pounds will look after themselves," was something she used to tell us. A bit of a waste of time really as we seldom had a penny and those Mother was so very careful with never seemed to build up into pounds. Also, "You must cut your coat according to your cloth". Same problem here as with pennies - no cloth!

Other sayings of hers which from time to time fitted a particular occasion were: "A drunk speaks a sober mind,"

"You can't make a silk purse out of a sow's ear" and "Force a man against his will and he'll be of the same opinion still."

Sometimes Mother used words that were peculiar to her, such as, "Don't moither me," meaning, "Don't bother me." Difficult people were known as 'Funny Ossities'. If any of us girls sneezed, she didn't just simply say "Bless you" but "Bless her, she's like our dresser, all drawers." When we or one of our friends had been clumsy in any way, such as dropping a dish, she would ask good-naturedly, "Are there any more at home like you?" She might say to a child who had outstayed its welcome, "Go tell your mother she wants you." She was quick with words. When we were assembled to go out, she might ask, "Are all those who are coming not here?" If we wanted to know how far away a place was when we were being sent on a message, she would say, "It is five minutes walk if you run." And, if we were out with anyone and there was a discussion as to who should pay, Mother might joke, "You pay whilst I fumble." Of anyone who constantly complained, Mother would say that the person, "Pulls a poor mouth." Or, "They are only happy when they are miserable." When any of us baulked when we were asked to do something, we were told to "Stop making heavy weather of it." "That doesn't become you" fitted both whether we were wearing something unsuitable or if we were sulking. Anyone who gossiped was a "proper News of the World."

A measure of her very happy personality, "We ain't got much money but we do see life." This is a line from a song. And whimsically, "We want for nothing we've got." I once asked her in later years how she managed to always be so happy and her response was, "I don't dwell on things." She was also capable of letting bygones be bygones, and that included herself - she didn't suffer from self-flagellation. She would say if there was a break in a relationship, or when anyone passed on that she was close to, "I have nothing to reproach myself for." At times she might enlarge on this and say, "You can only do your best. What more can you do? I've nothing to reproach myself for." She didn't allow many things to disturb her natural serenity - she believed in 'Anything for a quiet life'. If you wanted one thing and she wanted another, she would invariably go along with what you wanted, saying, "Have it your way - anything to save my breath". Pat, one day musing on this characteristic of Mother's, wondered whether that was the reason she had so many children.

One of Mother's homilies was of the man who told another in need that he would help him when he had something to give. The other man said, "You've got two sheep, give me one of those." Receiving the reply, "Ah but I have those." The message being, we fail to give from what we've got, whilst talking grandly of what we would do if in the future we had anything. Mother liked to talk of "the Widow's Mite." Once she saw a destitute man picking up cigarette butts in the street - she was a widow then but went into a shop and bought him a packet of Woodbines. Woodbines could be bought in packets of five only and that was all my Father had been able to afford to buy during the Depression. They were known as 'coffin nails'. Another time, downtown, Mother saw a fish-wife pushing a huge wooden barrow near the market and obviously struggling, so she went to help her to push it. These fish-wives, as we called them, were always dressed in black. Some of the streets in Liverpool were cobbled, and they may well have been outside the market which was a cavernous, gloomy edifice. Mother had a well-developed social conscience and was quick to criticise any display of social injustice. She told us of the poor boy who had been hanged whilst the son of a rich man got off - both having committed murder.

Though she didn't talk directly to us children about politics, she was politically aware. For some reason or other she didn't like Lloyd George, but I've now forgotten the comments she made about him. But I remember what she said about Queen Victoria - "When that fat woman was on the throne, people were starving." Mother, who claimed to be no royalist, could reel off royal lineage and history with no problem at all. She did like the Duke of Windsor and said that he was known as the Workers' King. Mother felt sorry for him - he fitted her dictum 'Uneasy lies the head that wears the crown' and she felt he should have married Mrs Simpson in a morganatic marriage and still kept the throne. She also felt for the situation of the Jews and held to the view that "He who harbours the Jews will prosper."

Mother had her quirks - one of them was always to leave a little on the plate. She had got this from her father who felt it was ill-mannered not to do so. When Mother was asked if she wanted more and didn't, she would say, "I have had elegant sufficiency." She did not eat a lot and believed in "Little but good." If she offered a drink to anyone whom she wasn't sure took a drink, she would ask, "Do you indulge?" Another quirk of hers was never to refer to toilet or lavatory except to members of the family; she would ask others if they wanted "to wash their hands." People didn't have bottoms, buttocks or bums (I can only think we picked up the expression 'bum' from our playmates when we called out rudely "Big Bum" to Mrs Davies) but derrieres or narratives; narratives being another word for 'tale' which was a play on the word 'tails'. When people were sick, they were more often than not referred to as being 'poorly', but to Mother, children were 'poorly', grown-ups were 'indisposed'. Neither expression was relevant to her as Mother was never sick; she always said that she didn't have time to be sick. In later years, clocks became 'timepieces' for Mother, though I don't remember her calling them that when we were growing up. Perhaps a clock was known as a timepiece in her childhood, and she merely reverted to calling it that in her later years. Otherwise, probably the only remnant of her early years when life was not so real and earnest was the fact that Mother liked dainty handkerchiefs of fine linen festooned with lace. To her a handkerchief was not just utilitarian but part of your dress and should reflect that.

    We were never allowed to feel sorry for ourselves, Mother didn't encourage grumbling or complaining of any sort. We might be told when we took to her any hurts that we had experienced, "You don't know you're born," or, "If you gave the person responsible for your troubles a good hiding, you wouldn't be able to sit down for a week." More generally and not specifically directed at one or other of us, "I cried because I had no shoes, then I met a man who had no feet." Though Mother was a shoulder for all and everyone to cry on, Ferg, Kath and I were invariably told to, "Count your blessings," if we took our problems to her. She seemed to think we were having it pretty soft and would say, "I was born too soon." Looking back and being able to see things from her perspective, it is not surprising, the problems we children had certainly paled into insignificance beside hers. So we learnt to keep things to ourselves. In later years she said to me, "You were a funny child, you kept things to yourself." One of the reasons was that I was fully aware from a very young age of the difficulties Mother faced in her situation, but also I feel that this was the result of her discouraging any discussion of a problem we might have had.

    None of us inherited Mother's aptitude for sayings and as children we were given more to retorts than sayings and these were common expressions amongst our playmates. We would ask anyone who stared, "Had a good look?" eliciting the inevitable response, "No, I've had a bad one." And if a person insisted on something they thought was so, they were told, "You know what 'thought' did, don't you, he thought but didn't think." And we wouldn't do such-and-such 'for toffee'. And even though we didn't swear or blaspheme, we did say, when exasperated, "Bloomin' Heck" and "Flippin' Heck." We spoke the local dialect, instead of saying "anyway," we said "any road." When we offered to pay, instead of saying "My treat," we would instead say "I'll mug you." We called each other "kid." When talking to anyone, even our own family, we would refer to our siblings as "our Ferg" or "our Kath" and so on, but when talking of Mother, we would say, even to each other, "my Mother."

Adults had their own stock sayings. For instance if they expressed a liking for the place they were living in would say, "When I leave here it will be feet first." To refer to a woman as 'she' would elicit the response, "She is the cat's mother." And if a person had a lot of wax in their ears it was said, "You could have planted potatoes in them." A common question from adults to children who were tall, "Is your father a policeman?" Those were the days when policemen had to be a certain height before they could join the police force

Even though we weren't given to sayings, Mother's expressions were also ours. In our house we 'teemed' the vegetables, we didn't strain them, and we 'wet' the tea instead of making it, and an apron was a pinny. An unpleasant odour was an 'Eau de kaniffe'. If people were the subject of criticism by others it was "They all had her/him 'decked' for it." If anyone left a door open and there was a draught, we would ask "Were you born in a barn?" If we shivered involuntarily we thought that someone had walked over our grave. And the dead would 'turn in their graves' if things happened that they would have disapproved of in life. A plain, lazy person was 'neither use nor ornament'. Acquisitive people were jackdaws. If anyone stayed in the lavatory too long we wondered if they were making their will. When we were ready to go out it was "Time to make tracks." Anything out of alignment was 'skew-whiff'.

 The main superstition that Mother had was that she didn't like thirteen to be sitting down to a meal at the same time. Some of the others were - a broken mirror meant seven years bad luck; Mother might say when her right hand was itchy that it showed she was going to come in for some money; an itchy left hand meant a visitor. Her lucky number was five and it didn't have to be a straight out '5', she added and subtracted at will to reach this number if the occasion warranted it. 32 was 5 if you added the two digits together and 27 also, if you took the first digit from the second. One thing Mother really liked was having her teacup read. If anyone came to the house and so much as suggested teacup reading, she was right into it. She also liked having her cards read. What was not liked at all was the Ace of Spades, the 'death' card. She once joined in a séance, but it was with friends and just to be sociable - she certainly didn't believe in them. Mother, however, was a believer in 'three knocks'. These were rare happenings but when she heard 'three knocks' she knew that someone had died. Also, when her father died, she felt a tap on her shoulder, and later when she heard of his death she found it had been at that very time.

* * * * * * * * * *

CHAPTER ELEVEN

In September 1939 Mother married Edward William Pugh. The first time I had met Pop was not long before I heard that he and Mother were to be married. I was with Mother at Granny and Granddad Elliott's house; Pop was a good friend of theirs. He was visiting England from South Africa where he lived. He gave me a shilling and told me to buy myself some sweets, but Mother had taken it off me and given me back one penny. When I returned from the shops, Pop asked me what I'd bought and I showed him. He said, "Didn't you get anything for your sister and brother?" I said, "I only had a penny." He said, "But I gave you a shilling." I replied, "Oh, Mother took that." He laughed and said, "Your Mother is quite a one." I know this conversation off by heart because Mother, when we got home, asked me to repeat it over and over. She seemed to think it very funny. It was not long after that she told us that she was to be married.

It must have been prior to the marriage that Mother started to throw out all her old letters. Pauline read through some of the letters as Mother sorted them. There were a number from a Texan, Cordy Massey, whom she had met during the First World War and referred to as 'Lofty'. He had wanted to marry her but she didn't even consider it as it would have meant going to America and she didn't want to move away from her parents. Pauline had been moved by the protestations of love that this Lofty wrote to Mother.

After she married my Father, Mother again didn't want to move away from her parents and go to Canada. He had been keen to emigrate there and made arrangements but Mother declined to go because of her parents. Another aborted plan was when my Father wrote to Uncle Sam, Auntie Georgie's husband, and asked about possibilities in South Africa. But it seems there weren't any. Mother would no doubt have been more amenable to going there as she would have been near her sister.

When my Father proposed to my Mother they were upstairs on a tram and he said to her, "You have made me fall in love with you," he then asked her to marry him. I asked her why she had said "yes" and she said, "Well, my brother was married to his sister and I thought it would be nice for the two families to be together." So it hadn't exactly been a love match on Mother's side. Mother's siblings and her parents were always enormously important to her. Mother was 19 and my Father 23 when they married on 15th May 1919.

Pop was born in Oswestry and his parents were first cousins. He had gone out to South Africa as a young man and had been around the world at least twice. In South Africa he lived in Krugersdrop in the Transvaal and worked as a building inspector with the local council. He had also done an apprenticeship as a carpenter. Mother said that it was strange that both her husbands should have been carpenters. She would add that all my Father left her was a bag of tools.

I can't recall the day of Mother and Pop's wedding and we didn't attend. It had taken place in a Registry Office. I don't know what she wore but it was probably the smart tailored suit and the Robin Hood hat with the very tall feather which suddenly appeared as part of her wardrobe after she was married to Pop. No doubt she would also have worn her fox fur - she had asked Pop for this instead of an engagement ring. But it is interesting that we would, after all, be going to South Africa as from the time Mother married Pop, we knew that that was to be our future.

When Mother and Pop returned from their honeymoon to the Isle of Man they brought me back a yellow dress and a black doll. The doll had a tag around its neck which said 'Toni' - I took this to be the doll's name and I was most disappointed that a girl doll should be called 'Toni', so even though I had wanted a black doll, I never took to it because I didn't like the name. But the yellow dress I really liked. It had a smocked bodice and a silky feel and it felt good when I wore it and was the poshest dress I had ever owned.

Pauline and Pat referred to our stepfather as Pop, we called him Dad in the early years, but when we were grown up we too called him Pop.

On the 3rd September, whilst Mother and Pop were on their honeymoon, World War II broke out. Pat and I were listening to the wireless and heard the announcement, "We are now at war with Germany." Pat sent me off to tell Mrs Carter and then instructed me to go on to the shops to buy some sugar. Mrs Carter hugged me when I told her about the war and said, "You poor child," but I really couldn't imagine why. I was nine years old.

Britain mobilised. Unless they were in a reserved occupation, men between the ages of eighteen and forty-one were called up to serve in the forces. Amongst the many that we knew, cousins, other relatives, friends and neighbours, there were Mr Morrisey who joined the air-force, Ronnie and Mother's brother, Arthur, who both joined the army. The saintly twins who taught Kath and I at Sunday School were also called up and wrote to us for some time afterwards, and then there came a letter to say they were being sent overseas and it would no longer be possible to keep in touch. Mother would say that if Deryk had been alive, in two years he would have been old enough to be called up. In some small way this was a comfort to her as she felt that at least he had been spared that. Ferg couldn't wait to go but he was only twelve years of age and no-one expected the war to last long enough for him to be eligible. Mother wasn't exactly a pacifist, but she often voiced the opinion that it was the generals who should be sent to fight the battles she believed they had started.

All women between eighteen and forty-one had to do some form of war work unless they were in a reserved occupation, such as teachers or nurses. They were also excused if they had a child under fourteen. Mother was excused because of Ferg, Kath and me. Amongst the many things that women could do to further the war effort were - join the forces, or work on the land, (the latter were known as Land Girls), or work in a factory. One young woman we knew, when called upon to do war-work, opted for a munitions factory and her skin turned yellow.

Pop went to work in the Censor's Office but never said anything about what he did. He was now marooned in England until the war was over. I find it interesting that he would have travelled from South Africa to England at a time when there would have been a lot of talk about the possibility of war.

School lunches were introduced - hot meals being served to the pupils each day because a lot of their mothers would be on war work. Mother briefly tried this job and then she found heaving around the huge food canisters too much and quickly claimed exemption, citing her three younger children. Children attending nurseries were given a daily dose of cod liver oil and orange juice. Many years later in South Africa I met a person who said that he had known pre-war Britain well and remembered the children with rickets and the large number who were undernourished but it had all changed with the war.

Next thing they were building air raid shelters in the schoolyard. Whilst they did so our school hours were curtailed and for a short period we only went for a few hours a day in one or other of the pupils' homes. They also built air raid shelters for the public along Kings Drive in case you were caught outside when the bombing started - of course they were a positive invite for nocturnal shenanigans. Ferg, coming home late one evening, heard a desperate cry from inside one of these shelters and released a young woman who had been locked in there by her boyfriend. Old cars were placed on the grass verges on either side of Kings Drive - we were supposed to push these cars onto the road if the Germans came. In no time they were stripped bare of anything useful or interesting.

I don't know when it was they gave us an Anderson shelter, except they first of all put it at the bottom of the garden and then, in the same way that we figured out about the boiler falling forward, they moved them close to the house. Anyway, it is what I thought was the reason they moved them. We slept in it for a while - it was fun, like camping out, but we soon became bored with that. The trouble was, ground water would sometimes seep into the pit in the middle where we were supposed to put our feet. Some people really fitted out their Andersons - had a little larder and bunk beds and put planks over the centre pit. But Pop didn't do that - it wasn't that Pop couldn't - he was a very good carpenter. He put cupboards in the house and did lots of things like that, even mended our shoes. He came equipped with a last - it appeared after he arrived on the scene so I presume he brought it with him. He put rings of rubber on the heels of our shoes, these could turn so that when we wore part of the heel down, we turned the rubber to an unworn section. Pop's thumbs and little fingers were permanently crooked and turned inwards - he said it was because they had become atrophied that way from holding tools - though he probably said 'stuck' and not atrophied - he would have known that word but I wouldn't. I learnt only recently that Pop's crooked little fingers could show he was descended from Vikings - apparently it has been found that many Vikings had this same genetic defect.

Elderly and handicapped people were given Morrison shelters. These were for indoors and were designed to double as a bed. The top was of heavy steel which people put their mattress on. When an air raid began, they merely slipped underneath. Granny and Granddad Elliott had one of those. Though, looking back, Granny Jackson didn't have one. Perhaps they didn't expect Barton to be bombed, or maybe she had refused it. It could be that she thought of them as one of those new-fangled things that she had no time for.

The school got into the spirit of the war effort and we were encouraged to bring our pennies to Monday morning Assembly when each class would line up and form a line in front of them with their pennies. This way they had the classes in competition with each other as each wanted their line of pennies to be the longest. The school also encouraged us to bring along our silver paper (silver paper was used as the inner wrapping on bars of chocolate) and we had to take this directly to the headmistress which gave us a sense of importance.

Barrage balloons appeared in the sky and our windows had cross-strips put on them for precaution against the blast of an explosion. And then there was the blackout - no street lights and people out walking would have little fluorescent badges which glowed in the dark to make their presence known on a pitch-black night. They came in different shapes, some like butterflies. I always wanted one of those but was never given one. Busses and trams had their windows pasted over and you had to know where you were going as visibility through them was very poor. I imagine that the pasting was mainly done to minimise the light seen outside and also to provide protection from flying glass should there have been an explosion. The busses and trams still drove with their headlights on, but they were shielded and directed downwards. When an air-raid was really bad the busses and trams would stop where they were. One night Pat was marooned on a tram and decided to walk home instead and saw a plane being shot down with the pilot baling out. She quickly ran home. On another occasion John told us that when the Jolly Miller at the top of Millbank was bombed, he was blown out of his bed by the blast.

Curtains had to be substantial enough to cut out all light at night and Air-raid Wardens were engaged to see that this was done; as they passed by in the road, if they saw a light they would blow their whistle and call out, "Put out that light!" Air-raid Wardens had a particular area they had to patrol when the air-raid siren sounded - Mr Hemming was the warden for our road. We became used to the sound of the air-raid siren and the sound of the 'all-clear'. We learnt to tell the difference between the British planes and the German ones - the German ones going 'chug-chug-chug' in a dull, staccato-like fashion. Searchlights, with their probing beams, would scour the sky looking for the planes of the Luftwaffe.

Posters appeared on the busses and trains, in fact everywhere, warning you about careless talk because 'The enemy might be listening', and 'Be like Dad, keep Mum'. We learnt that the Fifth Column could be anywhere. 'Is your journey really necessary?' greeted you at the railway stations. Children were cautioned not to pick up toys or cigarette cases or lighters which they saw on the road in case these were booby-trapped. We were asked to conserve hot water; the King, we were told, only had 5" of water in his bath. But these things all came at different times, not together, and I have no idea of their sequence. One day they were not there, and the next they were.

The war brought food rationing and we were given a set number of points per month for jams, dried vegetables, dried fruits, biscuits, flour, nuts, glace fruits, oils, sauces, etc., and tinned goods such as preserved meats, condensed milk, stewed fruits, fish, beans, etc. Just because all these things were on points, didn't mean that they were available, some things were still difficult to get. There would be a different number of points required for different items. Everyone was allocated a specific ration of the following per week - butter or lard 4 ozs; tea 2 ozs; sugar 12 ozs; meat 6 ozs; bacon or ham 4 ozs. We were allowed, I think, 6 ounces of sweets a month and 1 pint of milk per adult per week and ½ pint a day for children up to the age of fifteen and 1 pint a day for babies and pregnant women. Ice-cream disappeared entirely, no more Wall's Ice-cream man cycling down the road. The van with the black puddings was also no more, as well as the 'salt' man with his horse-drawn flat-tray cart with the enormous blocks of salt, though salt was never rationed. Perhaps the salt man was now serving at the front.

Eggs became non-existent, except for babies and children who received a limited allocation a week. Dried eggs appeared and were available on points. We particularly liked dried eggs, and would re-hydrate them with either water or milk (I've forgotten which) and then soak our bread in this mixture and then fry it - scrumptious. Spam, a great favourite fried or otherwise, also required points. They were not needed for fresh vegetables or fruit, and there was never any shortage of things like potatoes, carrots, turnips, cabbage, onions, etc. Tomatoes became hard to get, as did fresh fruit, and if you saw a queue outside a vegetable shop you automatically joined it and bought whatever it was they were selling. Fruits that needed to be imported, like bananas, disappeared entirely and didn't reappear again till after the war. Also things like tinned peaches and pineapple. Mother's sister, Georgie, would, on rare occasions, send us a food parcel and this would invariably contain a tin of pineapple, which was always in chunks and not in slices. I remember how delectable our minute portion was when it was shared out.

Saccharin tablets appeared to replace the sugar in one's tea. However, Mother wouldn't touch them and continued using two spoonfuls of sugar, which she was able to do as the rest of us didn't mind the substitute so there was sugar to spare. Mother also wouldn't eat margarine which now replaced butter but as we also didn't mind that, she was able to use our butter ration as well. On occasion when there was no shortening for a cake, liquid paraffin was used and soya bean icing stood-in for almond icing. We never went hungry, when there were a number in the family it was easy to cope because, when your rations were pooled, they were adequate, but for people living on their own or only a couple, it was much more difficult. Invalids received an extra amount of milk and when Pop was recovering from pneumonia, Mother was able to buy glucose for him.

I once had my sweet ration card stolen. I had just come out of a shop where I had purchased my allocation of sweets and still had the card in my hand. A person who happened to be passing snatched it from me in the twinkling of an eye. I had to go to the Food Office and apply for another card which I received in no time at all.

Clothing and shoes were also rationed. We received about 60 coupons per person per year. A coat required eighteen coupons. One could appeal to the relevant authority if, for instance, you had a child who outgrew its clothing in a matter of months and would be given some extra coupons.

Mother once applied for some for me - I remember accompanying her and being given extra coupons to buy shoes, but I don't remember getting the shoes!

Fashion in general changed - cami-knickers appeared - these were singlet, slip and knickers combined - and women wore blouses that consisted of a front with a net back and no sleeves because their jacket would cover those areas. Under-slips were cut on the cross and Liberty Bodices disappeared. Young women, and older ones, painted their legs to look as if they were wearing stockings, some to the extent of painting in a seam up the back. Prime Minister Churchill made the Siren Suit popular; this was an all-over tunic similar to a boiler suit, which one stepped into and zipped up the front. In touring bombed areas he was invariably shown wearing one. Slacks for women became commonplace - they were no longer a sensation as they had been when they first came out many years before the war. Mother said that then the first woman to wear them in Liverpool was jeered at as she walked down the street.

A lot more peroxide-blonde-haired women were to be seen with plucked eyebrows - women had left the confines of the scullery and had become more fashionable. The turban came in vogue - this, I think, because women working in factories needed to keep their hair out of the way and a turban did this. Also snoods - a heavy open-webbed covering for the hair. Hats with a veil which could be pulled down to cover the face seemed to have had their day. Pixie hoods appeared and also balaclavas. Pauline knitted Kath and me an Elizabethan-style hood each. All women knitted then - girls were taught as early as possible to knit and this is what we did after tea of an evening, in fact during every free moment. Our wool came in skeins and we held them for each other as they were wound into a ball. One jumper I knitted was grey, with red and blue stripes of one inch width after every four inches of grey, the stripes being ruffled by knitting in double stitches when you came to the stripe and then casting off the extra stitches again when you continued with the grey. I topped these stripes off by knitting little bows and adorning the middle of each stripe with these. Unfortunately something went wrong when I knitted the neck and it practically choked me. Pauline said, rather unkindly, how could I expect it to fit around my fat neck. My later to be diagnosed colloid goitre, was then beginning to make its presence felt. Mother took to knitting carpets with string, weaving in pieces of rag which she had cut into pieces of even length. If we found some part of our wardrobe had gone missing, it was almost certain because Mother had knitted it into one of her rag rugs.

Clogs were occasionally seen - Betty Heathcote had a pair and I longed for a pair too but Mother wouldn't buy me any. People learned to make sheets, curtains and even clothing out of flour sacks, but no amount of washing or even dyeing would remove the flour mill's name from the cloth. Mother got some flour sacks from her brother, Hugh, who worked for a flour company and made curtains of them. Pauline made me a coat out of a grey army blanket. We learnt to make-do as we had done when Mother was a widow. It is rather ironic really, just when there was an increased income in the household due to Mother having married Pop, we went from the frugality of Mother being a widow, to the frugality of rationing.

Household linen, furniture and kitchenware were in short supply; saucepans were unavailable. You couldn't just go into a shop and buy any of these things, though newly-weds were allocated coupons to buy a certain amount to be able to set up home. Furniture became far more flimsy, due no doubt to the shortage of materials. It was very difficult to rent a house and the chances of newly-weds being able to set-up home on their own, were severely limited. Most had to move in with their parents or grandparents. Auntie Cissie's son and daughter-in-law lived with her.

At the railway stations the heavy iron 'penny-in-the-slot' machines which gave either a wafer-thin bar of chocolate or a packet of 5 Woodbine cigarettes for a penny, were 'Not in use'. If you were travelling by train and wanted a cup of tea at a station kiosk, you had to provide an empty jam jar to have it in as crockery also became in short supply. And on the station platforms, happy children with buckets and spades all set for a day at the seashore, gave way to troops leaving and tearful farewells.

One day we were all given gas masks. I received a green bag from some member or other of the family to put my gas mask in - it had a plaited handle and looked really nice. I liked carrying my gasmask around in this green bag. Sometimes at school we had practice drill in putting on our gas masks. Later we were given an extra snout to screw on to the first one - the powers-that-be had become concerned about another gas that might be used. Otherwise school was as boring as ever and the only escape was when the air-raid siren sounded and we could go home. What is more, there was even more school than before. The schools kept open over the holidays because so many mothers were on war-work. Even though Mother did not go out to work, she sent us anyway even though it wasn't compulsory for pupils to attend. There was no 'reading of the register' and no lessons as such and we did things like painting pictures and writing compositions and the whole atmosphere was more relaxed.

But even in wartime, peacetime activities go on and, some time in 1940, Mother took Kath and me on holiday to Colwyn Bay with her friend, May Sanderson, and her son, Tony. May had been Mother's friend since they were both seventeen. I would have been ten at the time and Tony was six. We stayed in a very big house and Tony, Kath and I shared the same double bed. One evening Mother and Auntie May (as Kath and I called her) had gone out and Tony, Kath and I sneaked out to the woods. It was there I was accosted by a man. Kath and Tony ran home where Mother and Auntie May had since returned, but I was able to fight the man off and fled back to the house. Mother and Auntie May tried to get me to tell them what had happened, but as I've mentioned, after my first experience of being molested, I refused to talk.

As nothing was able to be replaced during the war, old trams were brought back into service - these were open upstairs with a roof only, and downstairs the poor driver was exposed to the elements. He would dress in heavy oilcloths and would stamp his feet to keep warm. The floors of these old trams were of slatted wood and the seats downstairs ran along each side opposite each other. Mother's friend, Mrs Burns, became a conductor on the busses and if we got on the bus when she happened to be on her shift, she would say when we proffered our fare to her, "Your Granddad's upstairs, luv, and he's just paid it for you."

Bicycles were at a premium after the war began, preferable to taking 'Shanks Pony', that is walking, which the posters implored us to do. When anyone left a bicycle anywhere, it had to be secured with a safety chain and padlock. However, Pat's bicycle was stolen from our backyard where she thought it would be safe. Petrol was strictly rationed, not that that affected anyone we knew in Liverpool as none of our friends had a car and the only relatives who did, such as Uncle Ronald, my Father's brother, lived in another city. He, according to one letter of Granny Jackson's, had been saving his petrol ration up so he could visit my Father's grave.

We began to see New Zealand, Australian, South African, Canadian, and later American military personnel when we went downtown. Kath had an autograph book and would ask for their autographs, they were always very obliging and some of them wrote very nice little jingles in the book. American sailors were known as 'doughboys'. We thought their bell-bottom trousers and white caps looked odd. The American military were not as popular as the other allied troops, as they sometimes seemed very patronising. It was said of them that they had Coca Cola at the front. I was once at the swimming baths along Prescott Road and some American troops had been swimming there. They later stood on the gallery above the baths and threw pennies to the children, we provided entertainment for them as we ducked for the pennies. After automatically ducking for one I stopped and felt humiliated.

An American Army Camp with all black soldiers went up somewhere not too far away from us - this was an era when the American Army was segregated. An Internment Camp also went up not far away for displaced foreigners and on one occasion a group of us kids went to look, thinking they were the enemy and wondering what the enemy looked like. We had no understanding of the difference between foreign nationals who happened to be in the UK when hostilities broke out between Britain and the country they were from, and those who were actually enemies. Some of them resented our curiosity and shouted at us and a solider guarding the perimeter, shooed us away.

Wireless programmes changed. 'Workers' Playtime' came into being and was broadcast during lunch-time at the factories. ITMA (It's That Man Again) with Tommy Handley was enormously popular. There was a cleaning woman in it, a Mrs Mop, who would always enter saying "Can I do you now, sir?" and the Colonel who, at the merest suggestion that anyone might be talking about a drink, would say, "I don't mind if I do." Some of the sayings, such as TTFN ("Ta-ta for now"), became part of the common language. ITMA was a great favourite with the family, particularly with Ferg.

There was also Lord Haw Haw (William Joyce) who broadcast propaganda from Germany in an effort to undermine British morale - he was regarded with some amusement. However, during one of his broadcasts he mentioned Mab Lane, saying it was going to be bombed; this was a country lane just on the edge of our suburb and there was amazement that it was known outside our area, let alone overseas in Germany.

Less remembered and only names to me now, are 'In Town Tonight' and 'Jack Hilton and his Orchestra'.

The news which had never been a big thing in our family, suddenly became so, at least to the adults if not to us children, and we were forever being told to "hush" when the news was on. Churchill's offering of only 'blood, sweat and tears' left us children uninspired.

Many haunting songs, all to do with war, became popular - some of them sung by Vera Lynn whose lovely voice added to the poignancy of them. The father of Pat's friend, Betty, thought Vera Lynn was fantastic (as a lot of people did) and he said I looked just like her. I was offended, but Betty assured me that, given how her father thought of Vera Lynn, it was the greatest compliment he could pay me. Some of the songs popular at the time were: 'There'll be bluebirds over the white cliffs of Dover'; 'Goodnight Sweetheart, till we meet tomorrow'; 'We'll meet again'; 'It's a lovely day tomorrow' and 'When they sound the last All-Clear'. There were also stirring, patriotic songs like 'There'll always be an England. We children sang more down-to-earth songs like:

We're going to hang out the washing on the Siegfried Line
Have you any dirty washing Mother dear ...

But the old favourites were still there - Gracie Fields with 'Sally, Sally, Pride of our Alley', and George Formby playing his banjo and singing, 'When I'm cleaning windows'.

The only wireless programme I can remember from before the war was the children's programme which had as its theme song, 'We are the Ovaltinies, happy girls and boys'.

We queued to see the film 'The Great Dictator' starring Charlie Chaplin. Ferg, Kath, Eric Gates and I saw this at a picture-house in Old Swan.

I can't recall now the actual year it came out, but we all went to see 'Mrs Miniver' - it was a great hit. It starred the American, Greer Garson, so very lovely and so very British; we all fell in love with this image of ourselves, the very epitome of the British stiff upper lip.

Words came into our everyday language which bespoke the war, such as 'U-boats'. If shoes were too big and looked like clod-hoppers, we said they were like U-boats. And 'Jerry' - I don't know which came first, Jerry for a German or Jerry for a chamber-pot, but it was our name for both.

Downtown in the docks area, some people began sleeping in the underground areas of railway stations. One night returning late we saw them lined up against the wall, sleeping. They had made themselves comfortable with blankets. I understand that they took it in turns to keep watch, which included waking up the loud snorers who might be disturbing the sleep of others. Apparently people walking by didn't bother them.

When the air-raid siren sounded, Mother would sometimes bring us three younger ones downstairs and we would go to sleep in the glory-hole under the stairs. Mother and Pop would sit on chairs on top of the coal in the coal-hole if things started to sound really bad, because that cupboard was also under the stairs. Sometimes, though, they would just sit in the kitchen with a candle under a chair to subdue the light. Pauline and Pat refused to budge from their beds. They would say, "If we are going to be killed, we might as well be killed in our beds." There were ack-ack guns in the woods behind the houses in Southdene Road, not far away at all, and the thunder of them going off rattled the windows. But I must say, for some reason, Ferg, Kath and I never felt afraid. One night, when everything had gone quiet, Mother brought us out of the glory-hole and put us to sleep under an eiderdown in front of the fireplace. Suddenly, we heard the approaching sound of a whistling bomb and it was so close, we instinctively pulled the eiderdown up over our heads - the deafening noise as it hit the ground would soon follow. The bomb had landed in the grounds of St Dominic's in Southdene Road, just around the corner from us, but had missed the building. Each day the Town Hall would put up a list of casualties from the previous night and one time there were 2,000 names on the list.

One night, when it was fairly bad, from the glory-hole we could hear Mother and Pop in the coal-hole - Mother was very upset and was saying, "I can't stand it anymore, Willie." Not long after, Mother and Pop with Ferg, Kath and me, went off to Thornton, which is near Blackpool. We boarded first with a Mrs Jackson, but then there was a falling out and we moved to board with a Mrs Owen. Mother resented Mrs Jackson saying of a night-time - "Let's go outside and watch the fireworks." Some nights, the air raid over Liverpool would be so heavy that the flames from the city could be seen as far away as Thornton.

Mr and Mrs Owen kept hens and I revelled in their country smell and watching them being fed. Also their house backed onto a field in which there was a horse which always came over when it saw me even though I never had anything to give it. I would tell this horse my troubles. Sometimes Mrs Owen would ask me to stop at the bakery on the way home and pick up a fruit tart, these were always very small, only saucer size, but delicious and I loved the smell of the shop. I shared a bed with Freda, the daughter, and she would make a joke of how I was always kicking her out of bed in my sleep. I found this very funny but for some reason or other, Mother didn't. Pauline wrote from Liverpool that she was lonely in the house on her own; I don't know where Pat was at that time, probably at Teachers' Training College in Hull, though she was also for a brief time evacuated to some place in the Lake District. So Kath returned home to keep Pauline company.

Ferg and I attended the school in Thornton. The school was very old-fashioned in its style - rooms leading into rooms - so different from the cold and impersonal, but well-planned, Liverpool school. Miss Hodgson was my class teacher and was marvellous to me and I did very well in her class. We had other teachers for some lessons, one of whom was irascible. One day this teacher dragged me out of my seat by my ear. Mother was livid and went down to the school and told her that she didn't mind my being disciplined, but not in that way. That teacher later brought me in to her classroom and hugged me. The headmaster was very gruff and we had to address him as 'Sir' - I kept forgetting as I'd had all female teachers at my school in Liverpool and had never had cause to call any male 'Sir'. He would reprimand me and I didn't like him at all. I had such a good relationship with Miss Hodgson that I told her about it and she clucked sympathetically. At one stage we were encouraged to knit mitts, socks and balaclavas for the troops. I knitted mitts and they came out all wrong. Miss Hodgson said, "Never mind, some farmer will be glad of them." It was the only time I ever enjoyed my school days, thanks to the wonderful Miss Hodgson.

One of the boys in Miss Hodgson's class would sometimes walk me home; we had to pass by his house on the way to where I lived and I was impressed by how posh his house looked. All the pupils were nice and I fitted in from the first day. I made friends particularly with a Jean Godbert. Some evenings I would go to the library which made me feel really grown-up. I would borrow books but the only one I now remember is 'Black Beauty', but what it was about I have now forgotten. We didn't go home for lunch as we did in Liverpool but took sandwiches and every now and then, as a special treat, Ferg and I were allowed to have a fish and chips lunch in a room at the back of the fish and chip shop.

I have forgotten how long we were at Thornton, but Mother eventually wanted to return to Liverpool and when she had decided, she was not going to wait, despite the fact that I had passed the Review in Thornton, and by having done this, was eligible to sit the scholarship for high school. (The Review was the preliminary exam which decreed whether you could sit for the scholarship). Miss Hodgson appealed to Mother to delay her return, and when Mother said she couldn't, she suggested that I be left behind, saying that the work in Liverpool would be different and I would be required to sit the Review again there. But Mother was not to be deterred, and so it happened as Miss Hodgson had said, and I didn't pass the Review in Liverpool.

The changes the war made to our way of living, coincided with the changes which came with Mother's marriage to Pop. Christmases were never the same after that. Pop believed in practical presents and I remember our enormous disappointment that first Christmas after Mother married him, to look in our pillowcases at the end of the bed and find only clothes. Our disappointment was obvious to Mother who then told us we could help ourselves to the foil-wrapped chocolate decorations on the tree.

Going to the seaside was not the same either. There was not that wonderful anticipatory build-up days in advance - now that Mother had Pop, we were no longer part of the planning. And when we arrived at the seaside, Pop and Mother would leave us to our own devices and go off together. Possibly some of the changes came because we were simply growing up. I remember my stepfather with love but tend to date things prior to, or after, his coming. He could be blunt to the point of rudeness. One friend of Mother's who came to visit when Mother happened to be out (few people had a telephone then and anyone wanting to visit had to take the chance of finding you in) was greeted at the door by Pop with, "Marion's not in, but if you hurry, you can catch the next bus." He was nowhere nearly as gregarious as Mother who enjoyed having friends around her. He was very set in his ways and liked the same armchair kept for him. If you happened to be sitting in it when he came into the room, he'd either cough meaningfully at the side of the chair, or yank you unceremoniously out of it. When he had a boiled egg, he carefully sliced a piece of bread into fingers and then dipped each finger in the egg. He had rice pudding almost every day. When Pop was going out, if he was asked when he would be back he would reply, "When I arrive." We were horrified when he would go to the front gate in his dressing gown and slippers - something you simply did not do in our district. One of the magazines he bought was 'Titbits' - this might possibly have changed its format since those days, but then it was eminently suitable for all the family to read. He shaved with an open, cut-throat razor, sharpening it on a leather strop. Other things I associate with Pop are Wintergreen ointment and Senna Pods, which he introduced into the household. Quink Ink only made its appearance after he arrived as well; it came in an interesting shaped bottle which you could rest partly on its side. He also brought shoe trees into the household which kept shoes in shape. They had a rounded heel and a formed toe with a metal rod in between which could be adjusted according to the size of the shoe.

It wasn't long after they were married that Kath and I were upset with Pop over something and were talking about him after we went to bed, obviously in quite loud voices, because he came in and gave us some toffee and we then felt awful that we had criticised him.

Pop had an aunt in Liverpool, Aunt Annie, and Mother would often go there to help her. Sometimes she would send Kath and me to see if Aunt Annie wanted anything. She lived in a very large house and, on one occasion when Kath and I were there, she told us to select any book we wanted from her extensive collection of books and we both chose a Bible - Kath's was backed with ivory and mine with oak. I still have mine.

Pop also had a sister, Edie, in Liverpool. She stayed with us for a while and I liked her a lot though she was a very restrained personality. We always referred to her as Auntie Edie. She shared the bedroom with Kath and me and of a morning would curl her hair with curling tongs which she had heated either on the gas stove or in the fireplace. Her white hair was singed brown at the ends. Auntie Edie had an account at George Henry Lee's, an exclusive shop. Pop used to say, "She has champagne tastes with a beer pocket." He said her former husband had told him, "She wanted me to buy her a car and I couldn't afford a bloody bicycle." She did put on airs. When Mother bought me a skirt at Marks and Spencer's, Auntie Edie said between her thin lips, "Oh, really, Marie. Fancy shopping there." And when Mother suggested that Auntie Edie invite her friends to visit her at our house, she said, "You don't think I would bring my friends to this district." Mother was rather hurt by that one.

Later on houses were going very cheaply and Mother suggested to Pop that they buy a house along with Auntie Edie. His response was that he didn't come all the way to Liverpool to live with his sister. There was one house in particular near Newisham Park, a four-storey place with a cellar, that Mother looked at and was interested in. Pop would keep her mind set on the future and talk about when they would go to South Africa. Future plans now began with, "After the War is over…"

Mother's sister, Georgie, who lived in Pretoria, was a friend of one of Pop's daughters, Baby, who lived in Krugersdrop where Pop used to live. I don't know what Baby's Christian name was, nor that of his other two children, Dolly and Sonny. All his children were known by their family pet names. Sonny was in the South African Navy and he once came to visit us when his ship had called in to Liverpool. Mother had actually met Pop many years before at her parents' house when he was married to his first wife, Maggie, and she was married to Cyril and had young children. She said he didn't make much of an impression on her then. Apart from being a friend of Granny and Granddad Elliott, he also knew Great-Aunt Nellie Morton and told us how he had once called on her in London. She lived in a large house and happened to be upstairs when he called, which meant that she had to come down to open the door for him. She greeted him with, "Did I come all the way down the stairs for you." Pop had met his match in bluntness in Great-Aunt Nellie.

On Boxing Day 1941, Pauline married Leonard Ernest Smith and Kath, Pat and I were bridesmaids. Pauline made Kath's and my dresses. They were green taffeta. Pauline made many things for us over the years, she was an accomplished seamstress from a young age - she was actually talented all round and always succeeded in whatever she took up. Mr Finnegan gave Pauline and Leon a mirror for their wedding present, this was made by the firm he worked for. Otherwise I don't remember too much about the wedding except that the organ broke down and John filled the breach by hand-pumping it. Mother warmed towards the mother of Pauline's friend, Olga de Jong, when she asked her, "Who is that very smart gentleman?" referring to John. Mother loved her brother John and felt a glow on his behalf when he received a compliment from anyone.

Leon was an Australian and we loved him - in fact all the road loved his wonderful outgoing personality. Mother and Pauline had been on tenterhooks when he was taken to meet Auntie Lottie, but his "Did yer?" went unnoticed by her and she was as charmed by him as he was by her. Leon used expressions which we had never heard before, such as 'Fair Dinkum' to confirm a truth, 'Bonza' for something good, and 'Good on yer', as a form of approval. Sometimes Pauline and Leon would go and watch the wrestling matches. One wrestler was called 'Pie' and the spectators delighted in calling out "Dirty Pie! Dirty Pie!", Pauline along with them, according to Leon.

When he was on leave, Leon took us three younger ones to the State Restaurant on a couple of occasions. This was a 'posh' restaurant downtown and it was here I first tasted a peach melba and a banana split. It would be hard to describe how marvellous that was to children who had never had such treats. Mrs Davies' brother, Matt, worked in the kitchens of a similar sort of posh restaurant and he said that if we saw what went on in them we wouldn't eat there - that he himself would go out at lunchtime and get himself fish and chips. It was probably Leon who also took us to the Kardomah Coffee House where people sat in booths and the walls were paneled. I remember going there and I couldn't imagine any other family member taking me; coffee was for Sundays and adults only. When Leon came home on leave he always had something special for each of us that he had been able to bring in. For instance, silk stockings for the older female members of the family - these were very hard to get in the U.K. and were guarded carefully, being invisibly mended if they got ladders. He brought Kath and me a dress each on one occasion. Leon had no trouble guessing what our sizes might be and they fitted perfectly. His best friend Bill Jones once managed to bring in a three-piece suite from a voyage to America. They said that if you had a fiver on the ready you could slip anything through the Liverpool docks. Leon was always open to a 'dare', which is why we ended up with a large, saucer-shaped ashtray with a funnel-like centre, souvenired from the State Restaurant. Leon once took us on board the ship he was due to sail on to have a look around. He told us at the end of a voyage all the left-over food would be thrown overboard - what Granny Jackson would call 'a wicked waste' and I would have agreed with her. Leon had a cousin in Liverpool whom we visited every now and then. Her six year old daughter had a wooden rocking horse, a huge one, such as I'd only seen in story books and always wanted and now I was too big to ride it. Such was life.

It was a source of amusement to us that Leon, who was Leon Smith, had a best friend called Bill Jones. Bill was engaged to May. May lived with her parents in a large house and as they had a lot of room, they were obliged to take in an evacuee from London. A young cockney lad was billeted on them who, it appeared by the tales they told, was quite a handful. He was very common so it was quite an adjustment for them.

I don't know how rigid were the rules on taking in those who had been bombed out, but we always had a houseful so there was no thought of our taking any more. For a night or two the Gypsy Field had people sleeping there, they had been bombed out of an area downtown and the authorities were still trying to find them accommodation.

It was not long after we returned to Liverpool that Ferg had to go into Broadgreen Hospital. He had been climbing up on the shed roof to pass Eileen something (she was reaching for it out of her bedroom window) when he slipped and grazed his shin. Some time afterwards Mother caught him dressing the wound, which at that stage was horribly infected. The doctor had him admitted to hospital and he was there for a while with a cage over his leg. Ferg was told that if it had been left any longer, he would have needed a plate next to the bone. The ward Ferg was in was so crowded that he was put on the verandah. When we first visited him, I unintentionally embarrassed him by saying, "You didn't say you had any lemonade." I had never seen a urine bottle before. The boy in the next bed was dying of peritonitis and the bed was shielded by a screen. He was delirious and would shout out now and then. His parents kept vigil at his bedside. The wards were a series of pre-fab buildings and there was a patch of lawn between each building. Each ward was divided into two sections connected by a porch which also provided a walk-way through to the next ward. Next to Ferg's ward was the T.B. ward and when I walked through the connecting porch I would hold my breath so as not to breathe in any germs.

T.B. was as active as ever. Eunice, the sister of Pat's friend, Betty, caught it and was hospitalised for a year or so. When we next saw her she had the most exquisite porcelain complexion and rosy cheeks; Betty said that it was the T.B. which gave her that complexion. Pat had a boyfriend who had a two-year old brother. His father had been hospitalised for twenty years with T.B. of the spine and had been let out of hospital thinking he was cured. However, he was only out long enough to father another child and then had to return to the sanatorium.

At some stage Pop became ill with double pneumonia and was admitted to the Royal Infirmary. I visited him there and the tiled walls echoed and the place was cavernous and cheerless and overwhelmingly dour. By contrast, Broadgreen Hospital had a cheerful atmosphere.

When Ferg was fourteen he went to work in an office, the idea being that he would stay there until he was sixteen when he would begin an apprenticeship at Birchall's. Before he had this position, he had worked briefly at the market, that is until Uncle Hugh, downtown one day, saw him pushing a barrow and told Granddad who was furious that his grandson should be doing so menial a task, so Mother took Ferg away.

Every couple of weeks Pat had to do air-raid duty at the school and often would take me along with her. We slept in a room at the end of the building. Pat was supposed to patrol the corridors at intervals but didn't, because it made no sense as, if the school had been bombed, we would surely have heard it. She was paid 4s 6d a night for this.

* * * * * * * * * * *

CHAPTER TWELVE

We were not back in Liverpool for long when Mother decided that Kath and I should be evacuated by ourselves to Wales. We were sent to Colomendy Camp in Loggerheads, near Mold in North Wales. Mother had first tried to get us evacuated to South Africa and we had the smallpox vaccination which gave me a bout of cowpox, leaving me with a number of scars on my legs. But we didn't go to South Africa after all because a ship taking children to Canada was either bombed or torpedoed and the overseas evacuation of children stopped. We would have gone to my Mother's sister, Georgie, in Pretoria. Though we had been looking forward to going, it had been the thought of the ship journey and seeing another country which had been the attraction; we really preferred being in the same country as the rest of the family, and to us Wales was the same country even if the Welsh didn't think so.

Colomendy Camp was in a beautiful situation at the foot of Cathkin Peak. There were girls and boys there but the boys' camp was situated way away from the girls', though we were each accommodated in the same sort of wooden buildings. In the girls' camp there were five dormitories - a sixth building of exactly the same design was used as a school room for the younger children. These buildings were situated either side of a footpath, the three on the left were for the older pupils and the two on the right for the younger ones; the third on that side being a schoolroom. Each dormitory held about fifty pupils. We slept in bunk beds with a locker between each bunk, the top and bottom bunks sharing the same locker. Our beds had to be made just so, the sheets and blankets tucked in, the corners mitred and the top, if not being taut enough to bounce a coin as in the military, headed in that direction. Every day, after we had made our beds and tidied our lockers, they were inspected.

All the dormitories were called after mountains in the vicinity - Moel Entlie, Moel Arthur and Moel Famau were to the left of the footpath, with Cefn Mawr and Vainol (I'm not sure of the spelling of this) to the right. The other dormitory, which was used as a schoolroom for the younger children, I think might have been Moel Cathkin. Moel Entlie held the oldest pupils of all and there was quite a rivalry between them and Moel Arthur. Once quite a melee broke out between the two. Moel Famau, the dormitory Kath and I were in, kept out of it. In actual fact, I was really not eligible to be in the more senior dormitory, only being 11, but an exception was made as I had a sister there.

At each end of the dormitory there was a small room on either side - three of these rooms housed teachers, the fourth was used for storage and was known as the 'Boot Room'. In the boot room we discovered a very old musical instrument, a tinfoil phonograph. We had to manually push the single cylinder around as the handle was missing. This rubbed the skin off our fingers. I can't remember now what tune the one metal cylinder played, it was probably not a recognisable piece to us anyway. Otherwise in the boot room there were just suitcases and other uninteresting things. We sometimes hid in there when we wanted to appear absent, such as when we should have been attending some boring thing the school was putting on.

In the middle of the dormitory on the right-hand side, a door led out to a lavatory. This was a seat placed on a large can and, we were soon to learn, strictly forbidden to be used as Mary the maid would carry on to the dormitory teachers if she had to empty this can. It is inevitable that if one is not able to go to the lavatory, the need becomes desperate. Many a night Kath and I tied our big toes together so that if one tried to go to the lavatory in the night, the string would pull on the other's foot and we would go together. We would go as quietly and as carefully as we could, hoping the boards wouldn't creak, but one of the dormitory teachers, known to us out of her hearing as Miss Prick because she had a pointed nose, must have slept with one ear open, as a good many times she heard us and we would be ordered to attend outside her door the next morning. This meant a berating - and how she could berate! Miss Prick loved to hear her own voice and would carry on endlessly at the slightest misdemeanour. It was usually to her that Mary, the maid, would complain if we had used the night lavatory.

In the room opposite Miss Prick was one of the other dormitory teachers, a Miss Thompson. She was tall and elegant with very pale skin and hair and was a somewhat remote personality. We preferred her being on duty rather than Miss Prick as she didn't seem to lie awake listening for the creaking of the floorboards, waiting to catch some hapless pupil going to the lavatory.

I can't remember the name of the teacher whose room was at the other end of the dormitory opposite the boot room but she was the one who decided to tell us the facts of life. It was shortly after Kath and I had arrived that this teacher came around at bedtime and asked if anyone wanted any towels. Kath and I said, "What's she talking about? We've got towels." At which the other girls giggled. They told this teacher that Kath and I didn't know what towels were and so she came to give us a talk one evening. Kath and I couldn't believe what we were hearing and were shocked. I was eleven and Kath was thirteen. We grew up innocent in those days. Those were the times when women who wanted to buy sanitary towels at the chemist, waited till the shop was cleared of men and even then only asked the woman assistant in a muted voice. So Kath and I had no idea what went on with the older females in the family as a girl was only involved when she had reached the age of menstruation.

Behind the older pupils' dormitories was the ablution block; the younger pupils had their own. Each morning the senior dormitories went in turn for ablutions and we would hurry to line up as we didn't want to have to wait for a washbasin to do our teeth, or wait for the shower. The ablution block was divided in two by an arch, lavatories being on the right-hand side, and the washbasins on the left. The shower room came off the room with the washbasins. There were a number of washbasins, back-to-back down the centre and along each side, but still not enough for fifty pupils. The shower only took twelve at a time. There was an adequate number of lavatories, these had a flushing system so there was no problem there with Mary the maid, except that we were not allowed to leave the dormitory at night to use them.

There was always a rush to get into the showers first. It took Kath and me a while to accustom ourselves to showering with others and we would wait until they had finished though Kath, who was modest to an extreme, surprisingly overcame her inhibitions in a relatively short time. I didn't, because before I went to Colomendy, Mother had bought 'coms' (combinations) for me; these were flannelette monstrosities that one climbed into and were a singlet and knickers in one - hence the name - with a flap at the back for when one needed to go to the lavatory - the legs also coming way down. I was so mortified at the thought of being seen in them that I waited for everyone to finish their shower. Fortunately I was not alone in having an insensitive mother, a girl called Sheila Spencer also had one and the two of us waited together to be the last in. Our 'coms' brought us two together and we became good friends. When we were alone we would swing on the pipes, back to back, one pushing the other outwards by placing her feet against the wall to provide the thrust needed to propel the other. On one occasion, this was done with such vigour that the one returning from her outward swing, came back with such force it sent the other's knees through the window, breaking it. Of course it was discovered what we had done and we were told to report at a certain time to Miss Thompson. I suggested to Sheila that we go and apologise before that fateful moment, but Sheila wouldn't agree so I went by myself. Miss Thompson listened to my apology and then didn't say anything, so I broached the matter, "Do you still want to see me?" I asked. She said curtly, "You know that you don't have to do that now you have apologised." Sheila was sorry that she hadn't gone and decided to go, but Miss Thompson said that she'd only gone because I had and she received some disciplinary action but I have forgotten what that was.

  The day started with going to the ablution block and then it was off to breakfast. We had to line up outside our dormitories for breakfast, lunch and tea, and be marched in pairs to the dining room under the supervision of one of the teachers. This was a more substantial building and was at the bottom of the path. The dining hall had tables running the full width and we sat at the table allocated to our dormitory. We raced to get the seats at the head of the table nearest to the servery, because all food was passed down by the pupils, the plates going from hand to hand till they reached the end. This meant that plates were waylaid on the way if the meal happened to be a good one, so only the smallest serves reached the end of the table, but the reverse was true if the meal happened to be awful, which was most of the time. The main meal was in the middle of the day and was always a hot meal with pudding. Two or three teachers would be on duty keeping an eye on us and they deplored the fact that some of us didn't finish our meals. They would say, "There are children in the world who are starving who would be glad of this food." We would reply irreverently "Send it to them then."

Though we lined up for breakfast, lunch and tea, supper was after school of an evening and we went to the dining room as soon as our class was finished, the younger pupils' classes finishing earlier than the older ones. Then we went to the servery individually and were given cocoa and a rock bun. Apart from suppers, Thursday was the only day that Kath and I found the food edible - it was a scouse-type stew for lunch, followed by roly-poly pudding. Breakfast and tea were also acceptable. At breakfast we would make a sandwich of the soggy fried bread; the fact that we found it delectable shows what point we were starting from. I've always had a warm spot for Thursdays ever since. One time Kath and I had a fight and I refused to go in at lunchtime so Kath, feeling remorseful, smuggled her roly-poly pudding out in her handkerchief to give to me. The teachers ate at a room at the end of the pupils' dining-room and most certainly didn't eat the sort of food we did.

There was a wooden verandah in front of the dining room, at one end of which was the Tuck Shop. This was only open on a Saturday morning. However, it was rare for Kath and me to have any money to spend there. Anyway, with sweets being rationed one had to be satisfied with things like carrots and apples - not that we wouldn't have been. I never did get to taste the flapjacks which the boilerman, who was very kind to us evacuees, once made for some of them in his boiler.

Pauline said later that before I went to Colomendy I had been very pasty and under-nourished but that when I came away, I was a different person health-wise. She said that even though she felt sure that Mother had sent Kath and me to Colomendy to get rid of us, it was the best thing that could have happened to me. Mother and Pauline didn't get on, but I must leave others to tell their own story. Mother had to cope on her own with a family of children who were strongly individual and who had competing demands. If there had been conflict with some and if she didn't always act in our best interests, she certainly did better than anyone I know would have done given the same circumstances.

On weekdays we had school in the morning and in the evening and in the afternoons we were taken for a two hour walk. The classrooms were in a separate block away from the dormitories. The teachers I remember most from Colomendy are Miss Delmarsh and Miss Cashen. The former was a wonderful person who taught english and nature studies and was imaginative in the teaching of both those subjects. In english she involved us in debating. For nature studies she took us on walks, made us aware of the sky by teaching us the names of the different clouds and how to identify them; she got us to collect leaves from various trees, having us compete with each other; whoever collected the most and was able to name them, being the winner. It was there I first came across the pussy-willow and was very taken with it. Miss Delmarsh also took us through the various stages of the frog - from the spawn through the tadpole stage, finally to the fully formed frog. There was a pond on the camp so we were able to observe all of these spawn-to-frog happenings first hand. She made us interested in the world around us and on top of that was warm-hearted and obviously had a genuine love for her pupils. In one debate which she organized, one of the pupils had to propose that it was all right sometimes to tell a lie and I had to rebut it, maintaining that it was never all right to tell a lie. I won that debate.

Our arithmetic teacher, Miss Cashen, was a fearsome person. She would rap the pupils over the knuckles if they talked in class. One occasion when the girl in the seat next to me and I were talking, she charged down the room and rapped the girl over the knuckles with a ruler and then walked away. The girl protested that I had been talking too and Miss Cashen said, "Jean can afford to talk, you can't." Arithmetic was one of my best subjects - right through school I had found it easy. In the dormitory where she had her room, the girls had a different image of her. They said that she would go around and tuck them in and kiss them goodnight; they loved her.

One teacher who taught us geography once put a map up on the blackboard showing where our troops were, saying, "Girls, we are being pushed back, back." She was obviously very concerned about this, but we weren't. The war the grown-ups were experiencing was a different war to that which we were and it never entered our heads that we might lose. War paled into insignificance in comparison to what was actually happening to us at the time, such as what awful thing there was going to be for lunch that day. However, there were times that we were very conscious of the war – such as the night the bombing in Liverpool was so bad the sky was lit up as far as Colomendy. Some of the girls cried, worrying about their parents, and climbed into each others' beds for comfort. Kath and I couldn't understand them, we weren't a bit worried, confident that Mother and Pop would be all right.

I never stopped to think whether the two hour walk we went on every weekday afternoon was enjoyable or not, it was just part of the daily routine, though we did try to avoid it if we could. To get out of going for a walk we had to be doing something else - which is why I opted to take part in the opera, 'The Magic Flute'. I was only in the chorus but I can still sing a few of the words - "Oh happy hearts in love united, unending joy be thine ..." One scene in particular stands out because I found it utterly ridiculous. Two characters go to opposite sides of the stage, their backs to each other, both saying, "... for fear he'll kill me, that's clear, I'd better go. Yes, I'd better go." I found this as silly as the scene from 'A Midsummer Night's Dream' where one of the characters wears a donkey's head. Whilst at Colwell Road School our class had been taken to see this at the Liverpool Philharmonic. One of the boys and one of the girls who took part in 'The Magic Flute' were later expelled, the boy having been found in the girl's dormitory and under her bed. This same teacher also put on Gilbert & Sullivan's, 'H.M.S. Pinafore'. Kath was in that and though I wasn't in it, I've disliked Gilbert and Sullivan ever since because we had to watch it being performed later.

The opera didn't last forever and I had to go back to the walking. Some walks were memorable. One evening when returning we crossed a heather-covered hillside as dusk was gathering. The scene was so beautifully mellow a group of us began singing, 'Just a song of twilight', which begins:

> Just a song of twilight,
> When the lights are low,
> And the flickering shadows
> Softly come and go.

We would cross over stiles and go through the farmers' fields. Along the roads the fields had stone walls, but inside areas were fenced with wire and we would sometimes come across tufts of wool where the sheep had come in contact. Once we came upon a row of dead moles strung along a fence to warn other moles not to burrow in that farmer's field. I was impressed as I had not known that moles could put two and two together.

On rare occasions we would go on an all-day hike, for instance to Moel Famau, and once some of the girls were taken there and picked bilberries on the slopes. This stayed in my mind because one of the girls went missing and they had to go back and look for her. Another time we were taken to pick rose-hips - these were supposed to materialise later as jam but they never did. I remember the smell of damp autumn evenings, the damson trees, the heather tumbling down the hillsides, the mystical light of the twilight - and how the local Welsh didn't like us. One time when the teacher was taking us to the pictures in Mold, the conductor shouted out when the bus drew up at the stop, "Welsh people on the bus first," and in the picture-house they made us sit on ordinary chairs right in the very front.

Apart from walking, there wasn't any other organised physical activity such as sports. With a vast area to roam and play in, we ourselves kept physically active. We had some spare time from the end of our walk until tea-time and sometimes we would go up into the woods behind the camp - strictly forbidden - and roam around there. There we found bluebells, crocuses, snowdrops, blackberries and crab-apple trees, and the disused lead mines with the coverings all rotting. Some of the mines were partially filled with water and we threw stones in and thought that the number of ripples the stone made was indicative of how deep the shaft was. Other mine shafts had not filled with water and when we threw stones into those we could hear them hitting against the sides and then the far-away sound as they hit the bottom. A story went around that once a girl had fallen in one that was filled with water and the boiler-man had had to rescue her, saying afterwards that he would never again attempt to rescue anyone if they fell in as the suction of the water pulling him down had been so terrible. We left our mark by etching our names on a tree. The woods were full of interesting discoveries, one dead tree we came across had an inner core that had a fluorescent glow. Once when we roamed further than usual, we thought we were on to something when we saw in the distance a hut, we wondered if it belonged to a spy but kept our distance, not wanting to find out for sure. War had made spies a realistic possibility. One day some soldiers came on manoeuvres in the woods and one of them received a gunshot wound, only minor, but we girls were very sympathetic when he was brought through the camp to the sick bay

Mother gave each of us a diablo. For this game, a string is suspended between two sticks and the diablo, which is a double cone, is placed on the string. The operator then twirls the diablo up and down the string, at times tossing it into the air and catching it on the string as it comes down. Kath and I became very adept at this and could toss the diablo quite high. Otherwise we had moved on from games like whip-and-top and marbles and were much more likely to do handstands and cartwheels (I didn't come anywhere near to mastering the latter) or act out plays. For a long time a group of us gathered together and improvised plays as we went along, each taking on a character. These took place outside in an area out of sight of the dormitories. In one play which continued over a number of evenings, I played a male called Johnny.

Every now and then in the evening we would be shown a film in the camp hall and once the film had a snake in it; we were scared to walk back afterwards to the dormitories fearing we might step on one. With school being in the evening as well, this kept us occupied, and after we had

had supper, there was only a brief time before it was prayers and lights out.

For the school concert Kath had me singing in a duet with another girl. We sang 'Sweet Sixteen', and at one stage I had to come in with a line and couldn't reach the high notes, so I said to my partner, "You sing that." I could see Miss Delmarsh at the side of the hall collapse in giggles. She was amazed that Kath and I were sisters and once told us this - Kath always so meticulously dressed, and I looking as if I'd been thrown together, as Miss Delmarsh put it. Kath once knitted a pair of socks. When she began them she had been going to knit a jumper, but changed her mind after the rib was done and turned it into a sock instead, with the result that one sock had a rib that trailed along the ground. Kath wouldn't wear them but I didn't mind.

When volunteers were sought from amongst pupils in the older dormitories to act as a guardian for one of the children in the junior dormitory, helping them with any difficulties they might have, I was only too happy to volunteer. I was put in charge of a seven year old. One of the things we volunteers were supposed to do was mend the clothes of our particular charge. Miss Delmarsh found it hilarious that I would take on the responsibility of doing this for someone else when I was so casual about my own dress. Miss Delmarsh was not a dormitory teacher but had a room at the end of the young ones' schoolroom and on a couple of occasions I went there just to talk with her.

Once a week we had to write to our parents and this took place in the school rooms after evening classes and before supper. For a long time Mother kept one of the letters I wrote her - I wrote words of love with gold paint and signed it, 'Your everlasting daughter'. By this time I had learnt to spell the name 'Pugh'. Not longer after Mother and Pop were married and I was staying with Granddad and Granny Elliott for a short period, I had written to them and addressed the envelope to Mr & Mrs Phew.

There was a mound in the vicinity of the headmistress' office, it was a marker in the general terrain and occasionally we would play on it. The verandah in front of the headmistress' office overlooked this mound. Once a girl who had lost all her hair came to Colomendy and we would sometimes see her sitting on this verandah with her head uncovered - she'd obviously been sent to benefit from the open-air. The headmistress was generally liked. It was said that when recalcitrant girls were sent to her for discipline, she would spank them with a slipper.

Before we went to Colomendy, Mother was given a list of clothes that we had to have. Amongst the items required were saxe-blue blouses. Mother bought some dye and dyed our white blouses 'blue'. Whether this was the required 'saxe-blue' I couldn't say. But it was all a bit of a myth anyway as, though we might have started off with saxe-blue blouses, in the end we wore whatever we happened to have. I can't remember what other clothing was on the list. When our shoes wore out we wore clogs. These we must have purchased at the camp as I cannot imagine a Liverpool shop carrying them and we certainly didn't have them when we went to Colomendy. I also had a horrible brown coat with no shape at all, whilst Kath had a well-fitted black one, and I think these were also purchased whilst we were at the camp.

The clogs we wore in Colomendy were not the lovely, green, Dutch-style clogs which Betty Heathcote had. These were raw leather things which came up the ankle and were laced together with thick leather laces. The leather did not yield to the shape of the foot, but formed folds which scraped the skin off our feet and caused horrible blisters; as we had no plaster strips to offer protection, we just had to put up with it. Kath suffered doubly because she would get the most awful chilblains. The clogs also had metal, horseshoe-shaped things, on the thick wooden soles - in winter the snow packed up in these and we would literally walk on ice. When we went into the dormitory we were likely to go a header on the oil-polished floors if we hadn't scraped the snow off our clogs first. We were meant to keep our footwear polished, we used Dubbin on the clogs and Nugget on our other shoes, always supposing we had another pair, which most of the time I didn't. In summer we wore canvas shoes which we whitened with Blanco, a white paste, which took an hour or two to dry, so we usually put it on the night before. If we laid it on too thickly, we left little puffs of white behind when we walked.

We were examined on a regular basis by Sister Jackson, a nursing sister, who was a very nice, motherly sort of person. There was a sick bay and we longed to be taken there if only to get a bit of attention. Once another girl and I gorged through a pile of berries that were still green and nowhere near ripe, hoping to get collywobbles and thus be sent to sick bay but, alas, they had no effect on us.

Kath and I had a wonderful relationship when we were growing up and I was happy that she was my sister. We were an enormous support to each other and I can't imagine my childhood without her. We were so close that each knew what the other was thinking to the extent that we would finish each other's sentences. I hate to think how devastating Colomendy would have been had we not had each other. When we first arrived we were absolutely miserable and the other girls bullied us, taunting us by sitting on our beds. There was one particularly mean-spirited girl called Freda, who had a dead white face and jet black hair. I shall never forget our feeling of wretchedness that first week - we would go into the ablution block, hide in the lavatories and sob our hearts out, clinging to each other.

Apart from Sheila, another girl we became friends with was Ethel. Ethel was an orphan and lived with an aunt and uncle. She had the most awful pyorrhoea and you could smell her breath from a distance. Ethel became a close friend and we got on well. She was one of the few girls who seemed very happy to be at the camp. Another girl was nicknamed 'Muggins' because she was so plain - she didn't seem to mind this at all. Everyone liked her, she was a lot of fun. Kath's friend Dorothy came to Colomendy because Kath was there, though she wasn't assigned to our dormitory. There were others with whom we became friends but I have now forgotten their names. Two sisters who were Catholics, came later and when we said our prayers of an evening, led by the teacher, they were allowed not to join in but to say their own - we would see them crossing themselves. They were very sweet and the other pupils more or less left them alone. Their parents had become separated and their father would visit them on Parents' Day bringing his girlfriend. They looked so posh and glamorous. We never saw the mother.

Visiting day was once a month on a Sunday, the dormitories rotating. Parents would bring their children all sorts of goodies, such as packets of breakfast cereal and pots of jam, which they would then take into the dining room for breakfast to supplement their meals. Even when it wasn't their visiting day, some parents would go to the bus taking the other parents to Loggerheads and send a parcel for their child or children. A cluster of eager children would gather around when the bus arrived, including Kath and me, but there was never a parcel for us. Even on visiting day, Mother never brought us anything, and didn't like to come on a Sunday, so got special permission to come on a Saturday. She only came for the afternoon, not arriving on the early bus as the other parents who came on Sundays did. Mother invariably liked to go to a farm near Colomendy Camp to buy some eggs, almost unobtainable in Liverpool. Once Pauline, Pat and Ferg came to visit us. Pat brought her boyfriend, Jack, with her and we were disgusted when he got a hedge tear in his trousers and made such a fuss about it. We thought he was very namby-pamby. On a couple of occasions Pauline sent us a parcel with some foodstuffs, and once she sent each of us a cardigan which she had knitted from the odds and ends left over from the woollens she made for a shop which sold babies' clothes. The backs and sleeves were grey, but for the fronts she cleverly made a pattern using all the baby pinks, blues, greens and yellows. Ethel was never visited.

After one visit by Mother, Miss Prick called together all the pupils in the dormitory just to tell them that Kath and Jean had the most charming mother and she couldn't understand why we behaved the way we did. From the time we went to school, Mother never missed things like Parents' Day and always took the opportunity then to talk to our teachers to see how we were getting on. Parents' Day at Colomendy wasn't intended for that purpose, our dormitory teachers not necessarily being our class teachers. However, Mother always managed to find one of our dormitory teachers to talk to.

When it was our once-a-month Saturday visit, Kath and I would wait at a vantage point where we could see Mother as she came around the corner of the driveway after passing by the Boys' Camp, when we would run down to meet her. One occasion in particular is emblazoned on my memory as this time she was dressed all in black, being in mourning for her mother who had died on Guy Fawkes' Day, 5th November 1941. Mother had written to tell us and Kath and I were broken-hearted and wept copiously. We also felt so guilty as we had been having such a good time on Guy Fawkes' Day, the camp having put on a huge bonfire. Mother didn't say anything then about Granny's last moments but in later years she told us that she had been with Granny at the time she passed away. Just before the end her mother had opened her eyes and said that she had seen a large crowd of people. Mother asked her, "Did you see Margaret?" (Margaret being Mother's oldest sister). Granny had replied, "No, but I saw my mother." We learned from Ferg that Mother had had to get special permission to attend Granny's funeral, as being strict Presbyterian, women were not allowed to go to funerals.

Mother's brother, Arthur, had been in Singapore with the British Army when he received the news of his mother's death. After the war he told us that when he had disembarked in Singapore he had received two telegrams, and fortunately he opened first the one telling him of his mother's illness, as the second one told him of her death. So he had some sort of forewarning. He took that bleak news with him into the prisoner-of-war camp when Singapore was taken by the Japanese in January 1942.

Pauline told us that after Granny died, Granddad came over one evening after having been drinking. He felt that Mother had not been to see him often enough so he stormed into the house waving his walking stick at her and dramatically bellowed, "Never call me Father again." "Hush, Father," Mother said, "The neighbours!" At which he retorted that he didn't care what the neighbours thought. Pauline said that, through all this, Pop remained supremely calm and just continued with what he was doing. He was quite unflappable.

When it wasn't your dormitory's visiting day, you were able to do what you wanted. Sometimes we would go along the brook which ran at the bottom of Cathkin Peak.

Along this walk there was a wonderful smell of dank undergrowth and I would spend ages watching the water as it rippled across the stones on the bed of the stream. Sometimes we walked up to the top of the peak by the path known as 'The Cat Walk' as it was so narrow. There was easier access from the other side. In Spring, the camp was a riot of daffodils. When one entered the double gates, the Boys' Camp was on the right and, on the opposite side of the path leading to the Girls' Camp, the ground sloped sharply upwards and in Spring was drenched with daffodils.

We were not supposed to fraternise with the boys but on rare occasions we managed to meet. For a while Ethel, Kath and I, with one or two other girls, met some boys at a hedge between the two camps. My boyfriend was called Arthur and he and I were egged on by the others to kiss each other. We probably met the boys only three or four times and then just to talk briefly.

Pop had a relative who was a teacher at the Boys' Camp; we had visited him and his wife in Liverpool. He said to call on him at the camp when we wanted to but we only once went. Though he was a nice person, he had a rather remote personality. He and his wife were Christian Scientists. I remember this because Mother was not the least impressed that his wife had had her child with no doctor in attendance, relying on the teachings of Mary Baker Eddy. Mother was put out by these women who spread it around that childbirth could be easy.

We had to go to church on Sunday morning. The closest was the Church of England service held in a hall in the Boys' Camp. We more often than not went there because it saved the long walk to the alternative, a picturesque country church some distance from the camp. The services held in the hall in the Boys' Camp were awful, we had to stand the whole time and our legs itched dreadfully.

Every now and then someone would try and run away from Colomendy, it was called 'Doing the bunk'. They were always caught. News of the escape and the subsequent capture, would sweep through the dormitories.

A song we sang in Colomendy was:

"There is a happy land, far, far away,
Where they get bread and jam,
Five times a day.
Bread and jam we never see,
Sugar is a scarcity,
That is why we're gradually,
Fading away."

Another song we sang was 'The Quartermaster's Store'. This had a chorus but the verses in between were improvised. A verse could go something like this:

There was cheese, cheese, just like father's knees,
In the store, in the store,
There were eggs, eggs,
Just like washing pegs,
In the Quartermaster's Store.
Then the chorus -
My eyes are dim I cannot see,
I have not brought my specs with me,
I have not brought my specs with me.

We went home for Christmas and when we returned we found that some Americans had heard of our existence and had sent the most magnificent presents to the children who had not gone home for Christmas. They came in beautifully decorated boxes, such as we had never seen before. We were a little sorry that we had missed out.

During the time we were at Colomendy, two of the teachers decided to take some of us on holiday to a Youth Hostel in Delamere. I don't know how we were selected, or whether it was open to anyone whose parents were prepared to pay extra for this treat, but we were able to go. I think in the end about twenty-five of us went. The Youth Hostel was in the back of yonder and was a building with a number of bedrooms, each able to sleep about eight in bunk-beds. Jobs were allocated, some had to work in the kitchen, others cleaning the bedrooms, and so on. Water had to be fetched in a large drum, I don't know where from, but the two girls assigned this task on the first day tipped the drum on one of the teacher's toes. The teacher spent the rest of the time hobbling around; she took this rather well. Of an evening we sat around the kitchen table with the teachers and just talked. In the daytime we went for walks in the lovely countryside round about. It was an idyllic few days and one of the highlights of my stay in Colomendy.

Another highlight was when Kath and I did the shopping for all the others in Mold. Once a month a couple of girls were allowed to go into Mold and shop for the others. The sense of freedom was absolutely wonderful. And to be able to shop made it doubly so. I don't imagine Kath and I had much money of our own to spend, I certainly wouldn't have had, but we had the pleasure of buying things even if they were for others. Mold was a lovely little Welsh town. Once when Mother visited us on a Saturday she took Kath and me into Mold and we had tea in a café above a shop.

Kath went home from Colomendy before I did. She had reached the age of fourteen and had to go out to work. When she left, one of the teachers who was arranging her departure, asked her if she would pay the money I owed. The dormitory teachers kept accounts for the pupils and would sometimes let you spend what you didn't have, though you had to pay it back eventually. Kath, frugal as ever, never overspent, whereas I was in debt. Kath could do nothing else but pay the money I owed. It was awful seeing her off on the bus from Loggerheads. When Kath reached home she begged Mother to let me come home too, but Mother wouldn't hear of it. However, about three or four months later I too went home. Not long afterwards it was Pat's 21st birthday celebration which took place at the State Restaurant; all I remember of it is a long table and a number of guests.

* * * * * * * * * *

CHAPTER THIRTEEN

When I returned to Liverpool I was sent to Fincham Road Senior School. It was out of the frying pan and into the fire. I had a dreadful woman for a class teacher who soon became known in my mind as Miss Howl, which was a play on her real name. Miss Howl was so obnoxious to me that Mother said she was going to see her but Leon, Pauline's husband, who was home on leave, said he would go instead. Leon was charm personified, to say nothing of his handsome Australian physique that spoke of the outdoors. Miss Howl positively melted. But not towards me.

There were A and B classes for each year and the four rows in each classroom were also graded, the top row being the cleverest, graduating down to the less clever row. Boy, where we ever going to know our place in the scheme of things! To engender even more division, each row operated as a team and there were merit points given or taken away for specific things. These were not connected with sporting prowess as we didn't play any sport - 'passing the bean bags', rounders, and vaulting across a wooden horse had disappeared after primary school. But one of the things which carried merits or de-merits was clean hands. Once a week, the time chosen at random, Miss Howl would get us to show our hands and she would then come and examine them and the nails to see if they were clean - we had to show each side. If they weren't clean your team lost points. One poor girl who came from a dreadful home always had dirty nails. She was very poorly dressed and as careworn as a downtrodden housewife. She would protest that she had to get all the younger children ready and do housework before she came to school, but Miss Howl wouldn't even be listening and would take points off for the state of her hands. This poor girl wasn't popular with her row as her dirty hands also dragged them down.

We had cooking lessons at Fincham. Food being rationed meant the selection of recipes was limited and concentrated heavily on potatoes. For one dish we had to first bake a potato in the oven with the skin still on, (the skin still on - what next!) and then cut it in half, scoop out the centre, mix that with cheese, tomato and onion, piling all back into the skin, then sprinkling with cheese on top and toasting it under the grill. We took to doing this at home as well. I found it difficult to get the family to eat any of my offerings which I brought home after cooking lessons, with the exception of Ferg who always enjoyed whatever I cooked. But he was at the age when he was growing so rapidly he could eat the table leg.

I can remember one Science lesson; though I have no doubt these were given regularly, it is only this particular one that has left an impression. During this lesson we had to fill a glass to the top with water, place a piece of cardboard on top, holding it in place as we carefully turned the glass upside down. Voila! The water didn't tip out when we removed our hand. That was if we had filled the glass to the very brim. I was impressed but hadn't a clue as to why this was so. Fortunately I was one day to marry my ability in science.

In Geography we were taught about Clive of India and Wolfe of Quebec. I remember Wolfe climbing over the wall into the French Fort and Clive and the Black Hole of Calcutta. As they held these lessons in quick succession without time for reflection, it was a long time before I sorted out Clive from Wolfe.

Remnants of the English lessons are having to learn poems by heart. Miss Howl knew how to choose poems. Amongst those we had to learn was 'Sea Fever' by John Masefield.

Then there was 'The Listeners' by Walter de la Mare which I particularly liked and it is still one of my favourites today. It has wonderful words like 'smote' and 'champ'd' and is haunting.

Another favourite was 'My Lost Youth' by Henry Wadsworth Longfellow. This poem was so long we only had to learn a few lines of it and went around the class in turn saying our little bit. Which was fine if you had been assigned the last two lines of each verse;

A boy's will is the wind's will,
And the thoughts of youth are long, long thoughts.

At home Kath and I were reading 'Wuthering Heights' by Emily Bronte and 'Jane Eyre' by Charlotte Bronte. 'Wuthering Heights' was by far Kath's favourite, but I preferred 'Jane Eyre'. Kath at this stage had also become fascinated with Joan of Arc who was something of a heroine to her.

When Ferg was at Fincham he had one teacher called Mr Winterbottom and another Mr Shufflebottom. Of course the pupils wrote a ditty about them. Mr Winterbottom and Mr Shufflebottom had obviously not thought to ameliorate their names as had a certain Mrs Sidebottom who referred to herself as Mrs 'Siddy Bóttome'.

Ferg was resentful when, on reaching sixteen, Mother insisted that he take up an apprenticeship at Birchall's. He wanted to stay in the office where he had been doing well, but Mother was adamant. This was something that did not help future relations between them as Ferg never liked the printing trade. His apprenticeship was as a stereotypist, this meant he worked with lead. Apparently they could have all the milk they wanted to drink which was supposed to go some way towards keeping the lead from their bodies. In his free time at work Ferg made metal soldiers in the style of those he had received as a child, some standing, some kneeling, all holding weapons. He made these for sale and they were a great hit with the local children.

It was thought that Kath might want to become a nurse and she was sent to a children's hospital 'over the water' in Southport. The staff lived in at the hospital and took their meals together. They were seated according to rank, those at the head of the table being the doctors and the matron, going in order down through sisters, nurses and other staff, till they reached Kath, the lowliest of all, at the foot of the table. Kath said as the platters of food started at the top and worked their way down, she would usually end up with just a small morsel of whatever it was.

Kath was so slightly built and short that they couldn't find an outfit small enough to fit her and the hat came right down on her forehead. One of her duties was to take six children with cerebral palsy out in a large pram, seated two together on each of the three seats. This was difficult as she said she could scarcely see over the pram handle.

Kathleen and the Pram.

Another of Kath's duties was to accompany the young children when they were taken in a pony and trap along the promenade. She found this an awful experience as she felt so 'conspicuous'. We happened to be visiting her once with Old Uncle Dave and saw her with the children being taken along the sea-front in a pony and trap, all dressed up in her nurse's garb. Kath had a habit of blushing bright red when she felt conspicuous, which didn't help.

Kath gave notice at the hospital as she was lonely living away from home and had a number of jobs after that. One was with Wetherall's, a fashionable boutique which made ladies' dresses, the hems having to be hand-sewn. Kath was always very particular when she did anything - her knitting was so neat it couldn't be distinguished from machine-made, each stitch was so even - so it wasn't surprising that she was commended for the neatness of her stitches at Wetherall's. Later Kath worked at Crawford's biscuit factory as general factotum in their office. (Their slogan was 'Crawford's Cream Crackers so Crisp and Creamy'). She hated it there as she was teased because she was so short. Kath's growth spurt came when she was sixteen, whereas I was fully grown at fourteen. I was going around feeling like Gulliver amongst the Lilliputians, whilst Kath was feeling like a Lilliputian amongst the Gullivers. It didn't help when we went to picture-houses that I would have to take her in if the picture being shown required children to be accompanied by an adult. She should have been taking me in.

Kath was still friendly with Dorothy whom she had known before Colomendy Camp and who had gone there to be with her. She went on a trip with Dorothy and her mother to the Isle of Man. Dorothy's mother was very fat and they couldn't find anyone to balance her on the opposite side of the plane, so she had to sit up front with the pilot. In those days it was necessary that the load be balanced on small planes.

Kath and Dorothy called on Ethel, the orphan girl we had been close friends with in Colomendy Camp. Ethel lived with her aunt and uncle in a very rundown area downtown. When they knocked at the front door, Ethel opened and she was very pleased to see them, but soon the aunt came shrieking for her to get back in the house so Ethel couldn't talk for long. It was obviously a dreadful household that Ethel lived in. No wonder she had liked Colomendy.

Some evenings Mrs Morrisey would come to our house to play cards with Mother and Pop and when she did, Ferg, Kath and I would go to her house. We had a wonderful time with Rosie and Gertie playing hide-and-seek in the dark and other games. Once Ferg put a sheet over his head and, using a torch, shone it from underneath onto his face, making an unearthly spectacle and half scaring us out of our wits. The Morrisey's had a billiard table and Ferg, by accident, ripped the green baize during one of our riotous carry-ons. Mrs Morrisey took it very well and it wasn't this that caused those evenings to come to an end but when Mrs Wainwright, who lived next door, complained about the noise.

Mrs Holme would also come to our house of an evening to play cards with Mother and Pop, these must have been pre-arranged as she never came at the same time as Mrs Morrisey. She was very deaf so we had to shout and later on Jim, her husband, had also gone deaf from working in the aeroplane factory. One day Jim left and went home to his mother and a Spanish boxer took his place. We always felt it was the best thing Jim could have done. Mrs Holme never brought the Spanish boxer over to our place but would come on her own. She would say, arms folded on top of her breasts, "He's so good to me." And then, as was her wont, she repeated everything she said, "I say, he's so good to me." I wondered what she meant, but had a strange inkling what she might have meant. Pop would say, "Are we going to talk or are we going to play cards?" This was Pop's response to anyone who spoke after a hand had been dealt.

Apropos of nothing - I recall when Mrs Holme was required by her doctor to bring along a sample of her urine, she put this in a whisky bottle and, on the way to the surgery, the bottle was stolen from her basket, whisky at that stage being almost unobtainable. Mother was once able to get a bottle of whisky which she took to a relative in Manchester who had become bedridden after being knocked down by a tram. Mother said she would say, "Enjoy yourself whilst you can as you don't know how your life can suddenly end." Another relative in Manchester was a taxi driver and on one occasion when Mother was with him, he pointed out a pedestrian with a very long nose who, he said, had an affliction in which the nose kept growing. He would hire this relative once a year to take him on his annual holiday.

When Mother and Pop were by themselves, they played crib. Mother told me that she developed a passion for crib before I was born and would sit with my Father playing it whilst she nibbled at raw rice kernels, one of those food fads that pregnant women get.

In November 1943, Eileen Finnegan died from meningitis - this was what my brother, Deryk, had died from when he was nine. Eileen was twelve years of age and had been a close friend of Kath's so Mother said that she would have to go by herself to see Eileen. It was the custom for a deceased loved one to lie in state in their home for a period of three days, during which time the curtains of the house were kept drawn and relatives and friends came to pay their respects. In those days if a funeral cortege passed, people stopped and men took off their hats as a mark of respect. Kath did as Mother said and went by herself to see Eileen. It was an ordeal for her as, though she loved Eileen, she was reluctant to see her in her coffin. When she arrived at the house, Mrs Finnegan told her to go on up by herself which made it even more of an ordeal. I went with Mother and I can still see Eileen now. She was dressed in a beautiful shroud and her mother stood stroking her face. On the left side of Eileen's face there was a vivid weal; Mrs Finnegan explained that that was the germs coming out. I remember Mrs Finnegan saying, "No-one can hurt her now."

Eileen was a particularly beautiful girl with jet-black hair, fair skin and blue eyes, typical Irish colouring. She had been enormously popular with the other children as she was somewhat of a scallywag, warm-hearted and generous to a fault. I once went with Eileen and a few of the other neighbourhood children on a walk down Mab Lane and we saw a man exposing himself. Eileen's response was, "Oh, the poor fellow." The rest of us had been disgusted. Another time I had been on a bus with Eileen and, at one of the stops, she had thrown some money down to some children waiting there. I've forgotten now how we knew, but they didn't have the money for the fare to get on the bus.

During the three days that Eileen lay in state at home, Kath moved in bed with me as her bed was against the wall where Eileen lay the other side. Mrs Davies went to buy flowers on behalf of the neighbours and I went with her. Someone later recalled having been on the bus when Mrs Finnegan had joined it at the Alder Hey Hospital at the time Eileen had died. Mrs Finnegan was weeping and saying, "My little girl." It is worth noting that the hospital would not have made arrangements for Mrs Finnegan to be taken home - she returned by public transport. Eileen had been so looking forward to the birth of Pauline's baby, whereas Kath and I had been so embarrassed for Pauline when she told us she was pregnant that we sat there in stunned silence, causing Pauline to say desperately, "Say something!" Eileen was not inhibited like we were and was over the moon when she first heard.

My inhibitions were rampant when I reached the age of menstruation (I was thirteen) and wanted to keep quiet about it, but Mother told Pauline in my presence and I was mortified and said, "Go on, tell the whole world." At this onset of menstruation I was confronted with the opposing views of Pauline and Mother. Mother believed you shouldn't bath at this time, saying it was bad for you. Pauline, on the other hand, believed that it was particularly important to bath at this time. Auntie Lizzie, when this momentous event was made known to her, was all on the side of Mother and said that if you bathed at this time, the blood would all rush to your head and you could go mad.

Not only was I inhibited, but I also became very self-conscious and this affected my legs. I went through a stage when, walking down the road, if I thought anyone was looking at me, my legs seemed to become wooden and it was an effort to put one leg in front of the other. Kath was also afflicted in the same way. Ferg told me, no doubt in jest but I took it seriously, that I had a bend in my nose and for a brief period I would put a peg on my nose for half an hour or so each day in an effort to straighten it. This was only forgotten when some other worry took its place. I was at that age. The self-conscious period disappeared as suddenly as it had come. Nothing to do with self-consciousness, however, was the fact that I had very weak ankles and it was not unusual for one or other of my ankles to keel over half a dozen times in the space of half a mile. I didn't give it a second thought and my ankles never became sprained.

Around this time I fainted for the first time. I had been queuing at Waterworth's for some hard to get item, probably tomatoes, we had an insatiable appetite for these at No. 32, when I suddenly felt dizzy and went outside. The next thing I knew I was coming around and a number of people were crowded around me as I lay on the ground. I was taken into the chemist and given a drink of sal volatile.

Mother took me away from Fincham Road Senior School and sent me to Skerry's College at 2 Rodney Street to take a commercial course. I did well there, becoming efficient at shorthand, typing, book-keeping, and a few other subjects. We were very well taught in typing by Miss Maddock, a no-nonsense sort with tightly-permed hair, who knew exactly how to turn us into efficient typists. The keyboard was covered so we had to learn to touch-type from the beginning. There was a rack above the desks on which a chart of the keyboard was placed. As one's eyes were pinned on the chart, it was the ringing of the little bell which told us when the carriage had reached the end of the line and we had to pull a lever on the carriage to return it back to the beginning. When we first began we had to type, in rhythm, to a record being played, 'The quick brown fox jumped over the lazy dog'. When we'd mastered that we could move into the main room and get on to some real stuff, the keyboard still being covered and whatever we had to type being perched above the typewriter. At this stage we were expected to know the keyboard off by heart so the chart was no longer there. We didn't stay on the same typewriter but had to use different makes and so I met Remington, Underwood, Olivetti and Smith Corona, mostly with a standard-size carriage for letter-size paper and foolscap. A few of the typewriters had double-length carriages to take wider sheets. These stretched our tabulation exercises to the limit. When we came to the end of a ribbon we had to change the spools around and use the ribbon again. We did this until it became so worn that we then had to turn it upside down and use the lower half. Some of the ribbons were half black and half red and if we wanted to underline something in red, we moved a little lever which raised the ribbon to the lower half. If we wanted to do more than one copy, we used carbon paper - the typewriter able to do about five copies at a time. If an error had been made, we rubbed it out - the erasers we used being hard at one end for the original and soft at the other for the carbon copies. To prevent the copies underneath from being smudged, we first of all would have to put little bits of paper over the offending word on each carbon copy and then work our way through the sheets.

We learnt how to operate the Gestetner duplicating machine for running off stencils, applying the thick black ink from a large tube. We had to be so careful not to over-ink. When cutting a stencil there would, of course, be no ribbon in place and this required a different touch as, if the keys were hit too hard, we knocked out the centres of 'O', both capitals and small, or sliced open the top of little 'e' and, to compound this problem, if one had over-inked the Gestetner, it would ooze out of these cavities and make an awful mess. This would cause Miss Maddock to become quite emotional. If we made a typing error when cutting a stencil we could correct it with correcting fluid - this was a dark pink and smelled of acetone - not unlike nail polish. There was only one small bottle of this circulating around the room and one tried to get it from the last person who had used it without attracting the eagle eye of Miss Maddock. We had to apply this correcting fluid carefully as too much would cause the stencil to adhere to the cardboard backing underneath and when we came to put the stencil on the roller and remove the backing, it would tug at the stencil, causing it to wrinkle and Miss Maddock's lips to thin.

We learnt Pitman's shorthand, beginning first with the alphabet, the dark and the light lines, the strokes on the line, above the line and through the line, and then going on to vowels and diphthongs and small circles representing 's' and larger ones 'sw' and so on and so on, until we graduated to the shortened versions of long words (logograms) and commonly-used phrases joined together such as 'In the meantime'. We learned not only to condense English into lines, squiggles and circles, but also to make it more business-like, so 'last month', 'this month' and 'next month' became ultimo, instant and proximo. So, for instance, we thanked people for their 'letter of the 1st instant'. I liked shorthand and, when I had become more proficient, in my mind I would take down in shorthand what people were saying as they were speaking to me.

There was one very unpleasant teacher, I forget now what she took us for, but one day one of the boy pupils stepped out of turn in her class and she called him up front and grabbed him by the hair and slapped his face from side to side, over and over again. One felt a twinge for him - but only a twinge - as he was a mean-spirited bully who lashed out indiscriminately when the mind took him at whoever was in his way. Once, just in passing, he punched me full on the breast for no reason whatsoever.

I became friendly with a very nice girl, Marjorie, and often spent the night at her house which was round the corner from the prison in Walton. I don't know whether it was true or not, but it was said that Brendan Behan spent time in that jail. Mother never approved of Marjorie because she thought she was common. I met Marjorie on what was our first day at Skerry's. We had to put our bags on shelves in the basement and I was already down there when Marjorie came down the stairs and stumbled. I laughed and so did she and we became friends from then on. Marjorie had a wooden suitcase which her father had made - her parents worked very hard to give her a chance in life. Once when I went to stay overnight, I noticed one of the windows was broken. It seems Marjorie's mother had been chasing Marjorie's younger brother to give him a hiding after he had done something-or-other and, unable to catch him, had thrown the stick at him, but he had ducked and it had gone through the window. We all laughed heartily at this, including the younger brother.

Another friend I made came from Runcorn. She sometimes came to spend the night at our house and I think she was very keen on Ferg. When we sat down together for a meal, he would make her laugh and we would both be unable to stop giggling. On one occasion Pat got very cross in the scullery later at what she regarded as our silliness and expressed her annoyance to Mother who merely said, mildly, "You were no different when you were that age."

I was at Skerry's for ten months. The school hours were rather odd, six days a week but with a half day off on Wednesday and Saturday. A lot of the teachers had obviously been brought out of retirement, there being a shortage of teachers due to so many young people having gone off to war. My maths teacher, an elderly gentleman, wrote on my report 'Her work in this subject is excellent'. I can't remember what the other teachers said about me, except for the general comment that I could do better if I didn't play around so much. Mother couldn't help but smile as this had been her own shortcoming when she was at school. One pupil was something of a rebel. She once left the tap on in the washroom on the top floor of the building and put the plug in the basin so that when we went next day, the water was streaming down the stairs. She was expelled and we got to go home for the day whilst they mopped up.

Sometime during 1943, Leon was reported missing - his ship had been bombed. We were devastated and Kath and I, after we had gone to bed and said our prayers, praying in particular for Leon, would sometimes sing the following hymn, the first verse of which is:

> Eternal Father strong to save,
> Whose arm hath bound the restless waves,
> Who bids the mighty ocean deep,
> It's own appointed limits keep,
> Oh hear us when we cry to thee
> For those in peril on the sea.

We would sing it right through to the last verse. I knew all the words of this hymn off by heart once. If I hear it today, I always think of Leon.

I don't know how long after it was, but one night we woke up to see Leon going through the chest of drawers (Mother always preferred to call the latter piece of furniture a 'tallboy') in our bedroom. I suppose we must have been told that he was no longer missing, but we certainly hadn't known that he was on his way home and so we were surprised to see him. We had lots we wanted to ask him but he was eager to get going to Barton where Pauline was staying with Granny Jackson awaiting the birth of their first child. When Leon reached Hull the last ferry had left for New Holland, so he grabbed a rowboat and started to row across the Humber. Of course he was picked up by a military patrol and the next thing Granny Jackson knew, a policeman was on her doorstep asking for Mrs Pauline Smith to come and identify her husband. Granny told him that she could do no such thing, that she was pregnant. How he was identified in the end I can't recall, but he was released.

Going Home

Pauline and Leon's daughter, Jacqueline Lesley, was born 22 December 1943. Pauline had continued teaching at Colwell Road School up until the last few months and then had gone to Barton. Whilst Pauline was at Colwell I once went to meet her at school and she left me in charge of her class whilst she went off to do something. The class went beserk as soon as she left. When she returned she only had to enter the room and her very appearance was enough to silence them. Pauline certainly had authority. A neighbour commented about her, "Every flag is her own," meaning that her determined stride was the pace of one flagstone.

We all went to Barton for Christmas to see her and the new baby, except for Kath who had broken out with chicken-pox. After having not got any of the same childhood illnesses that Ferg and I had, she now had the chicken-pox at the age of fifteen. The doctor said that he wasn't worried that she might pass it on to the baby, but that she might infect Pauline.

The two doctors in Barton were husband and wife, the Drs Kirk. If you needed them at night-time and you weren't on the phone, which most people weren't, you had to go to the surgery and call them through a tube which had its mouthpiece next to the front door. I presume it was one of the Drs Kirk who delivered Jacqueline. Mother was a bit annoyed at Pauline because she downplayed how difficult childbirth was, she had found it easy. She also didn't approve of the fact that Pauline only stayed in bed a week. In Mother's day, a women stayed in bed three weeks after giving birth and was only fed a thin porridge. She said it was the only time a woman had a chance to rest.

Pauline had a midwife stay with her over the confinement. There was an on-going tussle with Granny about whether the window should be open or shut. Pauline, who was a great believer in fresh air, had to contend with Granny who believed that lactating mothers were in danger of milk-fever from draughts. Granny said that she herself had got milk-fever after the birth of one of her children and it had been caused by a draught. So Pauline would get the midwife to open the window, and Granny would come in later and close it. Even Pauline with her strong will was no match for Granny Jackson.

The midwife shared Pauline's double bed - in those days that was quite acceptable. She had many tales to tell of her midwifery experiences but the only one which I now remember is of the time she was working in a hospital and a baby had been born covered all over with hair and looking like a mole. The doctor decided to let the baby die by not feeding it but lactating mothers in the hospital would sneak along and feed it, as they felt sorry when they heard it cry. Whilst Pauline was in bed we all gathered around it and played cards on the counterpane. I used to comment that when I was born, the first thing Mother said to me was, "It's your deal."

Pauline came to Liverpool for Jacqueline's christening at St David's Church. Pauline's friend, Olga de Jong, and Pat were the two godmothers. When Pauline had taught at Colwell Road school, she had become very friendly with Olga de Jong, one of the former teachers of Kath and me. It was difficult for us when she became a friend of Pauline's to start calling her by her Christian name, she having been that far-removed being, a schoolteacher.

Auntie Ida and Uncle Dave came from Barton to be at the christening, Auntie Ida stayed with us and Uncle Dave stayed with family friends, Gertrude and Stan. Even No. 32 couldn't cope with so many extra people. Auntie Eve also stayed overnight, even though she lived not too far away, but Uncle Arthur was then a prisoner-of-war of the Japanese and it was no doubt a chance for all the family to be together. In the days following the christening, we would all go out en masse. It was the custom in those days for one of the men in a group to pay every-ones' fare - taking it in turns. Those were also the days when a smoker, taking out a packet of cigarettes, would offer them to all in the group who smoked, this had continued despite the fact that cigarettes were hard to get during the war. Someone would then light all the cigarettes, though it was considered unlucky to light three from the same match, a carry-over from the First World War when, in the trenches, the third man to get his cigarette lit was also liable to get his head shot off by a German sniper who, by the third light, would have had time to take aim. Cigarettes were frequently referred to as 'fags'.

Sometime during that year Mother picked up a little boy on Kings Drive who had been run over. His head was shattered but Mother, who cringed at the sight of any injury, picked him up without a second thought and rushed him into the doctor's surgery which was nearby. The child died and Mother had to go and tell his mother. It was his birthday and he had been given a ball. This had gone into the road and he had run after it, not thinking of anything else but getting his ball, and a lorry had run over him. There used to be a traffic warning which read, 'Remember, a rolling ball is always followed by a child'. Mother got some blood on her coat and when it was later turned into one for me, the stain was still there on the lapel regardless of it having been dry-cleaned.

The most important thing in my eyes around this time was the pair of green shoes that Mother wouldn't buy me. I longed for green shoes but Mother insisted on black, sensible ones, which also meant lace-ups. I protested, but to no avail, and when she took me along to buy me a pair and asked whether the black lace-ups I was given to try on fitted me, I said yes, though they didn't at all and I paid dearly for it. In no time at all I had a nasty infection on my right foot and it was only when Mother warned me that it could be serious enough that my foot could be in danger, that I reluctantly went to the Foot Hospital. This was a large edifice on the way into town which, I discovered, didn't deal with infections. However, they dressed it for free but worried me even more by saying that it was imperative that I see a doctor. I went off post haste to do just that. I don't know what the doctor did, but my foot eventually healed though I had five small scars for many years.

Apart from the Foot Hospital, there was also the Dental Hospital in Liverpool. This was where we could go and have all sorts of things done to our teeth, paying no more than five shillings a session. The reason for this was that they were all dental students. One filling I had done, the professor after looking at it, advised the student to do it again. This happened a second time. I am amazed at how unruffled I was - especially in those days when they only had treadle drills and there was no novocaine given for fillings. I have to say, however, that that filling is still with me and has given no trouble. Leon went there once and came out looking as if he'd gone three rounds with Joe Louis. He was quite unruffled as well. We all agreed, it was a very good service.

On my fourteenth birthday, Mother took me downtown. She was taking me to have a brassiere fitted, fourteen being the age for this and also the age when one began to wear suspender belts instead of holding up one's stockings with elastic bands. There is a photo of her and me as we walked in front of Lime Street Station that day. Mother was wearing a turban, a smart suit with the lion's claw brooch which Pop had given her, and her fox fur. I was wearing a blazer, blouse and the skirt which Mother had bought at Marks and Spencer's and which Auntie Edie had disapproved of, not the skirt, but the fact that it was bought at Marks and Spencer's. Mother had a penchant for having her photo taken and there is another photo of her and me, also taken outside Lime Street Station, not long after this. On this occasion Pat was with us and she insisted that I walk behind and not be in the photo, saying, "I'm not having a photo taken with her, she looks a mess." The ensuing photo shows me walking behind looking fed-up, which Pat found hilarious. On that day we went to a posh restaurant where it was full silver service and

Pat was horrified when at one stage I picked up the wrong piece of cutlery.

If Pat was horrified by my not knowing what piece of cutlery to pick up first, Mother was equally aghast at my hair, which she seemed to think always looked a mess. Pauline rushed to my defence and said that I needed a perm - I don't think Mother had reckoned on this as she had to pay for it. So I was taken along for a perm - full head. There was a choice of half or full head; 12/6 for half head and 25/- for full head. A half meant that only the bottom half of your hair was permed. Strands of hair were put in curlers, after having been pasted with some sort of lotion, then these curlers were attached to plugs at the end of long wires, giving one a striking resemblance to Medusa; after which you were then 'plugged in'. You stayed like this for about an hour. After that the hair was washed and then set. My perm took so well that I went from hair that wouldn't stay in place to hair that stiffly bristled.

My very first boyfriend was Philip. Kath and I had met him and his friend when we had gone over the water to New Brighton. Philip lived over the water. (We always referred to going across the Mersey to the other side as 'going over the water'). Philip wanted to see me again but I wasn't sure as I didn't know what Mother would say. But he followed me home without my knowing and the next thing Mrs Davies was handing a letter to Mother that he had written to me. He'd got the address wrong and also had just put Jean on the envelope as he hadn't known my surname. As her daughter was called Jean and was younger than me, she had opened it and then realised it must have been intended for me. Far from being annoyed, Mother was amused and said that if I wanted to go out with him it would be all right. So I wrote back and arranged to meet him outside the Eagle and Child. We were to go cycling together. When I got there I asked him how long he had been waiting - it appeared he had arrived half an hour before he needed to - the reason being that he hadn't liked the thought of my waiting outside the Eagle and Child. Its reputation, it seems, was now known over the water. Philip was a baker and worked in Manchester during the week. He was eighteen and I was fourteen. On another occasion he took me to the pictures and we saw Monty Woolley in 'The Man Who Came to Dinner' at the Trocadero. I was so embarrassed to be going out with a boy and almost died inside when I was conscious of him looking at me. He wrote me very nice letters, in one of which I recall him saying that he appreciated how very young I was so he wouldn't tell me just how much he loved me but would wait until I was older before he talked to me like that. I couldn't bear it and threw him over.

I much preferred infatuations to the real thing and at the time I was infatuated with a boy called George whom I only ever saw from a distance, but he claimed my every romantic thought for some time. What exquisite agony it was to catch a glimpse of him every now and then.

It was about this time that Kath and I sent off for a book advertised in the columns of the newspaper which promised to tell you all about sex. They would, they said, send it in a 'plain, brown, wrapper'. Addressed to us or not, Mother opened it and no doubt read it before passing it on to us without comment. It was all very straight-forward clinical stuff which we already knew. We had expected a lot more romantic view.

Until I was in my early teens, we mainly went to either the Granada picture-house at Dovecot, the West Derby picture-house in Tuebrook, or the one at Old Swan. Apart from the Trocadero, the ones downtown were the Hippodrome, the Palais de Luxe, Paramount and the Majestic.

When Kath and I went to see 'Gone with the Wind' we had to queue for ages and we took along something to eat as it was unheard of for a picture to be so long. It reached Liverpool about 1944. In one of the picture-houses, I think it was the West Derby, they had a Wurlitzer organ which played in the intervals between sessions. It would be being played as it came up from beneath the stage, a symphony of coloured lights. Most picture-houses had continuous performances. If there were a queue, which was more often than not, it moved as there were always seats being vacated. Of course this meant we often saw the main feature from halfway through and having seen the ending, had to wait to see the beginning. Mainly we stayed to see it right through from beginning to end and sometimes stayed and saw the whole programme twice over. However, there were eagle-eyed ushers waiting to pounce to tell us to leave if they thought we were doing that, and we'd have to scrunch down in the seat when they shone their suspicious little flashlights along the row looking for faces that had been there too long. There were invariably double-features showing and always a newsreel, Gaumont British News.

Women wore hats in those days and would keep them on in the picture-house, sometimes blocking the view of the person behind. People also smoked in the picture-houses and you could see the blue smoke in the light beaming the picture onto the screen.

Amongst the film stars of the day were Betty Grable, Susan Haywood (Pat's favourite), Esther Williams (Ferg's favourite), Patricia Roc, Clark Gable, Margaret Lockwood, Phyllis Calvert, James Mason, Stewart Granger, Humphrey Bogart, Orson Welles, Rita Hayworth, Deanna Durbin (Kath's favourite), Merle Oberon (Mother's favourite) and many more. Who could forget the sultry Joan Bennett with her pouting lips and without a hair out of place no matter what. Or Laurence Olivier as Heathcliffe in 'Wuthering Heights'. Or the debonair Franchot Tone. Bette Davies was my favourite and I saw 'Now Voyager', in which she and Paul Henreid starred, a couple of times. When I passed through the age of infatuation, the theme song of this film, 'Wrong, would it be wrong to stay, here in your arms this way, under a starlit sky', allowed my day-dreams to flourish. In those days they knew the romantic pull of a cigarette; the handsome hero would light two cigarettes at the same time and then hand one to his woman friend. Such unspoken intimacy. All intimacy then was relayed by looks and gestures and when things as blatant as pregnancy had to be portrayed on the screen, it was so subtle there was no physical evidence of it apart from the dress just being a bit loose. Arthur Askey was a popular comedian and his picture 'Ghost Train', memorable. There was a particularly quotable line in this picture. One character says to the one played by Arthur Askey, "I want to go to Liverpool." He corrects her and says, "No-one **wants** to go to Liverpool. You mean you **have** to go to Liverpool."

* * * * * * * * * *

CHAPTER FOURTEEN

After I left Skerry's, it was some weeks before I got my first job at Baxendale's as work had become difficult to get. When the war was in full force, it was all hands on deck, but now that the war effort was winding down there was a surplus of workers as peacetime production hadn't yet got going. Married women had returned to the workforce when their country needed them and they were now competing for jobs. Granddad tried to help out by getting me an appointment with someone at ICI, but I lost my way trying to get there and so I didn't keep that appointment. He also arranged an appointment for me at Cunard. Before I went for that interview, Granddad got someone in the office at Birchall's to talk to me and advise me of what to do when being interviewed for a job. One of the things I was told was to 'look confident'. The woman who interviewed me at Cunard was very pleasant and said that if I were to go back to Skerry's and increase my shorthand speed, they would be able to give me a job. But I didn't want to go back to Skerry's and I'm not sure Mother would have agreed to that anyway.

Every day I would look in the newspaper and then go to the places where a job was being advertised. There was no such thing as an employment office and, like most people, we didn't have a phone, so I couldn't phone ahead for an appointment but just went and joined the queue along with others who were after the same job. That was how I came to get the job at Baxendale's. I had to sit a test first to see that my shorthand and typing were everything I said they were. I wasn't the only one doing this test but fortunately I was the one chosen and the boss was very nice. He said that he wanted to give a young person looking for her first job a chance, and he advised me to try to stay in the job for a year to gain experience so it would be easier if I then wanted to better my position and go after another job. For the first month I was on trial and earned £1/2/6 a week; after that £1/5/- a week. Mother gave me back 5/- a week and took the rest. The 5/- was also to pay my tram fare, which worked out at 2/6 a week. To save money I sometimes rode Pat's bike to work (Mother had bought her another after her first one was stolen). Also, on occasion, I would ask for a scholar's fare on the tram - I was never refused but sometimes the conductor might say good-naturedly, "How is the old man?"

Baxendale's sold everything to do with plumbing. Also pots and pans, one of the brands being 'Judge' enamelware. There was also a lesser make, but I've forgotten the name of that. Pat's friend, Milly, asked me to try to get her a set of pans - these were very difficult to get. The manager in charge of that section, as a special favour, let me have a set of the lesser brand for her - it cost £3/15/-, or thereabouts. The Judge-ware I think cost £5 a set. I carted this huge carton on the tram back home and Milly didn't offer me anything for having done so. Pat took her to task for it and I think she might then have given me a shilling.

There were a number of us in the one office, all the typists being lined up alongside the windows, each with their own small desk. The book-keepers sat on tall stools, their long desk being higher off the ground than a normal desk. At separate tables there were two comptometer operators. There was a switchboard tucked away in a corner behind the book-keepers. This was operated by a woman whose fingers were so riddled with arthritis, her hands had practically drawn themselves into claws. There were two or three other clerks dealing with general office work. Presiding over all this was the woman in charge. She sat in a glassed-in office, which was perched on a platform at the top end of the office, where she had a birds-eye view of everyone. You could never be seen not working, which meant if we typists ran out of work we had to type forms. These could easily have been done on the roneo, but it was important that we be kept busy. The woman in charge had a brother and sister-in-law who were deaf mutes; they would come into the office sometimes to see her and she would talk to them in sign language. Doreen, one of the typists, was a close friend and we sometimes went to each other's houses, always staying the night when we did. Doreen had rings and other pieces of jewellery which her father made out of perspex from his work.

    I had some opportunity to use my shorthand. I had to do the letters for one of the senior staff and I coped very well as they were somewhat repetitive and I soon picked up his way of expressing things. However, I was somewhat in awe when the head of the Paint and Dispatch section insisted, when his secretary was on leave, that I be sent down there to do his secretarial work. This particular person had a fearsome reputation - they said he had an explosive temper. Even the tough delivery crew were in awe of him. I wondered how my shorthand would stand up to this new experience. At the beginning of May, 1941, Liverpool had been blitzed and during three or four days of devastating bombing, the city had taken a pounding. Blackler's and Lewis' had gone up in flames and during that time Baxendale's also went and their dispatch and paint section had then to operate in temporary premises. These were barn-like and cheerless. My boss had a little office there. Though all the workers went in dread of him, he couldn't have been nicer to me, bringing me a bun to go with my tea during break-time. I was glad though when I could return to the main office.

    It was during the time I was at Baxendale's that I was treated for a colloid goitre and had to go once a month to Alder Hey Hospital to see the specialist there. I had to get permission every time from the Managing Director to take the morning off - this was never a problem. The specialist, a very warm and friendly person, would measure my neck. She treated the goitre by giving me thyroid tablets and I also had to take iron medicine, in the form of oil - a tablespoon a day. I was very thin indeed. The enormous swelling on my neck went down and I began to put on weight. Betty, Pat's friend, had been the first one to point out to Mother that she thought I had a goitre - Betty herself had one. Mother had taken me along to the local doctor but as she was away I was seen by a locum. He said it had to be operated on. Mother was horrified and took me to the Alder Hey Hospital where a specialist saw me and said that it was nonsense to talk of operating at my age, that tablets would bring it under control. I was fortunate to have a mother who didn't think that either teachers or doctors were ultimate oracles.

Doctors then were organized into panels and a doctor couldn't have more than one thousand patients on his/her panel. One still had access to the outpatients at public hospitals where there were not only general practitioners, but also specialists. Some of these specialists were top in their field and gave some of their time on the honour system to those patients attending public hospitals.

Baxendale's was on the same street as the Royal Infirmary. We would occasionally see a patient who had been shell-shocked, making his way there, his head shaking violently from side to side. The war entered the office one day when the fiancé of one of the girls was killed whilst on active service. She was so broken-hearted that she stayed away from work. The supervisor of the office went to her home and encouraged her to return.

Another good friend I made at Baxendale's was Marilyn. She was a general factotum which included also being on the switchboard. I often spent the night at her house - she lived near the gas works and you could smell them. Marilyn was an excellent swimmer and, up until then, I couldn't swim; so she taught me. Pauline had made some attempts to teach me, but for some reason I didn't have the confidence in her that I had in Marilyn. Maybe it's because Pauline couldn't dive off the 20 ft. high diving board which Marilyn could. Sometimes we would go to the swimming baths in Dovecot and sometimes to those near Marilyn's house. They were not a patch on ours and were a left-over from a previous age when people didn't have baths in their own houses and had to use those provided by a public facility.

On one occasion Marilyn took me to see her brother's fiancée who was in hospital with T.B. and was skeletal thin. Her mother was with her when we visited and she was talking animatedly to her about the holiday they would both take to the Isle of Man when she got out of there. A couple of weeks later Marilyn passed on the news that she had died.

One weekend I went camping to Colomendy with Marilyn, one of the comptometer operators, and a couple of boys who worked in the rear area of Baxendale's handling the goods which the firm sold. I don't know who provided the two pup tents we took with us. When we arrived at Colomendy we just pitched them in some farmer's field. It poured with rain the whole two days. Just before we were to catch the bus to return to Liverpool, I spied a kitten on the doorstep of a farm and, shame on me, I popped it under my coat. This was shades of my childhood all over again. I was a scrupulously honest person, except when it came to cats. I was besotted with them. I kept the kitten under my coat all the way on the bus back to Liverpool.

I became very conscious of my hair and would spend ages getting it just right. There was a variety of styles in fashion at the time. The one I favoured most was combing the front up high in a wave, tucking the ends under a ribbon (making sure the ribbon didn't show) and letting the rest of the hair hang loose and turned under at the ends in a pageboy style. Later on Veronica Lake's hairstyle became popular - the long, slightly wavy hair, hanging provocatively down one side and covering that side of the face up to the eye. Pauline favoured combing all the hair upwards towards the top of the head, culminating in a cluster of curls. As she often wore dangling earrings, this showed them off to effect. When we wanted to curl our hair we used strips of rag, rolling the hair up around them and then tying them. Rags never went to waste in our house; they also often served as sanitary towels.

I had my photo taken, in fact twelve. This was a new method. One sat in a seat and moved one's head this way and that as the camera clicked away. From a sheet of twelve different poses in miniature, it was then possible to select those one wanted blown up to a bigger size. I could only afford the twelve in miniature.

The war had wound down - no more sirens - no more 'All-clears'. But there was evidence of the war everywhere - rubble from bombed buildings was still there. When Ferg was returning home from work one day he took a shortcut across a building site which had been bombed but not yet cleared. He tripped and broke his arm and it was in a plaster-cast for some time. When it came time to remove the plaster, he said the doctor cut it from one end to the other and then distracted Ferg's attention by saying, "Oh, look at that," pointing to something in the opposite direction; and in that brief moment, whilst Ferg's eyes were averted, whipped off the plaster taking all the hairs off his arm with it. I once walked through the Anglican Cathedral's war-shattered graveyard amongst the tottering headstones and the thick fleshy plants with red stalks which grew out of the cavities in the ground - all very surreal.

Ferg joined the army as soon as he was eighteen, he had turned eighteen in the April and V.E. Day was May 1945. Mother and Uncle Billie joked that now Ferg was in the army the war would soon be over. His boss at Birchall's said that he would be able to make application for Ferg to finish his apprenticeship before being called up, but Ferg wouldn't hear of it. He was sent to a Signals Unit at Aldershot. During his visits home I would help him practise Morse Code and became adept at it myself, but I have forgotten it all now. He was very careful about ironing his uniform, he would pay me to do it and then not be satisfied with the result and would re-do it. One of the things he got me to do when we were younger was test his geography. Ferg had an intense interest in geography and would hand me an Atlas to select a place anywhere in the world and he had to say where it was. He always knew. However, geography was my worst subject, and all this looking up for him never improved my own knowledge. Ferg would have liked to have gone on to further education, once saying that he wanted to be a chemist. Ferg was very good at art, though he said he was better at copying a painting than creating it. Mother kept a painting he did of a tiger for many years. He was skilled in many areas and his general knowledge was superb. He could have gone far but the opportunities were not there for him. In later years, Mother said she felt for Ferg being the only male in the house, having lost his father and his only brother.

Ferg had actually wanted to go into the Royal Airforce to serve as a gunner and was particularly keen to be a rear gunner on a bomber, but they wouldn't have him because he wasn't medically A1. He also applied for the Palestine

Military Police, but once again was rejected because he wasn't A1.

We moved to Granddad Elliott's house at Millbank, Tuebrook, between V.E. Day (May 8th, 1945) and V.J. Day (September 9th, 1945). I remember looking out of the front bedroom window on the evening of V.J. Day and seeing a jolly group of revellers going down the road who waved and called out to me.

When we left No. 32 we mainly took only our personal things with us and one or two items of furniture because Granddad's house had more than enough furniture of much better quality than ours. Auntie Jean's piano came with us; this was virtually being returned home, Mother having inherited it when Granny died. We threw all the books from the cockloft out of the window to waiting neighbourhood children. There went 'Sinbad'; there went 'Rupert'. I have an image of the double bed from our bedroom with its iron, railing-like bed ends adorned with brass knobs, leaving the house - I think a neighbour bought it. I don't know what happened to the wot-not. Certainly the black wardrobe my Father had made didn't follow us to Millbank. I also don't know what happened to the Philco wireless or Mother's precious china that she wouldn't allow us to wash - the fruit set with the bronze-shot-silk effect and the green, fluted fruit set. The chocolate-coloured Grecian-style vases that stood on either end of the mantelpiece didn't come with us, nor the plaster-of-paris elephants which stood all in a row, going from large to small and taking up the rest of the space on the mantelpiece. The silver dish shaped like a shell which was always on the sideboard came with us; many years later Pauline inherited it. I don't know what special memories that dish had for Mother that she would want to take it with her to Millbank. The pair of Wedgwood candlesticks that Bert

Large, her former fiancé, had given her when they were courting, came with us. Mother rarely spoke about this first love in her life and I don't know what was the cause of the engagement being broken. Once when she mentioned him it was more to do with a row she had had with her father, after which she had escaped to her fiancé's home. Her father soon found her there and brought her home and Mother described the furious rage he was in because, in his view, by involving others she had brought shame on the family. He was so furious that he raised his fist as if to strike her, but in the end didn't. Later, after she married, one of the Wedgwood candlesticks also bore the brunt of rage; my Father attempted to break it when he thought that Mother still loved Bert and not him, hence the piece out of its rim. I inherited the Wedgwood candlesticks for a brief period many years later after Pop died, and then Mother, fed-up with me, asked for them back. I don't know where the candlesticks eventually ended up.

I must say, thinking back, I find it interesting that a young man would give a young lady Wedgwood candlesticks when they were courting. Mother was a particularly beautiful young woman and one would have thought that she would be given perfume, or something else just as frivolous. It gives an insight into the personality of the young person Mother was before she became that shadowy person (to her children that is) a mother. On reflection, Mother knew all about antiques and appreciated beautiful china and furniture. Her upbringing would have given her that. Undoubtedly, Granny Elliott came from a background that was cultured. Bert Large must have also appreciated fine things.

The lion made from the lava of Vesuvius, a memory of my Father, came with us. He had brought it back when he served in the Royal Navy in the First World War. I also inherited the lion and I still have it to this day. But where the blue milk-jug with DUMBARTON in white lettering on the side? Where the bubble-glass sugar bowl with the silver band around the rim? There were no regrets then but I wish now that I had more than the lion as a memento of the house at No. 32.

Not long after we moved to Millbank, the kitten disappeared. Perhaps one move from Wales to Liverpool was enough, or then again someone might have done to me what I did to the kitten's previous owner.

The picture-houses began showing newsreels of the horrific scenes in the Nazi concentration camps. At one picture-house I went to, someone was collecting for Mrs Churchill's 'Aid to the Russians Fund'. The war was over but rationing didn't suddenly stop. However, there were shades of things to come. At work one day there was great delight - a shop nearby was selling ice-cream! We all rushed to get some. Starved though we had been for ice-cream, it was a huge disappointment. We became part of the outside world again; Sonja Henie, the famous ice-skating film star, came to Liverpool, causing quite a stir when she wistfully wished for a large steak.

By this time one often saw returned servicemen bearing placards saying that they had fought for their country and now they couldn't get a job. One evening, after having been to the pictures with Kath and a friend, I was stirred enough to give one of them our tram fares, which I happened to be holding - much to the dismay of Kath and friend as this meant we then had to walk home.

Granddad had retired from Birchall's - finally. When he had first tried to retire he hadn't been able to stand the inactivity and so had gone back to work. But it wasn't long before he found he couldn't cope anymore and, after falling asleep on the tram one night returning from work causing him to go way past his stop, he finally gave up work. It was a difficult adjustment and Mother said that he aged overnight.

Granddad was still working at Birchall's whilst Ferg was doing his apprenticeship, but Ferg said that Granddad was not popular with the workers under him. Near to Birchall's were the Goree Piazzas, this is where slaves who had arrived from Africa were chained awaiting shipment to America. One could go through the back entrance of Birchall's to the Red Trawler where Ferg said they would often go for their lunch.

For a short period, straight after Granny died in 1941, Mother and Pop had moved in with Granddad for a month or two, helping him to sort things out. Pop and Granddad treated each other warily. Once, when Mother was visiting us in Colomendy, she had left a rice-pudding cooking in the oven and told them both when they should take it out. They had both gone to sleep and when they woke they couldn't see each other for smoke. Granddad had exclaimed angrily to Pop, "You beauty!"

Later Mother had tried to get Granddad a live-in companion, one who would also look after him. I can't remember the name of the person she eventually found, only that he was a wonderful old gentleman. Mother went along to visit one day and was concerned that the companion looked ill so she arranged for him to go to hospital. It turned out that he had pneumonia from which he died not long afterwards. Mother had tried to persuade her father to visit him but he said he found hospitals too depressing. Mother retorted that he would want someone to visit him if he were in hospital. In the intervening periods, John and Granddad coped by themselves, no doubt with a lot of help from Mother who was always very caring of her father. John needed no assistance, he was a very capable person and kept a clean and tidy house - Granddad could not have managed without him.

An image I have of Mother in Millbank is of her on her hands and knees scrubbing the floor and her father complaining about something or other with Mother just saying mildly, "Now, Father." She always addressed him formally as 'Father'. There seemed to be a particularly strong bond between them. Mother said that when she was three, she had almost died of pneumonia and her father had been beside himself. I can only once remember her getting exasperated with her father and that was when he told Old Uncle Dave that he was coming to the house too often. Mother was very upset and said that Uncle Dave was welcome any time he wanted to come, but Old Uncle Dave gently chided her and said, "You must remember he is an old man now." Mother said, "But you are old too and you don't talk like that."

However, Mother was often tense with Kath and me when we moved to Millbank. She would snap if she found us sitting down, "Haven't you got something to do?" Once she and Kath had a spat, Kath had answered her back and Mother, uncharacteristically, had gone to slap her.

Pat, in particular, was pleased we had moved. We were less conscious of the undesirability of a Huyton address. Pat told us of a friend of hers from Dovecot who had heard two women talking on the tramcar with one saying to the other, "Where are you living now, luv?" The other had replied, "Huyton." "Not that awful area," the first women had said, shocked. The two women had been unbelievably common and her friend had been shattered. Mother, on the other hand, in later years would say that she had spent some of the happiest years of her life at No. 32.

It's hard to imagine how we all fitted into the house at Millbank. There were only three bedrooms of which Mother and Pop had the main bedroom, Granddad and John had the second, while Pat, Kath and I shared the third, and smallest bedroom, all sleeping in the one bed. Ferg slept in the parlour when he was home on leave; he used a bed with fold-away legs. Kath and I were skylarking on it one day, I was pulling her off it by her feet when she called out that the bed was collapsing. I thought she was just fooling and went on pulling until the iron bed-end collapsed onto my big toe, causing the nail to drop off shortly afterwards.

We sometimes ironed in the parlour. John came home one night from his job as an usher in a picture-house and found one of us had left the iron on and it had just about burnt through the ironing-board cover. We had not long graduated from sad irons to electric and it didn't have an automatic shut off.

People still came to stay with the same frequency as when we lived at No. 32. A friend of Pat's once came for a few days with her small daughter from her estranged marriage, together with a boyfriend who was in the air-force and whom she wanted to marry. She was trying to get a divorce - not easy in those days. Apparently her husband would not divorce her for adultery, which was one of the few grounds for divorce, and she was trying to divorce him for desertion, but just before the time elapsed when she could have started proceedings for desertion, he asked her to return to him. It would have been unthinkable in those days for her just to go off and live with her boyfriend in a de-facto relationship. Not if you were a nice girl. A boy was not expected to be nice. Those were the days that hotels asked proof of identity from couples that they were married (to each other that is) before renting them a room.

We also had as many visitors coming for a meal, or for the evening, or for the day. Granddad was as outgoing as

Mother and enjoyed company. Once a Belgian was brought to the house and we were all charmed by his gallantry; he kissed all the ladies' hands in turn. It amazes me, looking back, that it didn't matter who came to stay, we could always fit them in and I never saw Mother flustered when she was entertaining no matter how many people there were that she had to cater for; on the contrary, she would be in her element.

Between Millbank and the shopping centre at Tuebrook, there was a very old thatched cottage. On one occasion, Ferg coming home late at night was walking by this cottage when the alsatian dog, which was kept on the premises, leapt on his back. The owner called out to Ferg that he was not to worry! Ferg said this was a bit difficult with a dog on his back.

One year Pauline and Leon rented a house at Scarborough over the holiday period and I went down to spend a week there. Ferg, generous as ever, when he saw me off on the train emptied out his pockets and gave me what he had; I being penniless as always and Mother hadn't given me any extra spending money over and above the 5/- pocket money she always gave me back from my pay. I had to change trains at Leeds and had very little time to do so without knowing which platform the train left from. One of the guards, in trying to give me directions and not getting anywhere, in the end actually took me to the correct platform. Some images stay in the mind and I can see Pauline and Leon waiting on the station to greet me when I arrived in Scarborough and I was suddenly overwhelmed by the warmth of their greeting and, feeling as gawky as only a fifteen year old can, was off-hand in my response.

It was a wonderful week. We went swimming in a pool which had a water chute but I could only be persuaded to come down this if Leon stayed at the bottom to catch me. I almost winded him with my feet on one occasion. Cousin Royce was also invited to come that same week and we went around a lot together. He had at that stage outgrown his devilment which had caused me years before to lock him in the chicken coop and we got on famously. We would sometimes hold hands as we walked along together.

During this stay at Scarborough I met a young man, Jimmy, who was convalescing at the Army Hospital nearby - he was a despatch rider and had been shot in the leg whilst on active service. When he recovered from his wounds, he was sent back overseas. I asked him the usual question, "What do Scotsmen wear under their kilts?" He wouldn't tell me. He was from Edinburgh and was very well educated and wrote sweet nothings to me in French, one of which was, 'Je vous aime trés beaucoup', which I had to get either Pauline or Pat to translate for me. The only French I knew was the 1-20 Pauline had taught me when I was about eight and which I still remember today. In civvy street, Jimmy worked for a stockbroker.

Whilst in Scarborough, Pauline needed to get something fixed in the house and contacted the military. Prisoners of war were given a chance to do odd jobs to earn a bit of pocket money. The person put in charge of the German prisoner happened to be a Swede. It was all very friendly, everyone having morning tea together before the 'prisoner' got on with the job.

Mother and Pop left for South Africa shortly after VJ Day. Kath and I were to follow as soon as we could get a berth on a ship. Meantime we would live with Granddad and John. Pat was also there and took over the running of the house.

During this time the corporation decided they would paint a couple of rooms in each house – all this kind of upkeep had gone on hold during the war. When they came to Millbank it was Pat who chose the two rooms to be done. A priority, she felt, was the double bedroom which I had attempted to paint and made a real hash of, even painting around an open door, leaving the section behind it a different colour. When Pat was showing the painter around, she felt she needed to explain and said, "My youngest sister has been painting it," and he looked at her bemused, obviously thinking she was trying to pass her own handiwork off onto someone else.

Not long after Mother had left, Pat and Ray decided to get married; they had been engaged for some time. Ray had not yet been demobbed and the marriage took place whilst he was on leave, so after the wedding and a brief honeymoon, he had to return to duty. We were living at No. 32 when Ray first began to visit. Our house was so small that when either Pauline and Pat had a boyfriend visit, it was difficult for them to have any privacy and we were warned to go straight upstairs when we returned from anywhere and leave the kitchen to them. When a girl and boy were romantically involved it was called 'spooning'.

When I was at Skerry's Commercial College, Pat would give me the letters she wrote to Ray to take to the Censor's Office to be perused and reduced in size. This happened to all letters sent to the military. A memory of Ray that stands out from those early days is that he liked a programme of orchestral music which came from a London hotel on Sunday nights. He was disappointed when he found out that the clapping was 'canned'. Ray was knowledgeable about music and could play the piano by ear. He was from Barton-upon-Humber and it was there that he and Pat had first met. When they first became engaged, Pat voiced her concern to me that Ray would not be as popular in the family as Leon was. But there was no need to worry. He might have been a different personality altogether to Leon, but he was very nice and we all liked him and were pleased he was to be our brother-in-law.

Pat was teaching at a school in Dingwall. This school was a far cry from Colwell Road School. She did her Prac' teaching at Colwell when I was still a pupil there and she happened to be given my class to take. She went home and complained to Mother that all I did was sit there and look at her fatuously. Pat once took me with her when she went to buy a pair of shoes at Saxby's, a really posh shoe shop in downtown Liverpool. I was agog that she paid something like £4 for a pair. Pat didn't have to hand over all her earnings to Mother as Ferg, Kath and I had to do, but merely paid board.

Ray and Pat were married on 24th November 1945 and Kath and I were bridesmaids. Pauline made our dresses in gold-coloured taffeta and we carried bouquets of large yellow chrysanthemums. Ray's mother came for the wedding and stayed at Millbank, but she was rather put off by some of Granddad Elliott's habits, such as first pouring out a cup of tea, then pouring it back into the pot, and then pouring it out again. Ray's mother drew me aside in the scullery to voice her distaste of this practice. Granddad took some getting used to if you didn't know him.

Very good friends of ours in Liverpool were Gertrude Brown and her mother, Mrs Longfield. The wedding was from Gertrude's house - she lived in a modern home in Childwall, an exclusive suburb. Pat borrowed Gertrude's wedding dress – not to save the expense, but to save the clothing coupons. The night before the wedding, Pat, Kath and I went to stay with Gertrude who lent me a piece of jewellery to wear and also fancy high-heeled shoes. Gertrude was fond of parties and often threw them. It was the sort of house I felt free to go to anytime I wanted and stay the night. Uncle Arthur, who had been a prisoner-of-war of the Japanese, was at Pat's wedding. It was the first time I had seen him since he arrived back in England. At the wedding, he had come up to me to say "Hello" and I looked at him blankly and he said, "I'm your Uncle Arthur." I'd been a child when he had left on active service.

Before her wedding, Pat had gone shopping for the decorations for her wedding cake - things like silver balls, frills, miniature silver shoe, all the usual paraphernalia. In those days of shortages, some shop assistants had taken advantage and no longer was it a case of the customer always being right, but quite the opposite; indeed sometimes it seemed the customer could do no right. When Pat went looking for her wedding cake decorations she was delighted to happen on a shop that had some and said, "I want such-and-such and such-and-such." Before she could get any further, the shop assistant snarled, "Want! What do you mean want? You should say, 'May I have such-and-such'." Pat then sweetly asked, "May I have such-and-such, and such-and-such, and such-and-such ..." going on and on until the assistant had just about everything she had on the counter. Then Pat said bluntly, "Now I don't want" and walked out.

Later, when Mother saw the wedding photograph of Pat and Ray, she said Ray had a pleased smile on his face as much as to say, "At last she is mine." Pat had a lot of boyfriends, some of them keen to marry her.

Pauline had invited Uncle Billie and Auntie Jessie to Pat and Ray's wedding. They came to Millbank prior to the ceremony and when I opened the front door my first question was, "Hello, who are you?" They found this very amusing and later would recall it. Some years before there'd been a break in the Elliott family and I had no memory of Billie (Mother's brother) and his wife, Jessie. Pauline, being much older, remembered them from the days when the family were still in contact with them. I have no idea what caused the break only that somehow Mother's brother, Hugh, and his wife, Winnie, seemed to be involved. It was not difficult to see, when the two couples were in the room together, that the atmosphere between them was tense.

 I didn't feel close to either Auntie Winnie or Uncle Hugh. I remember Auntie Winnie as being small and dainty with black hair and tightly-compressed lips; she spoke in a controlled manner. I remember Uncle Hugh mainly for his having to give himself insulin injections for his diabetes. He said his bottom was like a pin-cushion. Sometimes he'd break out and take that forbidden piece of cake and have to give himself an extra injection. In later years he and Auntie Winnie participated in competitive ballroom dancing. They lived in the vicinity of Tuebrook where Pat would sometimes visit Auntie Winnie and they seemed to get on well. Auntie Winnie's elderly blind father lived with them and Granddad would, on occasion, go to their house to take him out for a walk. Once I boarded a tram which Uncle Hugh was already on. There wasn't an empty seat next to him, fortunately, as I would have felt obliged to sit there. As he alighted he nodded to me, and the thought crossed my mind that it was odd to think that he was my uncle yet I felt so remote from him. He wore a bowler hat and in his stature and dress was very much the English gentleman. He may very well have had a 'furled' umbrella when the weather was inclement, as Mother would say when it was raining, and no doubt Hugh would also.

 I saw a lot of Auntie Jessie and Uncle Billie after they re-entered the family and would often go to their house, most times staying the night. They were both excellent card players and taught me to play solo. They told me that after they were married they often went to Whist Drives where the prize would sometimes be a three piece suite which they had twice won. Uncle Billie became one of my favourite relatives. They didn't have any children, their one and only child having been stillborn.

Auntie Jessie was very artistic and did a lot of decoupage, so pictures that she made had all sorts of things sticking out of them and were very imaginative but sometimes, to my conventional eyes, rather odd. She also liked to work in wax and all around the house there were wax butterflies, stuck on the lamps and other protuberances. She kept a model of a head which she would dress in wigs and hats and earrings, making up the face with lipstick and eye-shadow, etc. As this was kept on top of a chest-of-drawers in the end bedroom, facing towards the hallway, it appeared to be looking at you as you came up the stairs and was a bit off-putting. When going out Auntie Jessie always wore a cape, not a coat, and a hat which was cone-shaped, both black. These went well with her jet-black hair and her very white face.

I was to discover that Auntie Jessie was highly superstitious. Anyone entering the house by the front door, had to leave by the front door, otherwise their spirit would be left behind. We couldn't look in the mirror at the same time as she did, or put our hands in the dish-washing water when she already had hers in. An umbrella was not to be unfurled in the house - but I was familiar with that one as that applied in our home too. No-one could pour out tea in her house until they had known her for seven years. There were so many things, that we walked a fine line when we visited Auntie Jessie. But having learnt all the ground rules and therefore not suddenly transfixed by a sharp shriek when a rule had been broken, we had a lot of fun staying with Auntie Jessie. She made the most superb Irish soda scones - serving the butter for them in curls, something until then outside of my experience.

Auntie Jessie had a sister, Kathleen, a very pleasant person, who sometimes came to visit with her husband. Auntie Jessie was just a wee bit jealous of Kathleen and once when I was there helping to get the tea after Kathleen had come, Auntie Jessie said to me in the scullery, "This bread is stale, but it is good enough for her." When I took it in, Auntie Jessie said, as if in surprise, "Oh, Jean, this bread is stale." I said, "You told me it was good enough for Kathleen" and Uncle Billie laughed and winked at me.

Uncle Billie and Ferg would sometimes go together to the football matches, but Uncle Billie was disgusted that Ferg was a strong supporter of Liverpool whilst he supported Everton, and would say, "How can you support that common lot?"

Mother's brother, John, was very keen on football and could name almost every player in every first division team in the U.K. However, he would have nothing to do with the football pools, either Littlewoods or Vaughans. Other male members of the family would try to persuade him to fill in a line on their coupons, but he would have none of it. Another interest of John's was collecting the octagonal, gold-coloured threepenny bits. When we came home, we had to sort out our threepenny bits from our other coins and John would exchange them for others of like value. Of a night-time we could hear him in his room counting them. Granddad and Granny kept on their wall a framed certificate which John had received from the RSPCA for an essay competition on the care of animals, which he had won. John had gone to a special school but the competition had been between all schools and had been keen.

Once John had been going to get married but the girl's parents and John's parents had got together and decided that it would not be for the best. John had cried.

Sometimes we would go to Auntie Eve and Uncle Arthur's for tea. Auntie Eve kept a 'parsimonious' table, as Mother would describe it. She was an attractive woman and sometimes bought her clothes from Wetherall's, the place where Kathleen worked for a while doing hand-stitching. She gave me one of the dresses that she had bought from there, a pale blue crépe with a crossover bodice. I much preferred the green dress I had bought from C & A Modes which had come with a gold-coloured brooch. Pat was a particular favourite of Auntie Eve and saw quite a lot of her. Auntie Eve was not from Liverpool but had come to appreciate Liverpool humour. She said that on one occasion when she was on a tram someone got on with a side of beef. The conductor just commented drily, "Why can't you bring sandwiches like everyone else?"

Pauline had been living in Barton for some time and had returned to teaching but came to Liverpool during the school vacations. At that time Kath was working at the Colwell Road School Nursery. Kath was very fond of young children and this was an ideal job for her, but Pauline was concerned that there wasn't a lot of future in this job, whereas she and Pat were teachers and I had been trained as a stenographer, Kath had had no formal training, so she promptly enrolled Kath in Greg's Secretarial College to learn shorthand/typing and sent Mother the bill.

The Colwell Road School Nursery came into being during the war and was for the children of mothers who went out to work. Some of the children came from homes that neglected them and Kath and her co-workers would have to look through the children's head for lice and vermin when they came in of a morning. They had a bowl of disinfectant into which they dropped the vermin when they found any, which was often. One of the staff who was there for a short while used to nurse in the slum area of Liverpool and had lurid tales of what she had seen there. She told of a child who had so many vermin that its head was covered with scab and the nurse would have to lift the scab to probe out the vermin beneath. She also spoke of working as a nurse in a hospital. When she and other nurses had to 'lay out' the dead, they became so hardened to doing this that they would sing songs like 'Roll out the barrel' as they stuffed cotton wool up the various orifices of the corpses.

The Government provided young children with cod-liver oil and orange juice and they benefited from these. There were also school lunches which meant many of the children were far better off in the nursery than in some of their homes. Kath would sometimes collect one of the children to spend the day over the weekend. Kath was there at Christmastime and I happened to go along at the time of their Christmas party, being told, out of the blue, that I was to be Father Christmas! The staff dressed me up with a red suit and beard, the whole paraphernalia; I went down well with the kids. I was even taken to the classrooms to meet some of the teachers.

Whilst at the nursery, Kath caught cellulitis. She had to be hospitalised at the Alder Hey Hospital where they kept her quarantined and we could only see her through the glass when we visited. Even the nurse donned a different gown when she went into the room. In those pre-penicillin days, Kath was treated with M and B tablets which made her very nauseous. Kath's modesty was put on trial at the hospital. She hated the thought of using a bedpan and tried to hold out but then became so constipated that she ended up having to have an enema, which was much more embarrassing than if she'd used the bedpan.

At around the same time that Pauline arranged for Kath to go to Greggs, she also wrote to the military regarding Ferg's allotment to Mother. Servicemen were required to allot a certain amount of their pay to their family. She informed the military that, as Ferg's mother was now in South Africa and not providing a home for him to return to, the allotment which was being sent to her, should instead be retained by him. Mother was not amused. Pauline also turned her attention to me. As I wasn't getting on at all well with Pat, Pauline suggested I return to Barton with her. I have to give it to Pauline, she did try to look after our interests - you just had to give her unquestioning obedience in return!

* * * * * * * * * *

CHAPTER FIFTEEN

I left Baxendale's where I had been for thirteen months and went to join Pauline in Barton where she and Jacqueline had been staying with Auntie Ida and Uncle Dave. I had Douglas' room as he was serving in the army in Gibraltar. This room had tray after tray of birds' eggs which Douglas had gathered during his growing up years.

I got a job, which I really liked, as a secretary to the Town Clerk. I could have had a job at the police station but you had to be eighteen before you could work there and I was too young. I earned £1/12/6 a week and paid £1 a week board. I'd never been so wealthy. There were no fares to pay out of my left over 12/6d. In Barton there seemed to be bus services only between neighbouring villages - I don't recall any local bus services, though maybe it is because I never had cause to use them. The council offices were on the High Street and sometimes I walked to work, while at other times I rode Pauline's bicycle. Whenever we arrived in Barton, we walked from the train station on Butts Road to Auntie Ida and Uncle Dave's house.

Mr Hartley, the Town Clerk, was my boss. I've always had good bosses and he was particularly nice. He was active in the Methodist Church, working amongst the youth. Mr Hartley always insisted that it was Barton-upon-Humber and not Barton-on-Humber. It was an interesting experience working there as I once had to attend a public meeting and take notes whilst sitting on the platform. I typed a lot of letters to do with the Humber Bridge, still in the concept stage. Many years later when I returned with my Civil Engineer husband and crossed over that bridge, it was a nice thought to know that I'd been there at the beginning.

The council offices were in a large terrace house which had been converted. In the other front room across the hall from where I worked, there was a clerk whose daughter (about twenty or so) was dying of T.B. She often popped in to see him. She was always smiling and cheerful but he looked sad.

Ratepayers would come in to the office for various reasons. Some elderly people came to pay off their grave plots by instalments of threepence a week, they didn't want to be buried as paupers so purchased their plots in the cemetery in advance. Others came in to see where they now stood on the waiting list for council housing. The waiting list was long. One of the councillors, a Mr Mustard, regularly came in to explode about something or other. He was as apoplectic-looking as his name and would come charging into the office demanding this and that. Along with other ratepayers, Granny thought he was fantastic as Mr Mustard stood up for the ratepayers who felt the rates were much too high. One young woman who came in just for a chat now and then was an American, married to a local. She didn't find the people in Barton particularly friendly. It could be because she was probably one of the few foreigners seen in those parts. Though one day I did see a German prisoner-of-war walking around quite freely; no doubt he was lonely too.

I shared the main front office with a woman who was in charge of accounts, her husband was serving overseas. She was pleasant enough but I never really got to know her. In the building there was a young man, about my age in years but to me seemed very juvenile; he and I were allocated a supply of chocolate milk powder which had added nourishment. There was a huge sack of this in one of the rooms upstairs and we could go and make ourselves a drink whenever we wanted. This must have been a local council initiative - probably applied to people in government service as well, as there was certainly nothing like that in Baxendale's for their young employees

I don't know how it came about but I once collected for a charity in Barton. Maybe the charity used the council office as a collection point and had roped me in as a collector. My area was the Cement Works and as I went through the building where the cement was being bagged, the workers all greeted me cheerily. I felt deeply for one of them who had a false nose as I wondered how he coped with all the cement dust with which the men were enveloped.

Barton was memorable for the beautiful fruit you could get there. You could buy gooseberries almost the size of plums, and red-currants and black-currants so fresh they had the smell of the leaves still on them. Unlike Liverpool, there was no shortage of fruit.

Sometime during this period, Pauline and I had become sick from eating fruit which had recently been sprayed with DDT. These were early days of DDT and no doubt we had not washed the fruit properly. I was in a worse state than Pauline so it was she who kept up the supply of dry crackers and made the soda water; Auntie Ida and Uncle Dave had their own siphon for making this. Cousin Royce happened to call in from Scunthorpe, he had been looking for sympathy as he had a boil inside his nose which was all swollen, but instead ended up waiting on Pauline and me.

Uncle Dave was a keen card player, as Mother would describe it, as were all her brothers. When we stayed at 'Venita' we would play cards at least two or three evenings a week. It was Uncle Dave who taught us the 'marching' fingers. The fingers of the right hand are curled under the thumb and released one by one onto a hard surface, knocking the closed knuckles on the table at the end of each cycle of four fingers to mark time. As we did all this, we 'walked' two fingers of the left hand in time to the beat.

Uncle Dave was a great raconteur. A tale he once told was of when he was in the Royal Navy in the First World War and the vessel he was on was sunk. He was left marooned in a lifeboat without any clothes and when he reached dry land, the first thing he was offered was a hat.

Later we moved to Granny Jackson's house. Pauline was very much Granny's favourite of all us siblings - I think because she had been so close to my Father. Granny, who was then approaching eighty, took care of Jacqueline whilst Pauline was teaching.

During this stay with Granny she took me with her when she was visiting a relative. This relative had elephantiasis, Granny said, and when her foot was tapped it felt hard like an elephant's hide. Doctors came from all over England to see her. Granny was full of tales like that.

Granny also took me with her on a couple of occasions to the Women's Bright Hour, a once a week gathering run by her chapel. There the ladies chatted and had tea together and it was touching that even from her sparse rations, Granny managed to contribute a little tea and sugar for the afternoon tea. For though the war was now over, rationing was still on.

The room I slept in was at the far end of the house and didn't even have a gas-light, so I had to use a candle. When I carried this candle along the hallway, I could see my face reflected in the top section of the door which was half glass, and I got a fright just seeing my own spectral-illuminated face coming out of the blackness. Granny didn't make it any easier because she would tell me of people who had died in that bed. When it came to the dark, my imagination ran away with me and I was scared stiff. The bedroom was really very nice, the window overlooking the fields and the railway line at the back of the house. There were crisp lace curtains on the window - everything in Granny's house was always spotless. Whenever anyone came to stay, Granny 'aired' the bed clothes, which meant letting them hang out in the fresh air for a day or so before being put to use.

We were with Granny at 'Nisida' when she turned eighty on 20th January 1946. Nothing special was done for this and Granny worked as hard as usual. She was brushing the stair carpet with a hand-brush when she took a funny turn and had to sit down. I said I would finish brushing down the stair carpet, which I did. But next day I saw Granny continuing where she had left off the day before and I protested that I had already done them. "Oh, you Towners don't know how to clean," she said, stating what to her was simply a fact and without any animosity.

I had a bout of sickness myself at Granny's house, I don't know what the cause was but I fainted. Pauline, concerned, wrote to Mother who wrote to me telling me to "pull up my socks."

Granny still had all her own teeth, though they weren't in good shape at all and she had bad pyorrhea. She said that the doctor told her that if she had her teeth out she could expect to live another ten years. She told me that she wasn't interested, as ever since Granddad had died, she had not wanted to live. She had then been a widow for thirteen years. At one time there had been a 'Darby and Joan' competition held in the region and Granny told Mother that she and Granddad could have entered it as they had never had an argument in all their married life. It was Mother's opinion, unvoiced to Granny, that it would be impossible to argue with Granny. Granddad, it is said, would hand over his pay-packet unopened to Granny every week, but one week it had been opened and Granny wanted to know why. It seemed he had needed some tobacco so had taken the liberty.

I wish I had asked her a lot more about when she was young and what her parents were like. I did ask her once where she and Granddad had gone when they were courting, she said they only met each other at chapel every Sunday. She once told me another young man wanted to marry her and began his proposal with how much he had saved up. She spurned him as she said he drank and she could never marry anyone who drank. This could have been a subtle moral message to me, not to marry anyone who drank. Granny was fond of getting across the evils of drink at every opportunity. Sometimes she could be unwittingly funny, like the time she related the tale of someone who had been drinking very heavily one evening and, on getting up in the morning feeling ill, had taken some Andrew's Liver Salts, upon which he had dropped dead. As Pat said, not a good advertisement for Andrew's Liver Salts.

Granny had a lawyer handling her affairs and one day she came home after seeing him saying, "I feel I am being cheated but there is nothing I can do about it." I was too young to be of any help, but there was no way anyone else could have been, she was too independent for that.

Every so often Auntie Edna and Uncle Billy would come over from Scunthorpe and stay with Granny for a night or two. Uncle Billy smoked; this was all right in Granny's eyes for he was a man. Granny always went to bed at nine p.m. and when Auntie Edna and Uncle Billy followed, Uncle Billy would leave his cigarettes on the table for Pauline. Staying with Granny she was not permitted to smoke. On other occasions when she did after Granny had gone to bed, she would open the window and waft the smoke out as Granny would be sure to be able to detect the smell when she got up in the morning. When Uncle Billy was staying, she didn't have to do that as Granny would think it was he.

Once when Auntie Edna was in Barton she preached at the Wesleyan Church and I went along with Granny to hear her. Unfortunately, I do not recall anything of her sermon, only that I was impressed. Royce at that stage was playing the organ at Sunday services in their home church. Auntie Edna explained to me once why the family had broken away from the Methodist Church and become Primitive Methodists. It was because they felt that the Methodist Church had become too snobbish and did not have anything to say to the working person anymore. They eventually returned to the Methodist Church. She and Uncle Billy preached at lunchtime to the workers in the factory at Scunthorpe - sometimes only two or three people turning up. In those days one occasionally saw at fairgrounds and other places where people gathered for special events, tents erected by evangelical preachers, sometimes with an invite writ large to 'Come and be Saved'.

Auntie Edna had been trained as a teacher, her first examination as a pupil teacher was in May 1919, when she would have been 13½. She passed with a distinction in Elementary Mathematics during her Pupil Teacher exams in December 1923 when she was then eighteen. But she gave up work on marriage, feeling as strongly as her mother the different roles of husband and wife; she felt that a wife's role was to support her husband and this Auntie Edna did by working in the post office-cum-shop which he ran.

Uncle Billy and Auntie Edna must have moved around a bit as at one stage they were living in Bridlington. Mother told me that she went to stay with them there for a while when my Father's job took him to various building projects in the region. It was before I was born and I don't know how many children Mother had at that stage, but she said that she and

Auntie Edna got on very well and that it was one of the happiest periods of her married life. Auntie Edna was a delightful person, and so was her husband, Billy.

It was from Auntie Edna that I learnt most about my Father. She was ten years younger than he was and obviously admired her big brother. She told me of the time when my Father was in the Royal Navy during the First World War and she dreamed that the ship he was on was sunk. She was very distressed but there was no-one to tell this to as she didn't want to upset her mother. As it happened, before the ship sailed my Father had gone into the gym and, in doing some exercises, had broken his collar bone and was unable to sail with the ship. The ship had indeed been sunk during its voyage and all on board had perished.

I was told that as children, they swam in the drain and once my Father was caught in the sluice gates and it was only his father opening them which prevented him from drowning.

According to Auntie Edna, when he was growing up my Father had got up to all sorts of mischief. He and his best friend, Charlie Robson from next door, had to walk three miles to school and had three routes they could choose from, the road, the Humber bank and the railway cutting. An old roadman worked on the road and the boys, Auntie Edna said, "played him up so much, overturning his barrow, etc., that they daren't not go that way and it seems they played up on the other routes also, so that it was a hazardous job going to school." In those days they lived near the brickyard and were surrounded by brick pits in which there were lots of frogs. She said my Father would slip a frog under Granny's washcloth when she was scrubbing the floor, so when she lifted it, a frog would jump out. He also played the frog trick on his sister, Ida, slipping one in her hat which she was about to put on ready for chapel. Auntie Edna said that her mother said she would have been greyer a lot sooner if she had known of all the escapades my Father got up to.

Granny and the Frog!

One of my Father's escapades with his friends, according to Mother, was to block all the drains in the road so that it flooded. Perhaps Auntie Edna didn't know of that one. Or of the time he and his friends stole the Christmas goose. Every year the butcher raffled a goose for Christmas and every year he, or a member of his family or a friend of his, won it. My Father and his friends had determined that this particular Christmas they wouldn't.

Granny told me that my Father was fond of eel and when he caught any would bring them to her to cook. She did this but didn't like it as she said the smell of eel filled the scullery.

I liked to hear these stories, it made him a little more real to me whose upbringing had been so different. Though I have no memory of him, as a child I would sometimes dream that he wasn't really dead.

Mother's sister, Georgie, had also liked my Father and found him very humorous. She told me many years later that he had found her something of a prude and made up this ditty about her:

Mother put a card in the window
For lodgings for a nice young man.
A kiss and a cuddle before breakfast,
Followed by eggs and ham.
Mother put a card in the window,
But Georgie took it out.

When he had been in the Royal Navy during the First World War, according to Mother, one of the trips he went on was to Russia during the Russian Revolution. She said he felt very sorry for the Russian people, they were so poor. He was stationed for a while in Pensacola, Florida. Also for a period in Singapore, in fact it was there he got malaria. After he married Mother, he wanted them both to go and live in Singapore. He also went to Naples. I don't know the dates of any of these journeys, but I do have the date of one voyage, he left Liverpool for America on 29th November 1918 on H.M.T. Exmoor. This is interesting; was it during his stay in port prior to sailing that he began to court my Mother? They were married on 15th May 1919. If only I'd asked my Mother all these things when I had the opportunity.

Auntie Elsie and Uncle Ronald (my Father's youngest brother) came every month for the day. Sometimes they would bring their two sons, Peter and Lewis, with them. Uncle Ronald gave them each a cigarette once a week as he didn't want them smoking behind his back. He had other strange ideas too - he didn't believe in higher education. Granny was particularly fond of her daughter-in-law, Elsie Elizabeth (neé Gibson), as she was such a dedicated housewife. Uncle Ronald was a commercial traveller for an office supply company.

Auntie Mary and Uncle Edgar (my Father's eldest brother) came only once during the time I was there. Granny never called her son 'Edgar' but always, 'Edgus'. I don't know what Uncle Edgar worked at, only that he had served an apprenticeship in something or other. I know that because he and Auntie Mary had wanted to get married earlier than they did but Granny Jackson would not hear of it until Edgar had completed his apprenticeship. Edgar and Mary (neé Hill) had three children but I can only recall their eldest, Gordon, who was born out of wedlock. Granny raised him until Edgar and Mary were married three years later when he went to live with them, but not for long, he was later returned to Granny who continued to raise him. He visited Granny whilst I was there, he was then serving in the Royal Navy. In later years Mother visited Gordon and his wife a lot, she seemed to be particularly fond of them. She and Pat spent Christmas one year with them and Mother said it was one of the best Christmases she had spent in years. Edgar and Mary had two other sons, Derick Lewis and Roy Thomas. Roy was killed during the Second World War.

Auntie Mary told me that every time she saw me when I was a baby, I was crying. I had already been told by Mother that I was a baby who cried a lot - she put this down to the fact that Maureen had died whilst she was pregnant with me and she had cried a great deal. Mother thought that what you did during pregnancy affected the unborn. She put the red birthmark on Pauline's nose down to the fact that when she was expecting her, she had had some dental treatment done and there had been blood on one of her fingers. Without thinking, she touched her nose with that particular finger. The dentist had tried to warn her not to do that, but it was too late and Pauline was born with a red birthmark on her nose.

One other person visited Granny whilst I was there. Granny said that he had been a great friend of my Father's and she added that, even all those years later, she could not mention him as his death had been too upsetting for him. How one wishes that one had been more curious when one was younger as now I would have liked to have asked him all sorts of things about my Father of whom I know so little. When I first arrived in Barton I was buying something at the grocery shop and the woman serving me said, "Are you Cyril Jackson's daughter?" I said that I was. She said, "I thought so, you look like him. I knew your Dad." I didn't ask her one question about him! How sorry I am that when I was young I was young and not a bit interested in the older generation; even the live ones were as good as dead after they had passed the age of thirty.

I fitted in straightaway to the life in Barton and went most Saturday nights to dances at the Oddfellows Hall. One of the young men who was invariably there was in a wheelchair. There was always a gathering around him as he was very personable. If you were new to the town, he made a point of talking to you. During the week, he would often just park himself in his wheelchair on the High Street and people would stop and chat. On a couple of occasions a hired bus would be arranged to take the young people to a dance in one of the other villages.

Leon had taught me to dance. He and Pauline were fabulous dancers and when they danced the tango to 'Jealousy', they were a sight to behold. Leon taught me to dance by simply taking me onto the floor and dancing me around, no such thing as learning the steps first. But it worked and I thank him today that I can dance. The war brought the 'jitterbug' but I never took to it and it hadn't really taken off in Barton at that stage.

It was wonderful walking home in the evening from the Oddfellows Hall in the brisk, bracing air of the countryside. When I stayed with Granny I would take a short-cut through the church yard and sometimes would hear the hoot of an owl. In the daytime, cycling or walking to the High Street, I would go through the council yard where the morgue was.

I made a number of friends in Barton and also fell madly in love with Bill who lived at the Maltkiln. When I told the young woman hairdresser with whom I had become friendly that I had seen this boy that I liked, she arranged a meeting between us. I can still recall with what anticipation I went to meet him at the telephone box in the town square, no doubt wearing 'Evening in Paris' perfume which came in a dainty, translucent blue bottle. However it was not to be and my heart was broken when he later threw me over. But despite the later heartbreak, could one ever forget the exquisite agony of the first time one falls in love? I don't know how I happened to meet one of the relatives of George William as Granny never had anything to do with that branch of the family. He and I arranged to go out one evening but when he came to collect me, Granny sent him away.

One girlfriend I made invited me and another friend to her home one evening. She lived in a very large house and the family were obviously well off. During the evening she was playing the piano for us when she suddenly stopped and went to the door and opened it, her mother was just standing there, staring rather blankly. Her daughter gently led her in and encouraged her to sit down. Later the other friend who had been invited along with me, told me as we walked home that the son of the house was serving time in prison. I have forgotten what for but it had obviously brought great distress to his mother.

I saw a fair bit of Ray's parents, whom I called Auntie Betsy and Uncle George, and I was particularly fond of Auntie Betsy. Ray was very clever and had been a brilliant student who had won a scholarship to Grammar School. His parents were not well off and a loan was offered to pay for other expenses. But they were much too proud and independent to take it, Auntie Betsy saying that as long as she had two hands she would earn her own money. So she went out cleaning to pay for the extra expenses involved in Ray's schooling. Auntie Betsy was such a meticulous housewife that she would even polish the doors.

Uncle George was disciplined in the extreme. When he came home from work of an evening, he did everything in exactly the same way every night. Next to his armchair he had a box in which he kept his cigarettes, matches, and other paraphernalia. Taking off his shoes and putting on his slippers, he would empty the coins out of his pocket and place them in the box. After tea he would light a cigarette, take two puffs and then extinguish it, putting it in the box for the next time he felt like a cigarette. He said that one didn't need more than two puffs to satisfy the need for a smoke.

Auntie Betsy and I would go to the Old Time Dances together. I learnt to do all the old time dances, liking in particular the lancers. Women invariably outnumbered the men at these dances and Auntie Betsy and I often partnered each other. Auntie Betsy would knit a pair of socks a week and sell them to get the money to pay for the entrance ticket as Uncle George didn't altogether approve of her going and she didn't want to be beholden to him. On a few occasions when Auntie Betsy passed by the council office, she'd pop her head in and say that she'd just bought some cakes and to "come on up." If I had cycled to work that day I was able to nip up to her house for a quick cuppa. There was always some mail I could deliver by hand on the way instead of mailing it, so it wasn't a problem for me to be out of the office for forty minutes or so.

Auntie Betsy took me over to Hull with her to stay with her sister for the weekend. I really enjoyed it and I met other relatives when they came over for the evening. They were a lovely family. We had a 'séance', sitting around a table with our fingers on a glass with the letters of the alphabet circled around. We had to concentrate when we called on the spirits to give us a name, and the glass supposedly spelt out a message going from one letter to the other of the alphabet. Later Auntie Betsy said that two of the relatives there that I thought were sisters, were actually mother and daughter, but that the daughter had been raised by her grandmother as she had been born out of wedlock. I think she was grown up before she actually knew that one of the sisters was in actual fact her mother. Life in those days was all about hiding these sorts of things. Next morning, it was a homely atmosphere in the scullery, the sister's husband had gone off to the pub for his usual Sunday morning pint, whilst the ladies of the house prepared the Sunday roast. Later on I went over again to stay with Auntie Betsy's sister for the weekend, this time on my own. I liked her and her husband a lot, also their daughter who would have been in her early twenties and who I thought was so sophisticated.

After six months or so in Barton, I returned to Liverpool. When I gave my notice in to Mr Hartley, he put his head in his hands, he didn't know how he was going to replace me.

* * * * * * * * * *

CHAPTER SIXTEEN

Back home in Liverpool I went to work at a shipping agents on North John Street. I think I earned about two guineas a week. The shipping office has not left much of an impression, except for the tedious 'bills of lading' that I had to do. Make one little mistake and you had them to do all over again, the forms were already franked so it was an expensive business. I was an accurate typist so it wasn't a problem but the job was boringly repetitious. What I learnt there is that a shipment could pass through a number of hands before it even left the dock. Olga worked in the office and she and I became friends. Her boyfriend lived in a tenement on Scotland Road and on a couple of occasions she asked me to meet her there. It was quite an experience walking through that area in those days. One time I was foolish enough to be wearing a coat with a fur collar and a couple of urchins came up and were tauntingly stroking the fur of the collar whilst I just kept walking, not knowing quite what to do about it. The boyfriend's mother had supported her two boys by money-lending when their father had walked out on them. He had later returned and there was now another child in the family. When I first met the mother I couldn't understand one word she said, she spoke such broad Liverpool; her son was a bit fed-up with me thinking I was doing it deliberately. Olga herself lived in a very old house at the end of a lane. It is probably a National Trust home now but they lived there then because it was all they could get. When I stayed overnight I shared her tiny bedroom at the top of garret stairs. Her grandparents lived with them and her grandmother was an old crone who sat hissing by the fireplace. Every now and then Olga's mother, who smoked, would light a cigarette each for both of them and the old crone would puff away. Olga's parents were very unhappily married and in between granny hissing insults, her father would be flinging barbed remarks at his wife. Olga was an exceptionally beautiful girl.

I started to take piano lessons again, but not for very long as I found them too expensive on my meagre pay. Another girlfriend I had at that time was Rita and she was taking piano lessons so I went to her teacher. I learnt to play the first few bars of Chopin's 'Tristesse' ('Sadness'). Old Uncle Dave loved to hear this and every time he came would ask me to play it, even though I could only play the first few bars with confidence. The piano lessons were part of the self-improvement phase I was going through at the time. I also read about Christian Science and, no doubt misunderstanding what it meant, threw away my thyroid tablets and then had to go to the doctor for more as my neck started to swell.

I sometimes spent the night at Rita's house. She lived in Dovecot. I was also invited to her sister's wedding, the reception of which took place in the local hall. Rita's mother told us that when she married she had no idea whatsoever about the facts of life so her wedding night was something of a great surprise.

The trams and busses were filled to capacity - production of these had gone on hold during the war and even though they had brought ancient ones into service to fill the gap, there were still not enough. One particular conductor would let as many get on as could squeeze in, even letting them sit on the stairs and stand upstairs. I was once on his tram when an inspector got on who was taken aback by this surfeit of humanity, asking meaningfully, "Have you taken the fares upstairs?" The conductor replied cheekily, "No, but if you can get up there, you can take them." Sometimes I would go to the terminus at Pier Head and catch the tram there - the queues were very long but sooner or later you had a chance of getting on a tram. I often walked the four miles home rather than join the long queues. Old Uncle Dave asked me which direction I took and I couldn't tell him. He said I should always take note of the name of the street I was on, something I didn't do then and still don't do, which is no doubt the reason I frequently get lost. A familiar landmark on the way home was Ogden's Tobacco Factory, this whether I could see it or not as the smell of tobacco was always in the air.

Though the war was now over, rationing was still in full force and we even had bread added to it. We now needed coupons to buy it - these were known as B.U's (Bread Units in actual fact). Uncle Arthur, in a light-hearted mood, once referred to them as 'Bloody Units' which we thought was very funny and daring as, in our district, it was unacceptable to swear.

When Ray was de-mobbed, he and Pat moved to other accommodation. The first place they stayed was in the same area where the well-known film star Rex Harrison used to live. We were most impressed. They just had a living room and bedroom and shared other facilities as most people had to do then. It was impossible to get a house all to yourself. They later moved to similar digs in Barn Hey Green.

Pauline, Leon and Jacqueline returned to Liverpool shortly afterwards. By this time Leon had also been demobbed and they were awaiting berths on a ship to take them to Australia. People were wanting to get out of England in droves but Leon, as an Australian had priority, as did Pauline classified as a 'war-bride'. Leon, not wanting to idle his time whilst they waited, took whatever job he could get and that was in a sausage factory.

During this period Granddad was so angry on one occasion when he felt his meal hadn't been cooked properly that he demanded, "Bring in the girl who cooked this!" Leon told him not to talk like that, whereupon Granddad grabbed the poker and leapt at him. I shot off to the phone box at the bottom of Millbank to telephone the police and blurted out when I got through, "Come quickly, my Granddad is running around with a poker!" There was loud laughter from the other end but soon a policeman arrived. Of course Granddad told him what he thought of him as well, but the policeman just mildly said, "Now, now Mr Elliott". Outside he said to us, "If I were you I wouldn't stay here." Anyway, there was nothing for it, we had to stay there.

Cousin Douglas came to Liverpool to work in a bank and stayed for a while with Auntie Eve and Uncle Arthur. I had started going to the Liverpool Palace Ice Rink. I was never very good at ice-skating, nor at any sport for that matter, but I enjoyed it and when cousin Douglas came to Liverpool, he and I went together a number of times. Pauline would get me aside before we went out and tell me to make sure he paid - Douglas was notoriously tight-fisted. Douglas had been in the army and had been stationed at Gibraltar where he had been the army radio announcer. He had a rich speaking voice.

I left the shipping agents to better my wages, going to work for a film renters; I was to be secretary to two bosses and was soon to discover that this would make three of us with scarcely anything to do. My wages went from £2/2/- a week to £2/10/- (with a deduction of 2/6 for something or other - probably tax). The office was in a four-storey building. I don't know what was on the ground floor but the first floor was occupied by a Frenchman and his small band; we were on the second and the V.D. clinic occupied the top floor. I know that ads said that the only person who caught V.D. from a lavatory seat was a liar, I was, nonetheless, a bit cautious about holding on to the banister when I went up to the office.

Our office was a large room with two desks - the boss, Mr Aston, and mine. There was another office with the boss over both of us. I have now forgotten his name but he was a very nice, elderly gentleman who ended up being dismissed. I felt very sorry for him because he was riddled with arthritis and told me that he didn't know how he was going to manage if he ever had to give up his car. The Frenchman often came into our office to bring me a cup of coffee. He was very debonair. Once he came in and said, "Stay, just like that. Look at her hands, Mr Aston, how beautiful they are." Well, you couldn't help but like a person who spoke like that. For some reason or other, he took me to lunch one day. His band played at various functions and a girl contortionist was the star of the evening. Mr Aston, out of her hearing, called her 'Legs 11'. From our office we could hear the band practising and this relieved the tedium of having scarcely anything to do. I went from churning out bills of lading to doing about a dozen letters a day. These letters were very repetitious and the monotony of them was only relieved on occasion when Mr Aston, fed up with something that Head Office had done, would fume "Take a letter!" And then he would let fly. A short while later, whilst I was typing it and Mr Aston had had time to calm down, he would say, "What do you think of that letter?" This was my cue to say, "Well, I think it is a bit strong." At which Mr Aston would respond, "Yes, perhaps. Let's re-do it then." And the letter that would eventually go off would be very mild.

  I did a lot of reading in that office to while away the time. I would sometimes pick up the Daily Mirror and plod through the news pages, trying to figure out what was going on in the world, in those days my knowledge was very limited. However, the 'Old Codgers' column was more in my sphere of understanding. I think it was from that column I first learnt the term 'Whacker', which I would one day name a Great Dane I owned. I once picked up the book of the picture 'Night at the Opera' starring Groucho Marx and had to suppress my laughter as I read it.

The films we rented out were all second features and dated from ages ago, long before my memory. Bobby Breen and such like. Even Little Lord Fauntleroy. You could rent these for 30/- up to £4/10/- for something really spectacular. We didn't actually do any deliveries, just took orders. All I had to do was write letters about them. Sometimes a very nice boy, who happened to be an albino, would pop in from one of the other film renting offices, but his office rented out much more up-to-date films than we did. He was very interesting to talk to and he also told me what it was like to be an albino. He said his happiest time had been his school days in a blind institute. He was conscious that he attracted attention in the street but it didn't bother him. Occasionally I would be given a ticket to attend a preview of a film - I could never go because it was always during working hours so I would give these tickets to Auntie Jessie. Another person I chatted to on a more or less daily basis, was the charwoman for the building. A sheer bundle of energy packed into a wisp of a body. She would scrub the three flights of stairs as well as all the rooms. She was a very happy person, always smiling, and had no teeth. She would tell me about her 'old man'.

Mr Aston had two or three friends who sometimes came in after they'd all lunched together. One of them was a 'tipster' selling his horse-racing tips. They were all keen on the horses. When the Grand National was on I asked the tipster what I should back. He gave me, free-of-charge, the name of a horse, which I have now forgotten, and I backed it one shilling each way. It came in second. I went by myself to Aintree to watch the race, making my way to Beecher's Brook where I had been advised to go. All I can remember about the race was a horse having to be shot. Some man near me kept saying desperately, "They are not doing it right." A well-known character in the town was an African in outrageous dress who also used to sell tips on the horses. A couple of times one of Mr Aston's friends brought a musical instrument - a ukelele or some such thing, and then Mr Aston would say it was okay for me to leave early. Mr Aston's wife once phoned me up to ask me if a certain woman ever came in to the office; I was a good secretary and said "no."

The office was not too far from the Adelphi Hotel and I would sometimes pass by it. The Adelphi seemed luxury indeed and I would look at this grand edifice and promise myself that one day I would spend a night there. Interestingly enough, many years later I discovered that Mother had had the same yearning and actually did spend a night there. I have still to do so.

In the evening I often went to the Grafton Rooms dance hall; on rare occasions I would go to the Rialto Ballroom but I didn't like it nearly as much. In those days when you went to a dance you just stood there until someone asked you to dance. It was a way of meeting the opposite sex. As I often went by myself it was quite an art to just stand there and not look too desperate. I met many boyfriends that way, amongst them Frank and Eddie. Eddie was serving in the Army and was on embarkation leave before being sent to India. He was from Ireland and a Catholic, but we both decided not to mention the latter to Granddad when he came to take me out, not wanting to test the waters. In civvy street, Eddie was a schoolteacher. I also had another boyfriend, Douglas, though I didn't meet him at the Grafton. I was out walking one day with Kath and we became conscious that he was following us. Then he caught us up and said, "How much further are you going to take me?" Douglas was actually named Cecil, but when I heard that that was his name, I refused to call him by it so we decided that he would be Douglas. When he met Ferg it was discovered that they had sat next to each other in Colwell Road School. Mother remembers him well from when she went with Granny Elliott on the school Parents' Day and she had asked the child sitting next to Ferg what his name was and he had replied "Cecil" with a bit of a lisp. Granny and Mother had had to struggle to keep a straight face as it seemed funny that Cecil was sitting next to Cyril (Ferg's first name). By the time Cecil and I met, his family had gone up in the world and was now living in Barn Hey Green.

I went out frequently with boys. One boyfriend took me around Wales on the back of his motorbike. I happened to be staying with Uncle Billie and Auntie Jessie that night (I sometimes stayed over at their house) and when I returned Uncle Billie couldn't stop laughing as my face was covered with grime from the long journey. When he'd got over laughing and the boyfriend had left, he expressed his disapproval of the boy; he hadn't liked the look of him.

I suppose the most memorable evening was the one I spent with Frank - we went over to New Brighton hoping to go dancing at the Town Hall there, but it was closed as there was a power blackout. This dance hall had strobe lights reflected from a central globe hanging from the ceiling and covered in a multitude of tiny mirrors. As you danced these lights sparkled around you and it was very romantic. But as we couldn't go there, we went instead to have dinner at a small café which was also suffering from the power blackout and so our dinner was by candlelight. I had never had a candlelit dinner before and found it wonderful. Frank was not eligible to be called up as he was in a reserved occupation, being a welder on the Liverpool docks.

I would rout around the house for some old dress or any other bits of material and make myself a blouse and skirt. I cut these from a 'block' pattern - one drawn from my own measurements - something I learnt to do when I had taken a course a couple of years previously at a Workers' Education sewing class. I even made myself a pillbox hat out of some fur I found lying around the house. Dirndle skirts were easy as I simply had to get a piece of material, gather it, make a waistband of the same material, and assemble the two parts. I made my own earrings from fancy buttons, attaching them to thin wire which I coiled in a ring to hold onto my ears. I was adept at making do and improvising. I still had the shell necklaces that Ferg, Kath and I had made whilst we were still in No. 32. We had gathered shells from the seashore, painted them in different patterns and then strung them on coloured cord, putting the largest one in the centre and in decreasing size either side to where it was fastened at the back with a hook and eye. We sold some of those necklaces to friends.

Another boyfriend I had for a brief period was Alan. He was my second boyfriend after Philip. He would have been totally forgettable except that I went with him and a couple of others to a house where a blind woman lived who told fortunes. We had to give her some item of ours which she held whilst she told us our future. I can't remember at all what she told me, but it was a suitably eerie performance.

Mostly your boyfriend came to the house to collect you, but sometimes it was more convenient to meet downtown and when this was so, we met under the clock at Lime Street Station. This was a popular meeting place and immediately recognisable; everyone knew where the clock was. I was glad when returning many, many years later to find the clock still there. Unfortunately the concourse has been taken up with a lot of structures and you no longer have a sweeping view to the platforms and the imposing glass roof.

In July 1946 Pauline, Leon and Jacqueline managed to get berths for Australia on the Wyrangi. Kath, Pat and I went to London to see them off, staying at the Strand Palace for three days. We had to queue for breakfast - it is one of those innocuous occasions that stays in the mind. On one of the days, as we were walking around, we saw a shop which had some peaches for sale. Absolutely unheard of! Pauline sent me in to buy some. On examination they turned out to be bad and she sent me back in to get her money back. The assistant wasn't interested in returning the money so Pauline charged in and in no time the money was refunded. Pauline had a manner about her that brooked no argument. Our few days together in London were hectic - we went by boat down the Thames to Rochester; visited St Paul's Cathedral and the maze at Hampton Court and finally, on the last day, we went to the zoo. On the 10th July, we saw them off on the boat train to Southampton. The last memory of Leon is of him at the railway station about to board the boat train. He was so busy hugging us all that the train started to pull out and he had to run for it - he stood on the step of the train and waved us a last farewell. We were never to see him again. How we all loved him.

Now that Pauline and Leon had gone, Kath and I were left alone with Granddad and Mother's unmarried brother, John. Ferg was still in the army. Our time with Granddad is a story in itself, it was turbulent to say the least. To avoid meeting him, we would come in the front door and go straight upstairs, making sure not to make a noise. Then we would try to come quietly down again to warm up our tin of meat and vegetables in the scullery, and sneak back up again, locking our bedroom door. We were glad that John was in the house as we knew he was on our side. However, John was always out of an evening due to his job as an usher in a picture-house, so he never came home till it was very late. Sometimes when he came in we could hear him and Granddad arguing. We tried to get 'digs' as it was called, in other words, a room in someone's house, but the two or three we saw were not suitable at all, not only did they cost far too much for our meagre income, but it would have meant room only with kitchen and bathroom facilities having to be shared. When we didn't go out, Kath and I would spend the evening in front of the gas fire in the bedroom playing the portable gramophone (the wind-up type) that Old Uncle Dave had given us. He also gave us some records of Grace Moore and Richard Tauber, which we liked, but also had our own favourites of the era. Mine were the Ink Spots, particularly 'I Covered the Waterfront' and 'To Each His Own'. Kath particularly liked 'Bless You for Being an Angel' by a singer whose name I can't remember.

    Despite the difficulty of Granddad, by no means do I remember it as an unhappy period; our evenings weren't totally spent in the bedroom, we still went out as much as ever, mostly individually. We enjoyed our independence and had a lot of fun. We had the main bedroom which overlooked the front. I remember how nice it was late at night whilst in bed to hear the click-click of the trams as they passed on the road below. The only unpleasant experience I can recall is when Kath went to the Grafton on her own and the boy she had met there took her home, but on reaching Millbank had dragged her into the entry and she had to claw at him to get away. She thumped frantically at the front door shouting to me to let her in. When I opened, she stumbled in shaken and dishevelled.

A month after Pauline and Leon had gone, Mother returned to England to finalise things. Ray had found it deplorable that Kath and I were to be left alone after Pauline had left and even before she had gone, unbeknownst to us, had written to Mother and told her so. But he needn't have worried about us, we were our Mother's daughters and well able to cope. Shortly after Mother arrived, Ferg came home briefly on embarkation leave prior to being sent to Egypt.

Some time during this period when Mother was home, a relative rolled up, a gentle and unassuming person. She'd had a breakdown and we learnt later that she had been in a nursing home and had run away. Mother opened her heart and her home to her. Mother never turned anyone away. One evening when we were all gathered together and were laughing and talking, this relative suddenly burst into tears. She said, "You are such a happy family." She had not been so fortunate. Mother tried to get her a job and had one lined up for her at a butcher's in Tuebrook, but she didn't turn up to it and then one day left as suddenly as she had arrived.

Not long after she left, Mother was shopping in Tuebrook and came across a woman, Mrs Boardman, crying. It turned out she had just been evicted by her landlady, so Mother brought her home to our house. She had never met her before, but Mother was like that.

Amongst the things which changed when Mother was back in the house was, she took over the housekeeping and we had to turn over our pay to her again and receive back pocket-money. Another thing was the curfew. Kath and I had to be in at a certain time of night. I said to Mother, "You don't trust me," and she replied, "I trust you, it's the boys I don't trust." One evening after arriving back home later than I had been told to do, she was waiting for me, very angry. I took off the shoes I had been wearing which I had borrowed from her, and handed them to her. She said nothing then, but next day she said how funny she had found that - being so angry with me and I was handing her something which she might well have thrown at me. Mother's sense of humour was never far away.

Mother was doing her best to return to South Africa but was having a lot of difficulty as the ships were full to capacity. I would go with her to the phone box at the bottom of Millbank whilst she made the many calls to the shipping offices, with no effect.

During the time Mother was home there was a lot of visiting to and from her many friends and relative. Auntie Eve and Uncle Arthur were within walking distance of Millbank and when she went there, we would pre-arrange the time she wanted to return home and I would go and fetch her. Even though the war was over the blackout was still on because of a shortage of coal for the power stations. Mother could not see in the dark whereas I had cat's eyes. On one occasion when I went to collect her, a friend of Auntie Eve and Uncle Arthur was there. She lived in the Chinese quarter of Liverpool and said that when she went home late at night, she was sure they were peering at her through the letterbox slots of their front doors. We had that area down as a den of 'white slavers'. Granny Elliott used to warn us, "Beware the Yellow Peril." Sometimes Uncle Arthur would try to tell us of his experiences in the Changi Prisoner-of-War Camp, but Auntie Eve would say, "We don't want to hear about all that." Mother would get annoyed and say, "But I do." When he was allowed to speak, he spoke of the prisoners never being allowed to lie down, weak as they were from starvation and the very hot weather. One day he fell on his bed exhausted and a Japanese guard came in and ordered him to stand up, then punched him across the face. They were forced to stand to attention whenever the guards entered their sleeping quarters. The prisoners were so hungry that they ended up killing and eating the camp pet dog. They also resorted to eating rats. Uncle Arthur was sent with other prisoners to Osaka, Japan, to work on the mines, but he was so ill that he went straight into hospital. He had given up and no longer wanted to eat. An Australian doctor who treated him said that if he didn't eat, he would be dead by the next day. The doctor got from his very limited store a small tin of salmon and gave it to him. Uncle Arthur said it saved his life. All this was just before the atom bombs were dropped on Hiroshima and Nagasaki. When the prisoners were liberated, they were taken on a Canadian ship to Canada. Uncle Arthur said that he cried to see clean sheets and friendly faces. In Canada they were slowly given food as their stomachs would not have tolerated too much too quickly after so long being starved. They were three weeks in Canada before being sent back to England. However, careful as the feeding had been, after the starvation diet he had lived on for so long, food left him bloated and Uncle Arthur's skin was pitted. He said that he had a lot of wind and the doctor asked, "Up or down?" Uncle Arthur replied, "Up, thank goodness."

That last winter we were to spend in England, 1946/7, was bitterly cold and there was a coalminers' strike so it was forbidden to use heaters or cookers except at certain times of the day. We went to bed dressed in more clothes than we took off and during the short time that stoves were allowed to be on, we would heat a brick on the gas flame, wrap it in a cloth and try to warm the bed that way. We also had a stone hot water bottle which we filled with boiling water. There was no heating in the office either, though as the city proper and industrial areas had to have power, it couldn't be switched off at their sub-stations, so people in offices located in those areas were on the honour system not to use it. I put newspapers around the leg-space in the desk to retain the heat that my own body generated so at least my feet wouldn't be too cold. I sat at my desk with my overcoat, slacks, pixie hood with its built in scarf, and gloves on, taking the latter off only when I needed to type. Mother had knitted the pixie hood which was sky blue and had a very long, wide scarf which could wrap around the neck a couple of times. Mother invariably had some knitting on the go. To keep warm she put on so much underwear, singlets and bloomer-type knickers in flannelette, it became a family joke. She told people that they were fools to be staying in England, that they should migrate. Once she begged a wooden barrel from the vegetable shop in Tuebrook and rolled it back home, so at least there was a fire in the grate for a brief spell. A neighbour of Auntie Eve and Uncle Arthur had frozen pipes which burst, resulting in a deluge, causing the ceiling to cave in.

Pauline had begun sending us newspapers from Australia and they frequently depicted some bathing beauty on the beach. Also, one of Mr Aston's daughters had married an American and was now living in America and he would sometimes bring in photographs of her to show me, we were both impressed with how advanced America was as his daughter was wearing purple nail polish. Oh, what a far cry America and its purple nail polish and Australia and its beaches were from Liverpool.

However, though the cold is foremost in my mind when I think of that winter, I remember also the fogs; I have always liked their eeriness. Sometimes of a morning there would be a heavy fog, and running down Millbank to catch the tram at the stop at the bottom, one could hear the click-click of the trams and see their muted lights through the mist.

Christmas 1946, was the last Christmas we spent in England before going to South Africa and we went to Barton.

Mother left for Barton a few days before we did; Ray, Pat, Kath and I all left together. Pat and Ray were to stay with Ray's parents and Kath and I were to join Mother at Auntie Ida and Uncle Dave's. When we reached Hull, Ray insisted that we stay overnight there and not take the ferry straight away to New Holland, he said that we needed to be refreshed when we arrived in Barton. So we stayed at an hotel and next morning Ray paid the bill for all of us. He was always exceptionally generous. In Barton, Pat and Ray joined us for all family get-togethers and we all went to Ray's parents for tea one evening. Christmas lunch was at Auntie Ida and Uncle Dave's and Granny Jackson came to spend the day with us. When lunch was over and we were sitting in the parlour, Granny Jackson gave each of us five shillings with the exception of Mother. Auntie Ida returned her five shillings, not liking the snub Mother had received. All my Father's siblings liked Mother, only her mother-in-law didn't. But then one never knows the history of these things and she was a very good Granny to us.

We spent either Christmas Eve or Boxing Day with Granny and she tried to make it special for us so we used the parlour. She gave Kath and me an apron each, she had asked Pat to buy them and she had bought serviceable plain, bottle-green, heavy cotton ones. Granny felt abashed at giving them and said that she had wanted Pat to buy pretty ones. But to us siblings, a pinny was a pinny was a pinny. We didn't regard them in the same light as the older generations and we avoided wearing them when we could. Often when I was working around the house, Mother would come behind me and slip a pinny around my waist. Like Granny, she was a believer in them and would run one up on the machine from any useful piece of material that she found.

Kath and I received slippers made of rabbit fur from Pat and Ray. Ray had cured the skins himself and had hand-stitched them, turning the fur to the insides so they were snug and warm. Pat had embroidered our initials on the uppers. They were beautifully made.

The journey home was eventful in that a couple of very crude, Liverpool fishwives came into our compartment and belligerently pushed themselves onto the same seat as Pat and Ray, edging their way in and leaving scarcely any room for them. Ray asked them, politely, if they minded moving up as his wife was being squashed in the seat. It was a mistake to even speak to such people and they berated him all the way to Liverpool. With types like that you couldn't win. We felt very sorry for Ray as he was always such a gentleman and didn't deserve such an onslaught.

With the troops returning after the war the world order had changed and one day when Mother was standing in the street, a man came up to her and said, bitterly, "You lot have had your day." Which in view of the enormously hard life Mother had had, becoming a widow and raising five children on a pittance, was somewhat ironic. But Mother, no matter what, always looked very much the lady she was.

Mother eventually managed to get a berth to South Africa. Kath was working at Lewis' at that stage and had mentioned to her boss that she would be going to South Africa shortly. He promptly sacked her saying that he didn't want to be training her for nothing. Kath was too scared to tell Mother and, as Mother was just a week or so away from returning to South Africa, Kath continued leaving home each morning as she normally did, but then spent the day just walking around. One day, when she was on the tram, she happened to bump into Mother who, surprised, asked why she wasn't at work. Kath replied that she'd been sent on a message by her boss. I only learnt all this after Mother had left because Kath said nothing to me either.

It came time for Mother to leave again and how Granddad Elliott clung to her when she kissed and hugged him goodbye. Mother was really the only one of his children, apart from John, who cared for him. She wanted him to go to South Africa with her but he was too old to move. When I look back, I wish I had been more tolerant of him as I now realise what a desperately lonely life awaited him after Mother had left. Once when Granddad had visited us whilst we lived in No. 32, Pauline, Leon and Pat had taken him, along with some of their friends, to the Eagle and Child for a drink. They warned him, that on no account was he to put his glass down as someone would be bound to take it. He hung on to it so firmly that when he went outside at the end of the evening, he was still holding it. Pat said that at one stage she felt very sorry for him, as he looked at them laughing and joking together and said, wistfully, "Oh, to be young again."

Though John never said much, he too would miss her. There'd only been Mother to share his pain.

Others came to say goodbye and Mother went to visit others for the last time before leaving. Auntie Kitty wrote to her later, saying, "I watched as you walked away till I could no longer see you, knowing I would never see your dear face again." Mother meant so much to so many people. Her father wrote to her, "You are the rock on which I cling."

I have never known anyone who had as many friends as Mother. She was not constrained by formality but had a natural warmth and was wonderful company. Most people who met her responded to her engaging personality. With her children she did keep an eye on the sort of friendships they developed, particularly with those of the opposite sex which might lead to a more permanent relationship. Once when she came home Kath had two boyfriends there. Mother ordered them from the house and told them bluntly that she didn't want Kathleen associating with types like them. They appeared to me quite harmless, but according to Mother they were 'common'. Mother never used the Liverpool term 'bucks' to describe undesirable boys, which was how they were usually referred to.

The day Mother left for South Africa, Kath came to the office where I worked and told me she didn't have a job. We had to survive on my wage alone until she found another - having to live on a very sparse diet indeed and I had to walk to work to save the threepenny fare. We were paying half the rent at Millbank. Our diet usually consisted of a small tin of meat and vegetables for tea (dinner) but even this became a struggle. We were driven to pawning our clothes. One person we phoned came to the house and offered us a pittance; Kath refused. The woman was persistent and said to me, wheedlingly, hoping I could get Kath to change her mind, "She's a good girl, isn't she luv?" She didn't know Kath's immovability. It was some time before Kath found a job.

Now that Mother had returned to South Africa after her longer-than-intended stay, Kath and I were once again left alone with Granddad and John, but this time we also had Mrs Boardman.

We went to Pat and Ray's every Sunday and had tea and spent the evening with them. It was our one decent meal of the week. Ray had a number of books which I would borrow. I read H.G. Wells' 'War of the Worlds' and 'Dr Moreau's Island', amongst others. Pat belonged to a book club and I read some of those too, but the only title I can remember is 'Put out more flags' by Evelyn Waugh. She also had a book by Ursula Bloom, but I remember the name more than the book. Ray also taught me how to play chess and we would always have a game, the winner playing Pat. I was never the winner.

Meantime a teacher friend of Pat's, Brenda, had moved into a house on Queen's Drive and wanted someone to share it with her, going halves with the rent, so Pat suggested Kath and me. So we moved there and one of the first things Brenda said was, "How about you doing tea (dinner) one week, and I'll do it the next week? You do it this week." The rent there was £2 a week, of which we paid £1, which left very little over. Thus we had to manage with scarcely any food for the other two meals so we would have enough money over to feed all three of us for dinner. And then, when it came Brenda's week, she said, "I think it would be better if we each fed ourselves!" When the electricity meter needed feeding with another shilling we hoped Brenda would feed it first. The gas meter wasn't so bad, it took pennies. I remember one evening sitting in the dark when both Kath and Brenda were out - I didn't have a shilling for the meter. Interestingly enough Kath and I never told Pat or Ray about our predicament.

Kath eventually got a job at Littlewoods counting all the football pool results. It paid well - £3 per week. Littlewoods had a day out to Blackpool for their workers and Kath took me along. We were a couple of bus loads and we had a sing-song on the way back. Some of the girls went to the Tower Restaurant to eat but Kath and I couldn't afford to do so. The restaurant was on a lower level; the Tower itself had been closed during the war and hadn't yet re-opened.

Before we moved out of Millbank, Mother had written to say that we were to bring to her a tray and one or two other items that had belonged to Granny Elliott, but when I removed them and packed them away, Granddad found out they were missing, demanded them back and grabbed Pat's bike saying that he would keep it until they were returned. In the furore I shouted at him "Damn you," at which he chased me up the stairs, with Mrs Boardman coming out of her room and dramatically standing between us and saying, "I won't let you lay a hand on this girl." Granddad could not stand swearing of any sort and "Damn" was just as bad as any other swear word. I went off to see Ray who came back to the house and said we were to return the things to Granddad. After all I'd been through to get them, I found this a somewhat defeatist attitude.

Mrs Boardman was supposed to look after Granddad when Mother returned to South Africa but she didn't stay with Granddad for long after we left - it appeared he declared his love for her one night and chased her around the table.

* * * * * * * * * *

CHAPTER SEVENTEEN

The waiting list of people wanting to get out of England after the war was very long indeed and every time I enquired of the Union Castle Line as to when we could expect a berth, saying that we were priority, I was told that there were thousands ahead of us, also priority.

After a great deal of letter-writing and not getting anywhere, I eventually wrote to the Chairman of the company and told him of our situation, two teenage sisters waiting to join our parents. I received a letter almost by return of mail saying that the company had been instructed to put us on the next ship, 'The Winchester', but if that was not possible as it was due to sail in a couple of weeks, we were definitely to be put on the 'Warwick Castle' which was next to sail after that. Shortly afterwards we were offered berths on the 'Warwick Castle' and had forms to fill in. I showed Mr Aston one of the forms that I had just completed and he pointed out that, where it had asked whether I was 'European' or 'non-European' and I had answered 'yes' to the latter, they were actually asking if I were white or black. I hadn't realised that Britain was part of Europe. I'd always thought of them as the 'others'.

Mr Aston asked me if I knew of someone who might want to take over my job. Some weeks before I had come across Marjorie in an office where I happened to go - I hadn't seen her since Skerry College days. We had renewed acquaintance and been out a couple of times together. I asked her whether she wanted to take over my job and she did as it paid better than where she was. Mr Aston was happy with the arrangement.

Old Uncle Dave came to spend one last evening with us at Queen's Drive. I asked Brenda not to smoke as Old Uncle Dave didn't like to see women smoke. She said she would do as she pleased. However, she didn't and later said,

"I just couldn't do it to him." He had that effect on people. Old Uncle Dave asked Kath and me if we had enough money. We didn't, so he lent us thirty shillings. Later, when Mother found this out as she had to pay it back, she was furious, but we really were very short of money, barely able to scrape up our fare to London and the bed and breakfast place there where we were to spend the night. When we eventually arrived in South Africa we had four shillings between the two of us. Mother took that.

On my last day at the film renters I came out of the office at lunchtime and found Old Uncle Dave standing there. He said, "I just had to see you again." It is only in later years I realised that, with our going, he was losing contact with our family. When Pat left, there would be no-one of our particular branch left and he didn't have the same sort of relationship with other family members. He was a treasured member of our family and one of the strongest influences in my life.

Old Uncle Dave was to continue working at the Presbyterian Mission until 1952, having been there since 1905. In later years we learnt that the Mission had been sold around that time. A letter dated 19 February 1952 states, "It is primarily for the benefit of the aged superintendent of this Mission Hall that my clients wish to keep it going as long as possible and they feel that the Corporation are forcing them into the position of having to terminate this superintendent's life work (if not his life also) before it is absolutely necessary. It does not in any way soften the blow to learn that the Corporation no longer require the premises for demolition, but only to obtain an income from them." Old Uncle Dave died in 1954; he was 83.

We spent our final evening with Auntie Jessie and Uncle Billie, taking to them all our left-over groceries. The bus stop where we had to alight when going to their house at

Oakdene Road, Aintree, was the other side of the main road and it was our habit to hop off when the bus paused before it crossed. I hopped off successfully but Kath waited too long and the bus gathered speed when she was in the midst of getting off, dragging her along. I groped my way back in the darkness looking for her (the blackout was still on, not due to the war this time but due to a shortage of power) and found her, distressed, amongst the strewn groceries. Her stockings were all torn.

Pat came to spend that evening with us at Auntie Jessie and Uncle Billie's. She cried when it came time to say goodbye to us. Auntie Jessie wrote to Mother and said that she felt Pat had cried because she had just discovered she was pregnant. I actually do think it might have been more than that, as now she was going to be the only member of the immediate family left in England.

By the time we left England, Ferg had not yet been demobbed from the army and was then serving in Egypt. In one letter from him he said that on his first walk up a street in Cairo his wallet had been stolen before he had reached the other end so he wasn't able to buy us anything. It was to be some months before Ferg was demobbed and then he got special permission to go to South Africa instead of returning to England.

Uncle Billie asked if we had gone to say goodbye to Granddad. I said that we hadn't and he said, wisely, "You are very young. One day you might be sorry you didn't." And I am now sorry that then I was too young to care. I realise now that Granddad probably had as much reason to be disappointed in me as I was disappointed in him.

No-one came to the station to see us off - we either took the tram or bus to Lime Street Station, I don't remember which. A taxi would not even have been thought of. The midnight train to London was packed but we managed to get a seat for the six hour journey, others sat on their suitcases in the corridors for the whole journey.

We deposited our suitcases along with Old Uncle Dave's portable gramophone which we were taking with us, in the Left Luggage and, taking only an overnight bag, went straight to Mrs Moffat's bed and breakfast on Bloomsbury Street where Pop had arranged for us to stay; he always stayed there when he was in London. We hadn't a great deal of luggage, clothing rationing had seen to that, but we did have a long, beautiful evening dress each, made of pale blue voile with a small floral pattern. A neighbour of Old Uncle Dave's had made them for us from material which Mother had sent so we would have something to wear at dances on board ship. Certainly we would not have been able to wear them at the Grafton or the Rialto.

After a wash and brush-up we set out for the London office of the 'Society for the Overseas Settlement of British Women' at 20 Great Smith Street, Westminster. Pop had arranged a meeting for us with them. They were very friendly and when we left handed us a letter which read:

6th May, 1947

TO WHOM IT MAY CONCERN

This is to certify that the Misses Kathleen M and Lena J Jackson are proceeding to the Union of South Africa to join mother and stepfather, Mr and Mrs E W Pugh, c/o Mrs Wood, Rapson Road, Morningside, Durban, Natal. They are sailing in the R.M.S. 'WARWICK CASTLE' on the 8th May, 1947. My Committee will appreciate any assistance afforded to these passengers".

(It was signed by the Secretary.)

Mrs Wood was Pop's daughter, Dolly. Pop was wonderful in the way he tried to help us. In South Africa Pop belonged to the 'Sons of England' and the '1820 Settlers Association'. He was also a Mason.

We had arranged to meet cousin Douglas who happened to be in London, and he took us to lunch. We were surprised that he did so as he wasn't known for his generosity. We were also surprised that when he said goodbye to us he seemed sad that we were going as he was around Pauline and Pat's age and had not been particularly close to us. He commented on our leaving England, saying, "No matter where you travel, you will always find that England is the best place to be."

After saying goodbye to Douglas, Kath and I went to Madame Tussauds. What a wonderful place it was in those days. We then returned to Mrs Moffat's and, after putting our hair in curlers (the usual rag ones), we fell exhausted into bed early.

When we awoke it was seven o'clock. We were very annoyed as we had asked the maid to wake us at six. After a quick ablution we took the curlers out of our hair, being mystified that it hadn't curled. We dressed quickly as we had very little time, the boat train for Southampton leaving at nine. I finished packing the overnight bag whilst Kath went downstairs to pay the bill. Then I followed her and was surprised to find her involved in an argument with Mrs Moffat.

"We haven't time for breakfast," I called out.

"Mrs Moffat says we haven't stayed the night," Kath said.

"Of course we have," I said firmly. "We stayed last night. Hurry up, we have to go. There is no time to waste."

Mrs Moffat shrugged and took the money Kath proffered and, as we walked up the street, we could see her looking at us from the window. We couldn't understand her odd behaviour.

We took the subway to Waterloo Station and on arrival hailed a porter to collect our suitcases from the Left Luggage. He did so and then said, "Where are you going?"

"The 'Warwick Castle' boat train to Southampton," we said.

"That doesn't leave till tomorrow," he said.

He was a typical cockney, very cheerful and friendly, and we thought he was pulling our legs.

"Oh, do stop joking," we said. "We haven't a lot of time."

"I'm not joking," he replied. "I tell you the train doesn't leave until tomorrow."

We took out our tickets and showed them to him. "It says here the boat train leaves on Thursday at nine o'clock."

"But today is Wednesday," he said.

"No, it's not, it's Thursday."

He looked flabbergasted. "I tell you, it's Wednesday."

"It can't be Wednesday," we said. "We left Liverpool on the midnight train on Tuesday night, spent Wednesday going around London, and then stayed the night at a hotel. So it has to be Thursday."

The porter gave up and called a policeman. After a similar sort of conversation with him, he called another policeman with the same result. That policeman called another and so on, until in the end we had five policeman and the porter all trying to convince us.

They thought that the only explanation was that we must have left Liverpool one day earlier than we thought, but we said that that was not possible as we had spent the last evening with family and they knew when we had to leave. Kath and I even wondered if there was a possibility that Liverpool was one day ahead of London.

In the end, one policeman had a brainwave. "What time of day do you think it is?" he asked.

"Morning of course."

"It's evening. There, look outside."

We did, and sure enough it was beginning to get dark.

We got the porter to put our suitcases back in the Left Luggage. They didn't charge us a second time but accepted that there had been a mistake. This was just as well as our worldly wealth could be counted in shillings and even the few pence would have made inroads into that. As we were leaving the station one policeman called out, "Take the straw out of your hair."

The worst thing was going back to Mrs Moffat's. We wouldn't have done so but we didn't have the money to pay for another bed and breakfast place. When we got there she was in the lounge with a lot of other people who went silent when we walked in as we had obviously been the subject of their conversation.

"We thought it was tomorrow," I said inanely.

Silence! And then some kind person said, "I suppose that can happen, can't it?"

Next day, when it really was Thursday, we took the boat train to Southampton and, on attempting to board the ship, discovered that our passports were in one of the suitcases that we had placed in the luggage van with a label affixed to it saying, 'Wanted on Board'. This meant that it would be going directly on board the ship and the next time we saw it, it would be in our cabin. But right then we needed it to get our passports. The guard in charge of the luggage van was most obliging in helping us locate the suitcase and rifle through it for our passports. And so we left England for South Africa on the 'Warwick Castle' on 8th May 1947.

I learnt on the 'Warwick Castle' that I am a very bad sailor. I was seasick a good deal of the voyage. Kath got really fed up with me on one occasion when I wouldn't go up to dinner with her and shouted at me what a miserable person I was. We later laughed at this as she said that all the time she was shouting at me, I just lay there ghastly white from the seasickness, unable to retaliate.

Seasickness notwithstanding, we had a marvellous trip to South Africa - the Union Castle Line ran the best passenger ships in the world - and our day stop in Madeira will stay with me always. During the war, passenger ships had been converted into troop ships which were then used straight after the war to transport migrants. Pauline and Leon had had an awful journey on one of these migrant ships to Australia - the men being separated from the women and children and all in dormitory-type accommodation. But the 'Warwick' was back to peacetime service and was wonderful.

When we docked in Cape Town we received a letter from Pop and Mother which they had written on Monday, 19th May 1947. Pop wrote:

Sea Breeze Hotel
Durban
Monday 19th

Dear Kath & Jean,
A hearty welcome to South Africa to you both. Your Auntie Marge will, I hope, be meeting you when you arrive in Cape Town and will perhaps take you out to their house. Now when you go to see the Immigration Officer on the ship you must tell him that you are going to live with your Mother at the above Hotel and that the Principal

Immigration Officer here in Durban knows all about your expected arrival here and he has written to the Immigration officer at Cape Town so that you will have no trouble whatever in passing through the Immigration people. Whatever you do see that you do not miss the boat on the day she leaves Cape Town. My Sister in Law Mrs Dunn and her daughter Phyllis will meet you in East London where you will stay for a few hours. And then we will meet you the morning you arrive here.

Mother continued the letter, she wrote -

My dear Kathleen & Jean,
Welcome to S. Africa dears & wishing you all the happiness & prosperity in your new country. Do hope you have enjoyed the trip. Give my love to Margie & Sonny & Dick. They enjoy a game of cards, so you should teach them how to play 'solo'. <u>Don't forget to look out for Mrs Cole and her sister in law Mrs Stickells, & Mrs Dunn at East London.</u> The latter is Dad's sister in law & she is very like Lottie Preece so you should recognize her. I'm on duty at 4 p.m. today so I'm just going to town with Dolly Mc Cann.
All my love. Your ever loving Mum xxxxx

Margie was the wife of Sonny, Pop's son, and Dick was their son. It was Dick who met us at the ship in Cape Town. We really liked him. He was so friendly and welcoming and spoke beautifully. Margie had made a wonderful lunch for us, such bounty after the austerity of England was unbelievable. We stayed overnight with them, causing some of the crew to become agitated as to where we were as we hadn't told them we would be spending the night ashore; they had been keeping an eye on us. The ship stayed two days in Cape Town.

When Mother and Pop had first arrived in South Africa they had gone to Pretoria where Auntie Georgie lived in Muckleneuk. Pop, at that stage of his life, did not like the altitude on the Rand, even though he had lived and worked in Krugersdorp for a number of years and owned a house there. So they moved to Durban where Pop's daughter, Dolly, lived. They were staying at the Seabreeze Hotel on Gillespie Street, one block back from the seafront. Mother was working at Madisons, a restaurant-cum-milk-bar-cum-sweet-shop-cum grocery. Mother was a cashier at the sweet counter and took the money there for the restaurant also. When she applied for that job she had said, "I haven't worked since I was a teenager and I have never worked in a shop, but I'm willing to learn." She was taken on. Mother, being a very active person who was always busy, had found living in a hotel frustrating as there was so little to do.

When we reached Durban we also stayed at the Seabreeze Hotel. In those days the Seabreeze was a charming residential hotel. Kath and I had a very nice room with a porch overlooking a back street which was a hive of activity.

It was at the Seabreeze that I met Maurice within a few weeks of arriving. He was also staying at the Seabreeze, having recently been demobbed from the army, and was working for the Irrigation Department in Durban. Maurice proposed to me three weeks after we first went out together and we were married seven months later. But that is another story.

* * * * * * * * * * *

The following poems, 'Lord Ullin's Daughter', 'The Wreck of the Hesperus' and 'The Inchcape Rock', Mother would recite to Ferg, Kath and me when we were children. She knew them all off by heart.

'LORD ULLIN'S DAUGHTER' By T. Campbell.

A Chieftain to the Highlands bound
Cries "Boatman, do not tarry!
And I'll give thee a silver pound
To row us o'er the ferry!"
"Now who be ye, would cross Lochgyle
This dark and stormy water?"
"O I'm the chief of Ulva's isle,
And this, Lord Ullin's daughter.
"And fast before her father's men
Three days we've fled together,
For should he find us in the glen,
My blood would stain the heather.
"His horsemen hard behind us ride -
Should they our steps discover,
Then who will cheer my bonny bride
When they have slain her lover?"
Out spoke the hardy Highland wight
"I'll go, my chief, I'm ready:
It is not for your silver bright,
But for your winsome lady: -
"And by my word! the bonny bird
In danger shall not tarry;
So though the waves are raging white
I'll row you o'er the ferry."
By this the storm grew loud apace,
The water-wraith was shrieking;
And in the scowl of heaven each face
Grew dark as they were speaking.
But still as wilder blew the wind
And as the night grew drearer,

Adown the glen rode armed men,
Their trampling sounded nearer.
"Oh haste thee, haste!" the lady cries,
"Though tempests round us gather;
I'll meet the raging of the skies,
But not an angry father."
The boat has left a stormy land,
A stormy sea before her, -
When, O! too strong for human hand
The tempest gather'd o'er her.
And still they row'd amidst the roar
Of waters fast prevailing;
Lord Ullin reach'd that fatal shore, -
His wrath was changed to wailing.
For, sore dismay'd, through storm and shade
His child he did discover: -
One lovely hand she strech'd for aid,
And one was round her lover.
"Come back! come back!" he cried in grief,
"Across this stormy water:
And I'll forgive your Highland chief,
My daughter! - O my daughter!"
'Twas vain; the loud waves lash'd the shore,
Return or aid preventing;
The waters wild went o'er his child,
And he was left lamenting.

'THE WRECK OF THE HESPERUS'
by Henry Wadsworth Longfellow.

It was the schooner Hesperus,
That sailed the wintry sea;
And the skipper had taken his little daughter,
To bear him company.
Blue were her eyes as the fairy-flax,
Her cheeks like the dawn of the day,

And her bosom white as the hawthorn buds,
That ope in the month of May.
The skipper he stood beside the helm,
His pipe was in his mouth,
And he watched how the veering flaw did blow
The smoke now West, now South.
Then up and spake an old Sailor,
Had sailed to the Spanish Main,
"I pray thee, put into yonder port,
For I fear a hurricane.
Last night, the moon had a golden ring,
And to-night no moon we see!"
The skipper, he blew a whiff from his pipe,
And a scornful laugh laughed he.
Colder and louder blew the wind,
A gale from the Northeast.
The snow fell hissing in the brine,
And the billows frothed like yeast.
Down came the storm, and smote amain
The vessel in its strength;
She shuddered and paused, like a frighted steed,
Then leaped her cable's length.
"Come hither! Come hither! my little daughter,
And do not tremble so;
For I can weather the roughest gale
That ever wind did blow."
He wrapped her warm in his seaman's coat
Against the stinging blast;
He cut a rope from a broken spar,
And bound her to the mast.
"O father! I hear the church-bells ring,
O say, what may it be?"
"'Tis a fog-bell on a rock-bound coast!"
And he steered for the open sea.
"O father! I hear the sound of guns,
O say, what may it be?"

"Some ship in distress, that cannot live
In such an angry sea!"
"O father! I see a gleaming light
O say, what may it be?"
But the father answered never a word,
A frozen corpse was he.
Lashed to the helm, all stiff and stark,
With his face turned to the skies,
The lantern gleamed through the gleaming snow
On his fixed and glassy eyes.
Then the maiden clasped her hands and prayed
That saved she might be;
And she thought of Christ, who stilled the wave,
On the Lake of Galilee.
And fast through the midnight dark and drear,
Through the whistling sleet and snow,
Like a sheeted ghost, the vessel swept
Tow'rds the reef of Norman's Woe.
And ever the fitful gusts between
A sound came from the land;
It was the sound of the trampling surf
On the rocks and the hard sea-sand.
The breakers were right beneath her bows,
She drifted a dreary wreck,
And a whooping billow swept the crew
Like icicles from her deck.
She struck where the white and fleecy waves
Looked soft as carded wool,
But the cruel rocks, they gored her side
Like the horns of an angry bull.
Her rattling shrouds, all sheathed in ice,
With the masts went by the board;
Like a vessel of glass, she stove and sank,
Ho! Ho! The breakers roared!
At daybreak, on the bleak sea-beach,
A fisherman stood aghast,

To see the form of a maiden fair,
Lashed close to a drifting mast.
The salt sea was frozen on her breast,
The salt tears in her eyes;
And he saw her hair, like the brown sea-weed,
On the billows fall and rise.
Such was the wreck of the Hesperus,
In the midnight and the snow!
Christ save us all from a death like this,
On the reef of Norman's Woe!.

'THE INCHCAPE ROCK' by Robert Southey

No stir in the air, no stir in the sea,
The ship was as still as she could be;
Her sails from heaven received no motion,
Her keel was steady in the ocean.
Without either sign or sound of their shock
The waves flowed over the Inchcape Rock.
So little they rose, so little they fell,
They did not move the Inchcape Bell.
The good old Abbot of Aberbrothok
Had placed the Bell on the Inchcape Rock;
On a buoy in the storm it floated and swung,
And over the waves its warning rung.
When the rock was hid by the surge's swell,
The Mariners heard the warning Bell;
And then they knew the perilous rock,
And blest the Abbot of Aberbrothok.
The sun in heaven was shining gay,
All things were joyful on that day;
The sea birds scream'd as they wheel'd around,
And there was joyance in the sound.
The buoy of the Inchcape Bell was seen,
A darker speck on the ocean green;
Sir Ralph the Rover walk'd his deck,

And he fix's his eye on the darker speck.
He felt the cheering power of spring,
It made him whistle, it made him sing;
His heart was mirthful to excess,
But the Rover's mirth was wickedness.
His eye was on the Inchcape float;
Quoth he, "My men, put out the boat,
And row me to the Inchcape Rock,
And I'll plague the Abbot of Aberbrothok."
The boat is lowered, the boatmen row,
And to the Inchcape Rock they go;
Sir Ralph bent over from the boat,
And he cut the bell from the Inchcape float.
Down sank the Bell with a gurgling sound,
The bubbles rose and burst around;
Quoth Sir Ralph, "The next who comes to the Rock
Won't bless the Abbot of Aberbrothok."
Sir Ralph the Rover sailed away
He scour'd the sea for many a day;
And now, grown rich by plunder's store,
He steers his course for Scotland's shore.
So thick a haze o'erspreads the sky,
They cannot see the sun on high;
The wind hath blown a gale all day,
At evening it hath died away.
On the deck the Rover takes his stand,
So dark it is they see no land.
Quoth Sir Ralph, "It will be lighter soon
For there is the dawn of the rising moon."
"Can'st hear," said one, "The breakers roar?
For methinks we should be near the shore;
Now where we are I cannot tell.
But I wish I could hear the Inchcape Bell."
They hear no sound, the swell is strong;
Though the wind hath fallen, they drift along,
Till the vessel strikes with a shivering shock.

Cried they, "It is the Inchcape Rock!"
Sir Ralph the Rover tore his hair,
He cursed himself in his despair,;
The waves rush in on every side,
The ship is sinking beneath the tide.
But even in his dying fear
One dreadful sound could the Rover hear;
A sound as if with the Inchcape Bell
The Fiends below were ringing his knell.

'The Golden Vanity' - is one Mother sang to Ferg, Kath and me.

'THE GOLDEN VANITY'

There was a ship came from the North Country,
And the name of that ship was the Golden Vanity,
And they feared she might be taken by the Turkish enemy,
That sailed upon the Lowland sea.
Then up there came a little cabin boy,
And he said to the Skipper of the Golden Vanity,
"What will you give to me?
If I swim alongside of the Turkish enemy
And sink her in the Lowland Sea?"
"Oh, I will give you silver
And I will give you gold,
And my only daughter your bride will be,
If you swim along the side of the Turkish enemy
And sink her in the Lowland sea."
Then the boy made him ready and overboard sprang he,
And he swam along the side of the Turkish enemy.
And with his auger sharp in her side he bored holes three,
And he sank her in the Lowlands Sea.
Then the boy turned around and came to the portside,
And he called out to the Skipper of the Golden Vanity.
But the Skipper did not heed, for his promise he would
              need,

And he left him in the Lowland Sea.
Then the boy turned around and came to the portside,
And he called out to his messmates and bitterly he cried,
"Oh, messmates, take me up for I'm drifting with the tide,
And I'm sinking in the Lowlands Sea."
Then his messmates took him up,
But on the deck he died,
And they lowered him in his hammock,
That was so large and wide,
Then they lowered him overboard
And he drifted with the tide,
And he sank beneath the Lowlands, Lowlands,
He sank beneath the Lowlands Sea.

****

Above: Mother – aged seventeen.

Below: Dad – (left) aged nineteen; (right) in Royal Navy (back row at right).

Twilight & Wallflowers

Above left: Granny Elliott as a young woman.
Above right: Granny Elliott with twins, Kathleen & Maureen.
Below: Granddad & Granny Elliott; Mother holding Jean; Auntie Georgie and Old Uncle Dave. 1930

Above: Back – Winnie, Arthur, Eve, John, Pat, Mother, Pop.

Middle – Lottie, Mr Kingham (?), Granny & Granddad Elliott, Mrs Kingham, Old Uncle Dave.

Front – Dorothy and Lorna.

Left: Granny & Granddad Elliott, fiftieth wedding anniversary. 1940

Twilight & Wallflowers 311

Above: Billy & Edna's wedding.
Back (right) - Granny & Granddad Jackson.
Front (l to r) – Pauline, Cousin Douglas & Pat. In front of 'Nisida'.
Below: Ida, Dave, Granny Jackson, Edgar, Mary, Ronald, Edna and Billy.

Back row: Lottie, Eve, Arthur, Marion (Mother), ?, Jessie.
Middle row: Mabel, Jim, Granny Morgan, Granddad & Granny Elliott, Old Uncle Dave, Billie.
Front row: Jean, Nellie (friend), Sam & Georgie, ?, Hugh.
Children in front: Pat, Margaret & Pauline.

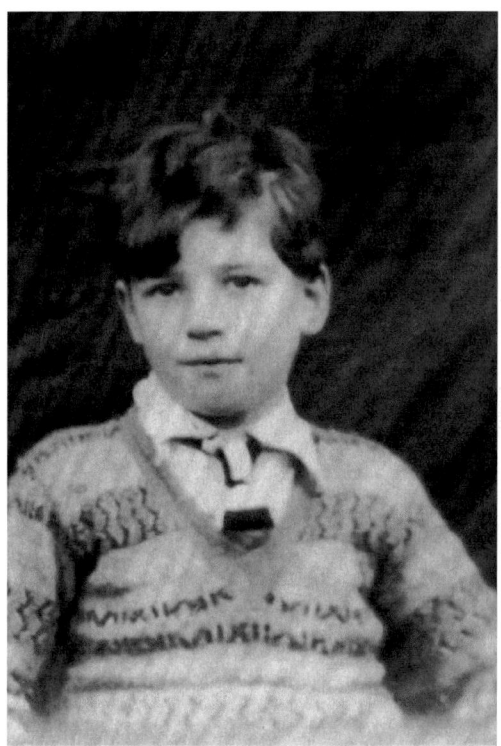

Above: Deryk, aged eight.

Below: Auntie Georgie holding Jimmy; Mother with Kath & Jean; Old Uncle Dave in background. 1930.

Pauline, Pat, Ferg, Kath and Jean outside No. 32. 1935

Above: The crescent row of shops.
Below: Jean with her children, Bronwyn & Lynn outside No. 32.
(Photos taken 1966)

Above: Colwell Road School, Hall at right.

Below: Schoolrooms, Colomendy Camp, Loggerheads. (Photos taken 1975)

Top: Dormitories, Colomendy Camp, Loggerheads. Moel Fammau dormitory front at left.
Middle: Tuck shop and dining room.
Bottom: Ablution block on left.
(Photos taken 1975).

Above: Pat, Jean, Pauline, Kath and Ferg. Loggerheads, North Wales, 1942.

Below left: Mother with Jean & Kath, Colwyn Bay. C1940.
Below right: Mother and Jean outside Lime St Station.

Above: Millbank (photo taken 1966).
Below: Mother with Pat, Jean, Kath and Ferg (who was on embarkation leave).August Bank Holiday, 1946.

Above: Pauline & Leon's wedding. Boxing Day, Dec. 1941. Old Uncle Dave back row left; Pop, Mother, Pat & Kath right; and Jean far left.
Below left: Ray & Pat's wedding, 24 Nov. 1945.
Below right: Mother and Jacqueline outside No. 32. Early 1944.

Above: Kath & Jean's first day in Durban, South Africa, with Mother & Pop. 1947.

Below: Jean & Maurice, shortly after their engagement, with Kath boating on the Amanzimtoti.

Jean & Maurice's wedding, 1948. Front (l to r) Maurice's parents; Maurice & Jean; Mother & Pop. Back: Ferg; cousin Val; friend; Kath; Margaret (Pop's granddaughter).